BEST PRACTICES IN PLANNING AND PERFORMANCE MANAGEMENT

From Data To Decisions, Second Edition

DAVID A. J. AXSON

BICENTENNIAL
1807
⟨⟩WILEY
2007
BICENTENNIAL

John Wiley & Sons, Inc.

For general information on our other products and services, or technical support, please contact our Customer Care Department within the United States at 800-762-2974, outside the United States at 317-572-3993, or fax 317-572-4002.

Wiley also publishes its books in a variety of electronic formats. Some content that appears in print may not be available in electronic books.

For more information about Wiley products, visit our Web site at http://www.wiley.com.

Library of Congress Cataloging-in-Publication Data:

Axson, David A. J.
    Best practices in business performance management : from data
to decisions / David A. J. Axson. — 2nd ed.
      p. cm.
    Rev. ed. of: Best practices in planning and management reporting.
c2003.
    Includes index.
    ISBN–13: 978–0–470–00857–7 (cloth)
    ISBN–10: 0–470–00857–1 (cloth)
    1. Benchmarking (Management)   2. Managerial accounting.
3. Business planning.   I. Axson, David A. J. Best practices in
planning and management reporting.   II. Title.
HD62.15.A97 2007
658.4'012—dc22

2006020341

Printed in the United States of America

10 9 8 7 6 5 4 3 2 1

To Mum and Dad
I miss you both.

About The Author

David A.J. Axson is the founder and president of the Sonax Group, a business advisory and research firm (www.sonaxgroup.com). He was a co-founder of the Hackett Group and is a former Head of Corporate Planning for Bank of America. He lives with his wife and two children in Bath, Ohio. He can be contacted at daxson@sonaxgroup.com.

Contents

PART TWO

Preface to the Second Edition

Since completing the first edition of this book in late 2002 much has happened in the world of planning and management reporting. The forces of globalization, technology and competition continue to redefine markets making it harder than ever for managers to rely on traditional budgeting, forecasting and reporting techniques—in fact the consensus of many is that those traditional processes are not only obsolete but dangerous. A reflection of these changes has been the emergence of a newly named but decades old discipline of Business Performance Management (BPM). BPM has come to embrace all the areas covered by the first edition hence the title change for this edition. Many best practices have moved from concept to everyday reality; technology is now coming close to fulfilling the promises made over the last half-century; and benchmarks have moved from simplistic cost and productivity measures to value-based measures that recognize that the real worth of effective performance management processes is not measured in terms of cost, cycle time, or accuracy but in sustained profitable growth or in many cases simply survival in an intensely volatile and fast-paced world. It is time for an update, so welcome to the second edition.

DAVID A.J. AXSON
September 2006

Preface to the First Edition

This book has its origins in my father's study during the late 1970s. Dad had bought one of the first Commodore Pet computers to be sold in the U.K. and was writing BASIC programs to automate the financial reporting for the family furniture business. I was his data entry clerk.

After staying up into the early hours of the morning writing programs and laboriously copying them onto cassette tapes—this being before the days of the first floppy disk—I would help him key in the day's transactions before leaving for school. Over the next few months, we developed a full accounting, budgeting, and financial reporting system for the business—complete with customer database, inventory management system and scorecard reporting system. We did not know then that this is what these features would come to be called, but they worked. Thus was my interest sparked in planning, management reporting, and the application of computers to business.

Dad sold the family business soon after and moved into computing full time; I left for university to study accounting and computer science. Twenty-five years later, I feel ready to document what I have learned in my journey through the application of technology to business planning and management reporting processes. Starting with my first job at Lloyds Bank (now Lloyds TSB) in London, followed by 18 years in consulting and moving on to research this book, information has been my career. Throughout that time, one of Dad's earliest pieces of advice to me has remained one of my guiding principles.

One night I was sitting in his study and we were talking about the potential of computers to change the world. I am sure Steve Jobs and Steve Wozniak and Bill Gates and Paul Allen were having similar conversations around the same time. As Dad and I discussed the potential applications to which computers could be put, Dad commented, "The real power of computers will only be realized when the user needs to know nothing about them in order to find them useful." He was right then and he is still right now. The full potential of computer technology to add value to life in general, and planning and management reporting in particular, will only be realized when the user does not need to have any computer knowledge at all to benefit.

Dad passed away in 1999. I hope this book follows his mantra of keeping it simple by explaining complex things in words people can easily understand.

DAVID A.J. AXSON
March 2003

Introduction

There is no doubt that that we live in the "Information Age." A typical weekday edition of the *New York Times* contains more information than the average person was likely to come across in a lifetime in seventeenth-century England. Consider how the average manager feels when asked to develop plans, build budgets, report progress, and make decisions in response to today's increasingly competitive, fast-paced, and volatile environment. Traditional planning and management reporting processes are simply too slow, too detailed, and too disconnected for today's competitive world. Managers are seeking new decision-making processes and tools that will enable them to shorten the cycle time to make and implement a decision.

This book summarizes the current state of the art with respect to best practices for business performance management or performance management, as I shall refer to the topic going forward. Best practices have been the subject of much discussion in recent years, and a growing body of knowledge has emerged that purports to define best practices and quantify their value to an organization. A lot of anecdotal evidence links best practice application to improved performance. This book seeks to establish a framework for identifying and implementing best practices in performance management.

The underpinning of the research and analysis contained in this book is my work over the last 20 years with over 200 different companies: first as a consultant with Deloitte and A.T. Kearney in London, then as a cofounder of The Hackett Group, as head of corporate planning at Bank of America, and now as president of my own firm, the Sonax Group.

This book illustrates how leading companies are rethinking the way they make and implement decisions. The aim is to provide a practical guide to managers and students of business on the processes and tools that can be used to consistently make and execute better decisions faster.

Part I makes the case for a radical change in the way managers manage performance. Chapter 1 explains the need for effective performance management in today's fast-paced world. Chapter 2 explores why many of the processes that organizations rely on today are completely unsuitable for the tasks. Chapter 3 provides a series of diagnostic tools and measures to help you size the improvement opportunity.

Part II describes the principal best practices for each element of the performance management process. Chapter 4 describes the approach for putting best practices into context and provides a brief review of the current state of the art. Chapters 5 through 8 describe best practices for strategic planning, tactical and financial planning, management reporting, and forecasting respectively. In this second edition a new chapter, Chapter 9, focusing on risk management has been added reflecting its emergence as a critical component of any effective performance management process. Chapter 10 describes the role of technology in supporting best practice processes.

Part III provides insights into the steps required to design a best practice–inspired process that is right for your organization (Chapter 11) and to understand the critical success factors for implementation (Chapter 12) and the importance of effective leadership (Chapter 13). Chapter 14 offers my own predictions for the future evolution of performance management updated for events of the last few years.

I have tried to use terms consistently throughout the book—not always an easy task. I have used the term "performance management" as shorthand for "business performance management" throughout. The terms "financial planning" and "budgeting" are used interchangeably since no adequate definition of the difference exists. Similarly with the terms "organization," "business," "company," and "firm" and the terms "user" and "customer" when describing the recipients of management information. Overall, I have tried to use the most descriptive term for the context.

This is a book for anyone who has questioned the value of the budget process, been frustrated at the inability to get good information quickly, wondered why so much time is spent developing forecasts that are always wrong, or been angered by the repeated failure of technology to deliver on its promises.

Acknowledgments

Numerous people contributed their knowledge and insight to the ideas developed in this book. One of the joys of consulting is that you have the opportunity to learn from many very smart people, both colleagues and clients. Thanks are owed to many current and former clients and colleagues who helped expand my thinking and challenge my stubbornness, including Doug Barton, Reuben Chaudhury, Carolynne Cox, Robert Craven, Stu Dressler, Mary Driscoll and all at *CFO Magazine*, Lou Eyermann, Mike Geltzeiler, Christine Gattenio, Greg Hackett, Jeff Holker and the Cognos Innovation Center, Greg Horn, Ian Hunt, Alex Jaime, Art Krause, Mark Krueger, Tim Murphy, Dave Paul, Steve Player and the team at the Beyond Budgeting Roundtable, Jeff Rosengard, Rick Roth, Lawrence Serven, Holly Snyder, Helene Uhlfelder, Mike Upchurch, Nic Walsh, and Liz Wenzel. Special thanks to Marc Oken, former CFO of Bank of America, for giving me the opportunity to put some of my ideas into practice.

Most of all I want to thank my family. My wife, Donna, proofread much of this book and offered constant support and encouragement. As always, she was the principal reason I was able to get the job done. My two children, Eleanor and James, provided much light relief as I struggled with various sections. Their smiles and love ensured I kept my priorities right.

Part One

Why Performance Management Matters

Chapter 1

Why Today's Management Processes Are Obsolete

Change is inevitable in a progressive country. Change is constant.

—Benjamin Disraeli

Disraeli's statement is as true now as it was when he was prime minister of Great Britain in the 1870s. At the time, he was focused on introducing many of the reforms needed to address some of the negative effects of the Industrial Revolution then raging in Britain. Legislation passed during his administration included the Artisans Dwellings Act (1875), the Public Health Act (1875), the Pure Food and Drugs Act (1875), the Climbing Boys Act (1875), and the Education Act (1876), all of which sought to adapt British law to the changing times. Today we have moved beyond the industrial age and are hurtling through the information age. The drivers of change are diverse, impacting everything from how markets are defined, to how companies are organized and how technology is utilized. The result is that managers must deal with unprecedented complexity, volatility, uncertainty, and risk. The facts speak for themselves:

- Mintel reported that during 2005, "a new product was launched every three and a half minutes. A staggering 156,125 new food and non-food fast moving consumer goods were introduced around the world."[1]
- Over 39,000 companies filed for bankruptcy in 2005, including Delta Airlines, Winn-Dixie Stores, Delphi, Refco, and another 80 public companies (see Exhibit 1.1).
- Almost 30 percent of public companies missed their earnings estimates during 2004/5, and there were over 1,100 accounting restatements in 2005, up from 600 in 2004.
- Nearly 10,000 acquisitions were made in the United States during 2005 with a total value of over $800 billion. In the last few years such revered corporate names as Sears, Gillette, MBNA, Fleet Boston, MCI, AT&T, Georgia Pacific, Hertz, Nextel, Compaq, and Texaco have succumbed to takeovers. Globally almost $3 trillion of deals were completed in 2005 (see Exhibit 1.2).
- The U.S. Justice Department reported that between July 2002 and March 2006, there were over 1,000 convictions in corporate fraud cases.

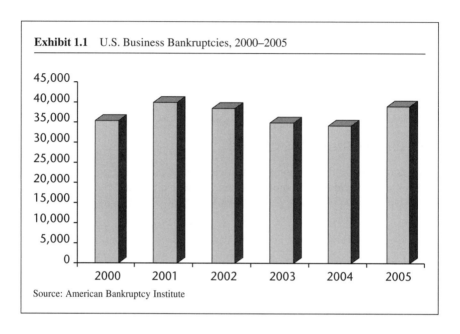

Exhibit 1.1   U.S. Business Bankruptcies, 2000–2005

Source: American Bankruptcy Institute

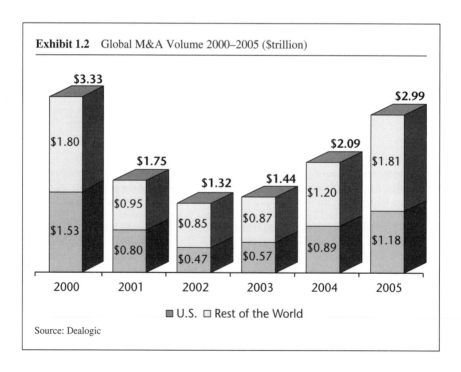

Exhibit 1.2   Global M&A Volume 2000–2005 ($trillion)

Source: Dealogic

The cumulative effect of these and other factors is changing forever the role of managers and more important the processes and tools needed to manage business performance: five-year strategic plans; static, detailed annual budgets; and purely financial forecasts of future performance are obsolete tools. Let's explore some of the major forces of change in more detail.

BETTER-INFORMED CUSTOMERS

I was going to title this section "smarter customers"; however, more knowledge does not always equate with more wisdom. Notwithstanding this nuance, there is no doubt that customers have access to better information than ever before when considering a purchasing decision.

The easy access to multiple sources of information and advice, not all of them good, has created customers who feel more confident, knowledgeable, and empowered. The balance of power between suppliers and customers has shifted irrevocably. For example, more than 80 percent of prospective car buyers research their purchase online before entering the dealership: they compare product and pricing information, assess financing options, and check the value of their trade-in all before they ever step into the salesperson's lair. The Internet has become the first stop for those seeking the best airfares or searching for a new job. Despite the wealth of new information available to customers, more information does not necessarily mean better decision making. Organizations need to understand the implications of dealing with a better-informed if not necessarily smarter customer base.

The Illusion of Competence

An interesting phenomenon presents a conundrum as companies seek to get ever closer to their customers. I call this the "illusion of competence" and define it as the "aura of misplaced confidence resulting from the assimilation of too much free information or advice of questionable quality." It manifests itself when people gain so much new knowledge that they mistakenly believe that they are now experts.

The Internet has given this phenomenon a powerful stimulus. Large amounts of information can be accessed easily. Examples include people who buy something on eBay for more than they would have paid at the local store and boast about the great deal they got, or those who plunged into managing their own investments, gave up their real jobs to become day traders, and boasted of having "got into Yahoo at $106 or Ariba at $75." These are probably the same individuals who started suing their online brokers when the market crashed in late 2000 or entered the Las Vegas real estate market in late 2005. Simply because customers can access millions of pages of free information and compare and contrast thousands of different products from the comfort of their armchairs does not guarantee that they will be transformed from suckers to seers.

Regardless of whether more information makes one smarter or just confused, there is no doubt that it is changing business. Organizations have unparalleled access to data about customers, suppliers, employees, and competitors that can provide managers with greater knowledge in order to make better decisions. Purchasing managers are able to ascertain complete pricing information for any item before entering into negotiations for suppliers. A human resources manager can compare the salaries being offered for different positions to ensure that the organization remains competitive; employees can do the same. Throughout the organization, people have access to better information; those who can take advantage can realize real benefits fast.

CHANGING MARKET AND BUSINESS MODELS

For anyone seeking to understand today's rapidly changing markets, a look back to the Industrial Revolution can be enlightening. The Industrial Revolution was founded on three significant changes:

1. A whole series of technological innovations broke the relationship between human energy and productive capacity. Prior to the Industrial Revolution, farmers could only be as productive as their own capacity to harvest their crops, and weavers were limited by the amount of wool they could weave.
2. Rapid advances in transportation allowed raw materials to be moved from their point of origin to a different location for manufacture into a finished product. It is no coincidence that the Industrial Revolution first took hold in Great Britain, the country with the largest and most efficient shipping fleet in the world at the time.
3. The recognition that these advances demanded new and different operating models, such as factories, in order to fully leverage these technological innovations.

In a relatively short time, the main underpinning of economic activity moved from the farm to the factory, and the population moved from the countryside to the town. This shift from a largely rural society to one based in urban areas was the defining social impact of the Industrial Revolution and was driven by the need to concentrate labor to exploit the productive capacity unleashed by the new innovations of powered machinery.

The dominant organizing factor was colocation of all aspects of the production process in a series of logical steps. Vertical integration reached its zenith with Henry Ford's massive River Rouge plant just outside Detroit, Michigan. Set on 2,000 acres by the Rouge River, the plant, completed in 1927, was the largest single manufacturing complex in the United States. At its peak during World War II, it employed over 120,000 people. The plant was self-sufficient in all aspects of automobile production, from producing a continuous flow of iron ore and other raw materials to finished automobiles. The complex included dock facilities, blast furnaces, open-hearth steel mills, foundries, a rolling mill, metal stamping facilities, an engine plant, a glass manufacturing building, a tire plant, and a power house supplying steam and electricity. However, the dominance of vertically integrated businesses was already beginning to wane even as Ford constructed his industrial age masterpiece.

Organizations found that the capital and skill set requirements needed to sustain excellence in all aspects of the process were too great. It was easier and cheaper to outsource much of the design and manufacturing process.

By the dawn of the computer age, the main elements of an integrated supply chain from raw material extraction to delivery of the finished product to the customer were well established. Unfortunately, one downside of this process was the creation of a series of cumbersome, bureaucratic paper-based processes to move the information needed to sustain the production process. Documentation of orders, shipping notices, invoices, and payments grew at a rapid rate, triggering the creation of paper factories alongside the real factories in most large corporations. The computer was perfectly placed to address this challenge by automating much of the basic accounting and transaction processing activities. As electronic communications improved, networks facilitating electronic data interchange (EDI) attacked the flow of paper between organizations. Emergence of Internet-based e-commerce made these capabilities easier and cheaper, fueling rapid adoption by almost all organizations.

While physical goods and services remain important, information-based services comprise an increasing share of the economy. In 1991, capital spending in the United States on information technology ($112 billion) exceeded spending for production technology ($107 billion) for the first time. By 2005, investments in information technology had grown to $489 billion, with software accounting for 40 percent of the total.[2]

Beyond basic transaction-processing applications, organizations increasingly began to use the same technologies to share other information, such as design documents and contract information. With the arrival of e-mail and the Internet, no exchange of information was out of bounds. No longer were organizations required physically to colocate all their people or operations. The level of flexibility is such that a company like Boeing can relocate its corporate headquarters from Seattle to Chicago, occupying its new facility less than five months after making the initial announcement. Philip Condit, the company's then chairman and chief executive, described the reason for moving as "to be in a location central to our operating units, customers and the financial community, but separate from our existing operations."[3]

Today, a call to a credit card company may be routed to a customer service agent in Des Moines, Dublin, or Delhi, and the computer systems may be running in Prague or Poona. Basic business rules are being redefined; new products and markets are being created. Who would have thought that eBay, essentially an automated flea market, could sustain a $35 billion market capitalization (up from $20 billion in 2002), Google $113 billion (as of August 2006), or that General Motors would employ less than 20 percent of its workforce in actually making cars? Such changes require ever more flexible performance management processes and demand new and different types of management information.

Technology is literally changing the physics of business. Barriers of geography and scale have been redefined. Booksellers do not need stores, telephone companies do not need networks, manufacturers do not need factories, and film companies do not need film studios. Amazon did not need to establish a physical retail presence to compete with traditional booksellers. E*Trade and Ameritrade did not need thousands of highly trained and highly compensated brokers to shake up the retail securities industry. Whether all these disruptive players survive is not the point; in each case, established players, such as Barnes & Noble and Merrill Lynch, were forced to respond.

Technology has enabled new entrants to enter markets with a new and differentiated service offering that has had a major impact on the traditional players. Companies are creating new products and services and inventing new ways to interact with current and prospective customers. Nike has created a $13 billion business and a very powerful brand based almost exclusively around design and marketing. Others, such as Dell and Cisco, have developed very successful product businesses while owning little manufacturing capacity.

Changing Market Boundaries or Arbitraging Harry Potter

In the summer of 1999, the third book in the hugely successful Harry Potter series written by English author J. K. Rowling was published. The launch of *Harry Potter and the Prisoner of Azkaban* was scheduled to follow a fairly typical rollout plan. To manage the associated advertising and promotional campaigns, the publication dates in each market were to be staggered throughout the summer in much the same way as for the opening of a new film. The initial release was to be in England, the author's home country, followed a few weeks later by release in the United States. Traditionally, this process had worked well, but this time things were very different.

The Harry Potter series had become a publishing phenomenon, doing for children's fantasy what John Grisham did for the courtroom and Stephen King did for the horror story. The level of interest in the new book was huge. CNN ran stories about the new book's publication; bookstores scheduled midnight openings so that eager readers could be first to snare their copies of the book. The hype, itself a function of the increasing global and instantaneous nature of communications, was unprecedented. There was also another crucial ingredient: A new medium was available—the online bookseller. What followed was a sequence of events that would have profound implications for the way new products were brought to market in the future.

Back in 1998, Amazon.com, the pioneering Internet retailer, launched a U.K. service, Amazon.co.uk, following its acquisition of online bookseller Bookpages. The difference with most other expansions was that in this case, now anyone in the world who had a computer and Internet connection could access Amazon's new U.K. Web site. The impending launch of *Harry Potter and the Prisoner of Azkaban* presented a unique opportunity. Devoted fans as well as some entrepreneurial individuals quickly logged on to Amazon.co.uk and ordered the new book. Soon there was a flourishing gray market in the United States for copies of the book. Many people were prepared to pay three, four, or even five times the cover price to secure a copy before the official U.S. publication date. Technology had decimated the traditional definition of a market and forever altered the planning assumptions associated with launching new products.

By the time the fourth book in the series, *Harry Potter and the Goblet of Fire*, was ready for publication in July 2000, the lesson had been learned. There was a simultaneous launch across the globe. Notwithstanding the logistical challenges of this launch, the hype was even greater. Television cameras covered the unique publishing event, and the launch was the most successful yet seen, only to be surpassed by the launch of the fifth and sixth books.

An organization's performance management processes must address the dual effects of simultaneously achieving much tighter integration up and down the supply chain combined with the effects of globalization and its impact on redefining markets. The need for timely, accurate information is much greater yet the organization's ability to mandate its provision is weakened. Similarly, planning is no longer an internal process; it requires the participation and collaboration of numerous players, some of whom also may be doing significant business with a firm's biggest competitors. It does not matter how many personal computers Dell manages to sell if its suppliers are unable to supply enough parts to meet the demand.

STRUCTURAL CHANGE IN THE ECONOMICS OF BUSINESS

The 1970s were a bleak time for the traditional stalwarts of the western economy. The three-pronged attack of sky-high oil prices, rising inflation, and aggressive competition from fast-growing, lower-cost Asian economies decimated whole segments of the North American and European economies. Some segments, such as consumer electronics, textiles, and shipbuilding, effectively disappeared. Others, such as iron and steel, automotive, and many manufacturing segments, were forever changed. In the space of a single decade, much of the foundation on which the Industrial Revolution was built was dismantled. If there was a positive effect of this brutal transformation, it was the increased focus on all aspects of productivity, quality, and cost management that took hold as management recognized that operational efficiency was a prerequisite for survival, let alone growth. Even successful companies were forced through a radical transformation. Exhibit 1.3 shows that, in 1980, General Electric derived 85 percent of its revenue from manufacturing; by 2000, this had been reduced to 30 percent, even as revenues grew from $25 billion to $125 billion.

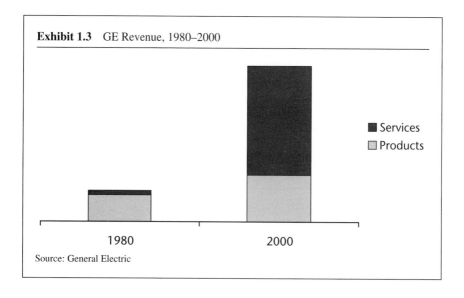

Exhibit 1.3 GE Revenue, 1980–2000

Services
Products

1980   2000

Source: General Electric

During the 1980s, the manufacturing sector led the way in realizing productivity gains as it fought for survival in the face of intense global competition. Process innovations using tools such as total quality management (TQM), outsourcing, and just-in-time (JIT) manufacturing drove significant change and productivity improvement. The results were impressive—between 1981 and 1991, manufacturing productivity as measured by the U.S. Bureau of Labor Statistics increased 34 percent.

However, as at GE, the focus of the economy was shifting—manufacturing was no longer the dominant segment. The U.S. economy no longer caught a cold just because General Motors sneezed. In 1950, manufacturing was the largest sector of the economy, accounting for more than 33 percent of all nonfarm employment. However, by the end of 1998, manufacturing had shrunk to less than 15 percent. While the manufacturing sector was declining, the service sector was rapidly gaining in importance, growing from 12 percent of all nonfarm payroll jobs in 1950 to 31 percent in 1998, and had supplanted manufacturing as the largest industrial sector. By the end of 2001, Wal-Mart had become the world's largest company with sales of over $217 billion. Farther down the list over half of the top 100 companies on the Fortune list were service companies. By 2006, Wal-Mart had lost its number-one spot to Exxon-Mobil but had still grown sales to almost $315 billion, and 60 of top 100 companies were primarily service providers.

Despite its rise to prominence, service sector productivity lagged behind that of manufacturing from 1981 to 2001. Between 1981 and 1991, service sector productivity improved by only 17 percent—half the rate of manufacturing (see Exhibit 1.4). Over the next 10 years, the rate of improvement grew to 24 percent but still lagged behind manufacturing, which achieved an impressive 46 percent improvement.

Manufacturing companies recognized that survival and competitiveness demanded continuous improvements in productivity and quality and reductions in costs. Fast-growing service companies were ready to embrace the new technologies that were fueling their growth. The result was an explosion in best practice innovation in core business practices. As the productivity data show, manufacturing led the way. Alcoa, Chrysler, Dow Chemical, and Honeywell (formerly AlliedSignal) drove substantial improvements in productivity throughout their operating processes and adapted many of the best practice techniques they developed in their core operations to back-office processes, such as finance and human resources. Service companies did not stand still; they began to translate practices developed on the plant floor to their own processes as well as driving technology-enabled improvements through critical areas of their business, such as customer service and support.

The combination of retrenchment in the manufacturing sector and rapid growth in services placed significant strain on traditional planning, budgeting, forecasting, and reporting processes and created significant impetus for innovation. During the first years of the twenty-first century, there were numerous signs that improvements in service sector productivity were accelerating. Many companies began to realize significant operating efficiencies as they deployed new technologies that targeted core service sector processes, such as customer relationship management (CRM), call centers, and customer self-service. Companies such as eBay, Google, Netflix,

Exhibit 1.4 U.S. Productivity, 1981–2001

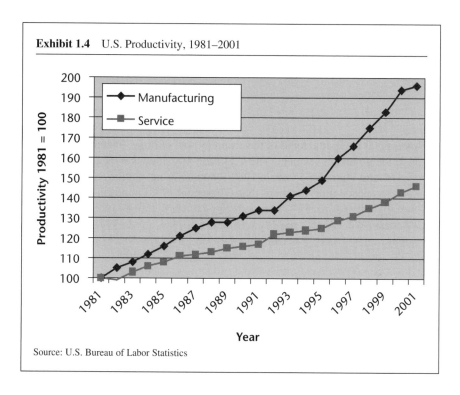

Source: U.S. Bureau of Labor Statistics

Vonage, and Skype (acquired by eBay in 2005) introduced new business models that were rapidly adopted. Further innovations such as Apple's iPod and iTunes, Tivo, exchange-traded funds, and craigslist began to disrupt traditional marketplaces and business models. The effect was to further imperil static, calendar-driven, financially focused performance management processes.

With respect to performance management, significant increases in volatility, competition, and globalization, combined with the increase in the amount of data being produced from new systems and the introduction of new tools to analyze and report the resultant information, has increased management focus. As we shall see later, the technology enablers have often proven to be double-edged swords.

REGULATORY REVOLUTION

The election of Margaret Thatcher as prime minister of the United Kingdom in 1979 and Ronald Reagan as president of the United States a year later ushered in a radically different regulatory environment on both sides of the Atlantic. Thatcher reversed over 30 years of tight regulation and increasing government ownership of major businesses. Whole industries, such as telecommunications and utilities, were turned almost overnight from monopolies into competitive markets. Rolls-Royce and British Airways were privatized and emerged as strong competitors in their respective markets. In the United States, the breakup of AT&T in 1984 triggered a transformation in the telecommunications industry that served as a precursor to subsequent relaxation of regulation in many other industries, such as financial services, gas, and electricity. Many other countries followed suit albeit at a slower pace. Even changes in political leadership, with the Democrats and Bill Clinton taking the White House in 1992 and Tony Blair and the Labour Party ending 18 years of Conservative leadership in the United Kingdom in 1997, did not reverse the trend. Although the merits of more or less regulation are not the subject of this book, it is clear that regulatory change has been a powerful stimulant for many of the changes that have taken place over the last 20 years. Changing regulation creates great opportunity but also great risks that an organization's performance management processes need to address. The U.S. telecommunications industry provides a chilling case study of the volatility and risk that regulation can create.

Before the passage of the 1996 Telecommunications Act, local telephone service was a simple, sedate, and very profitable business. Long-distance service, while less profitable, was dominated by three large players, AT&T, MCI (soon to become WorldCom), and Sprint, companies that together commanded 85 percent of the market in 1995. Deregulation changed the picture overnight. The intent of the act as defined by the Federal Communications Commission (FCC) was "to let anyone enter any communications business—to let any communications business compete in any market against any other." Local markets were opened up to competition, ownership restrictions were relaxed, and a number of other provisions were designed to facilitate greater access to different telecommunications markets by both existing and new players. For the first time, local service providers had to focus on customer service, competitive pricing, and productivity improvement to remain competitive. Overnight, a relatively stable, slow-moving industry was transformed into a Wild West shoot-out. Compounding the effect was that the act was passed at precisely the same time as the Internet was exploding. Americans seemed to have an insatiable thirst for communication capacity, or bandwidth. The number of companies seeking to participate in the market exploded from 3,000 in 1995 to over 4,800 by 1999. During the same period, over $2 trillion was invested in the telecommunications sector. Stock prices of new entrants, such as Winstar and Global Crossing, soared. Equipment makers Cisco, Lucent, and Nortel all reported record sales and earnings. A true revolution was under way. Unfortunately, it was all a house of cards. In a collapse reminiscent of that in the railway industry a century earlier, the bubble burst in less than two years. Winstar, Global Crossing, and WorldCom filed for bankruptcy. Qwest, Lucent, and Nortel saw their stock prices decline more than 90 percent, losing their chief executive officers (CEOs) in the process. Paper losses of over $2 trillion were recorded as the industry's collective market capitalization dropped by over 60 percent. During the boom, an estimated 39 million miles of fiber optic cable had been laid in the United States; by early 2002, less than 10 percent of that cable was being used. Subsequently even the established players succumbed as AT&T, MCI, Nextel, GTE, Ameritech and others all were acquired during another major wave of industry consolidation.

How many of the participants in this process saw the warning signs? Did their strategic planning processes ever contemplate that the demand for all the capacity that was being built was simply not there? Did their reporting and forecasting processes provide any advance warning that revenues were never likely to grow to a sufficient level to service all debt taken on, let alone make a profit for investors?

We learn from this and other examples, such as the fallout in the energy industry from events at Enron, that the positive and negative effects of changing regulation must constantly be considered in any organization's planning process.

GROWTH THROUGH ACQUISITION AS THE NORMAL COURSE OF BUSINESS

Mergers, acquisitions, and divestitures have long been part of the commercial world. Many of the early twentieth-century powerhouses, such as Standard Oil, General Motors, and Westinghouse, used acquisitions as a vehicle for growth. In the 1960s, often termed the age of the conglomerate, companies including ITT and United Technologies hit the acquisition trail. However, it was not until the 1980s that mergers and acquisitions (M&A) became an everyday business activity. Easier access to capital through junk bonds and the like fueled a boom in hostile takeovers and leveraged buyouts. In 1981, there were just 1,000 such deals completed worldwide with a total value of about $90 billion; by 1999, the number of deals had increased to more than 32,000, and the value was an astonishing $1.1 trillion. The economic boom of the 1990s combined with changing regulations in many industries sustained the wave of activity. Volume declined during 2001 and 2002 but by 2005 was back to record levels.

Cisco completed 50 acquisitions in the three years from 1998 to 2000, 23 of which came in 2000 alone. Thereafter the pace slackened somewhat, but the company still completed 12 deals in 2005. For many companies, acquisitions became a way to acquire new products or market access without having to do all the work themselves.

Despite the increasing popularity of M&A activity, the track record has been very uneven. At the outset, every deal promises significant benefits to investors and shareholders—that organizations will become leaner and more competitive, and tremendous synergies will be realized, delivering significant cost reductions. However, the reality is often very different.

Larry Bossidy described what he found on becoming CEO of Allied-Signal (now Honeywell) in 1991, a company created through a series of acquisitions made in 1980s:

> Allied-Signal had no productivity culture . . . . Individual businesses were allowed to have their own identities.[4]

I was a consultant to the company at the time and could recognize the truth in Bossidy's statement. Employees described themselves as working for Bendix or Garrett or one of the other acquired companies, rather than for Allied-Signal. Each business had its own set of financial systems and its own unique planning and reporting processes. Those systems and processes did not survive for long under

Bossidy's focused leadership. One small action early in his tenure set the tone: He removed the hyphen from the company name. Allied-Signal became AlliedSignal, a single company focused on operational excellence.

Even in situations where the postmerger integration pain is less, companies often find that new acquisitions create significant cultural, operational, and technological challenges. Problems range from getting diverse organizations to work together, to integrating the patchwork quilt of systems that most acquisitions create. Notwithstanding the variable track record, the use of acquisitions as a normal part of business has increased, introducing a whole new set of planning variables and information needs. Traditionally, M&A analysis has been handled outside of the core planning and management reporting process. This works fine until the level of activity reaches the point where day-to-day operating decisions are impacted by the level of M&A activity. Many high-technology and pharmaceutical companies fuel their research and development processes by taking stakes in or acquiring smaller companies.

The ability to continually scan the marketplace for potential acquisition targets—to develop sophisticated valuation and funding models to assess the real worth of any transaction—and the need to include acquisition-driven growth in strategic, tactical, and financial plans are all driving new planning and information requirements. Bank of America has grown from a small North Carolina bank to the rank third on *Fortune* magazine's Global 2000 list for 2006 with sales of $85 billion, profits of $16 billion, and assets of $1.3 trillion largely through a 30-year program of acquisitions. Two of its most recent deals, the acquisitions of FleetBoston and MBNA, went from concept to public announcement in less than two weeks, which reflects the need for timely and rapid analysis to support decision making.

REDEFINING ASSET VALUES

Traditionally, an organization's assets were tangible, physical things. Property, plant, equipment, and inventory made up the bulk of the assets of any organization and were reflected as such on the balance sheet. However, as the economy has evolved from a manufacturing focus to a service focus, the ability to relate an organization's true value to its hard assets has become much more difficult. Organizational success is increasingly tied to intangible assets, such as intellectual property, brands, skills, and customer franchises. While the valuation of such assets is problematic, no one can doubt that Coca-Cola or Nike's brand, Nordstrom's service levels, and NASCAR's loyal fan base are not valuable assets. Even a faded intangible asset can have considerable value; when SBC acquired AT&T in 2005, it considered the tarnished brand to still possess such value that it took the AT&T name.

The challenge for many organizations is that their performance management processes are much more closely aligned with the older tangible assets model than the newer intangible assets model. How many plans or reports clearly identify the return expected from investments made in proprietary intellectual capital, brands, customer franchises, or talented people?

CHANGING DELIVERY CHANNELS

Just as the introduction of postal service and telephones created new channels for selling and service, the Internet has created a new channel between suppliers and customers. Companies that were comfortable using one or perhaps two primary channels for getting their products to market are now dealing with multiple channels through multiple intermediaries. Traditional sales forces are learning to interact with Web-based direct selling. Companies are managing potential conflicts between selling their products directly to their customers over the Web and upsetting long-standing retail partners or internal sales forces by introducing an alternative channel that bypasses them. For example, Levi-Strauss encountered significant resistance from its traditional retail partners when it started selling its products online but barred them from selling Levi's and Dockers on their own Web sites. After months of high costs and poor sales, Levi's pulled the plug on selling from its own Web sites and developed partnerships with J.C. Penney, Kohl's, Macy's, and others to sell Levi merchandise on their sites, a change that solved the initial conflict issue. Charles Schwab solved the conflict between its retail offices and its online presence by ensuring that retail offices received full credit for all online business conducted by clients in the territory of each office. Best Buy turned another potential channel conflict into a marketing campaign by advertising that anything bought online could be returned to a store for a full refund—solving a problem that many other multichannel retailers initially failed to address adequately.

Increasing channel complexity adds yet another layer to the variables that need to be addressed by a company's performance management processes. Managers have to be able to develop plans that reflect multiple combinations of product, channel, and customer and the complex relationships between each.

COMPRESSED CYCLE TIMES

The need for increased speed has been one of the dominant themes of the last 200 years. In transportation, the evolution from horses, to stagecoaches, to trains, to planes has progressively shortened the time it takes to move people and product. In communications, the corresponding progression from mail, to telegraph, to fax, to broadband connection speeds data across the globe at ever-faster rates. The ability to execute flawlessly at great speed has become a distinctive competitive weapon. Drive-through windows at restaurants, banks, and dry cleaners, E-ZPass tollbooths, Disney's Fastpass, FedEx's Custom Critical, and Domino's Pizza have all successfully used speed as a distinctive product feature. It seems that everything in the business world is being driven by an insatiable desire for speed.

In their 1990 book, *Competing against Time: How Time-Based Competition Is Reshaping Global Markets*, George Stalk and Thomas Hout provided a powerful argument regarding the role of time in competitive success.[5] In the years since the book was published, little has occurred to weaken their fundamental proposition that time is a key driver of competitive advantage.

Despite the increased focus on speed and cycle time, most companies have relatively few time-based measurements in their plans or standard management reports. Typically targets and measures focus on broad areas, such as product development cycles, on-time delivery rates, and processing cycle times. Many organizations have little understanding of the trade-offs among speed, cost, and service quality that must be managed.

Elements of Time-Based Competition

- Time to market for new products and services from concept to realization
- Time to deliver products and services to the customer
- Time to close the books
- Time to hire new staff
- Time to deploy new staff
- Time for new staff to achieve full productivity
- Time to make key decisions
- Time to complete major business transactions
- Time to obsolescence for equipment and products
- Time to integrate acquisitions
- Time to respond to competitive actions
- Time to realize value from new technology investments
- Time to enter a new market

VAST NEW INFORMATION SOURCES

Peter Drucker talks about information replacing authority in organizations, Bill Gates describes the digital nervous system, and Australia even has a National Office for the Information Economy. The sheer volume of data now available is staggering. Samuel Taylor Coleridge, in the classic poem "The Rime of the Ancient Mariner," wrote: "Water, water, everywhere, nor any drop to drink." Many executives feel the same way about data. Plagiarizing Coleridge, the phrase "Data, data everywhere, nor any information to make a decision" accurately reflects the feelings of many business managers.

A study conducted by the School of Information Management and Systems at the University of California at Berkeley in 2000 estimated that the world produces between 1 and 2 exabytes of unique information per year, which is roughly 250 megabytes or the text of 250 books for every man, woman, and child on earth.[6] (An exabyte is a billion gigabytes, or 1,018 bytes.) The numbers are beyond comprehension, and they are getting bigger. Today all businesses rely heavily on information to drive every aspect of their operation. Wal-Mart has grown to be a $312 billion behemoth in a seemingly mundane industry: retailing. Although the company's success often has been attributed to the culture associated with its founder, Sam Walton, and its commitment to "everyday low prices," a more significant contributor has been driven by its use of computer systems that allow it to better manage inventory and track customer demand. FedEx, another success story of the last 30 years, redefined another simple business: package delivery. Again, a key element in FedEx's success has been the innovative use of technology to manage the flow of millions of individual shipments every day. Spend a few hours in the company's main Memphis, Tennessee, hub and the power of technology in enabling the business is clear. For a period in the late 1990s, the company built much of its advertising around its ability to tell users precisely where their packages were at any point in time. FedEx was using its ability to provide information about package delivery rather than the basic service itself as a selling point. Both Wal-Mart and FedEx have been able to profitably redefine seemingly mundane businesses through their ability to better manage information and turn it into better business decision making, allowing them to outpace more established rivals.

Conversely, too much information can be an impediment to effective management. On becoming CEO of General Electric in 1981, Jack Welch found that detail dominated the planning process. As Welch describes in his biography, *Straight from the Gut*: "These [planning] books were the lifeblood of the bureaucracy . . . . I never wanted to see a planning book before the person presented it. To me the value of these sessions wasn't in the books. It was in the heads and hearts of the people who were coming into Fairfield [GE's headquarters]."[7]

The task of managing the vast amounts of data coursing through the veins of the modern business is not going to get easier any time soon. The digitization of much of the information flow between suppliers and customers and between companies and their associates is providing a major opportunity to capture the meaningful insight they need. The driving force behind the development and deployment of best practices in planning and management reporting is the desire to leverage the data effectively without overwhelming the recipient.

RIGHT TECHNOLOGY

The final and most potent ingredient is technology. As with the inventions that triggered the Industrial Revolution in the eighteenth and nineteenth centuries, technological innovation is the yeast in the recipe of economic growth. Born in England in the second half of the eighteenth century, the Industrial Revolution was the result of a confluence of new ideas and inventions, including the spinning jenny (1765), Richard Arkwright's water frame (1790), and James Watt's steam engine (1782), that transformed the cotton industry and made the factory method of production possible. Aided by further developments, such as the railway, the ingredients were in place for a transformation of the once-agrarian economy to a factory-based economy. The same scenario has clearly been repeating itself during the early years of the twenty-first century.

The pace of technological change continues to be frenetic. Less than 20 years ago, the personal computer (PC) was in its infancy, databases were rudimentary, and the Internet was merely a government and academic network. Computers were housed in specially constructed buildings, and reports consumed vast quantities of green-and-white lined paper that spewed endlessly from industrial-strength printers. Today computers transact billions of dollars' worth of business every day, and corporations tap vast reservoirs of data housed in multidimensional databases. It seems that as soon as an organization starts deploying the latest new system, it is immediately made obsolete by the next generation.

More specifically, the convergence of three distinct technologies has fueled a transformation every bit as potent as the Industrial Revolution:

1. Improvements in the price/performance ratio of technology
2. Development of integrated package software offerings
3. Availability of high-bandwidth, low-cost communications

The dramatic improvements in the price/performance ratio of computer and communications technology have made it economical to place computing power wherever it can add value, from the supermarket checkout to the truck cab. Moore's law, named after Gordon Moore, one of the founders of Intel, encapsulated the exponential growth in performance. In 1965, Moore observed that the number of transistors per square inch on an integrated circuit had doubled every year since the integrated circuit was invented. He predicted that this trend would continue for the foreseeable future—and he was right (see Exhibit 1.5). The reduction in the relative cost of computing power is even more startling. By 2006, a Dell 3.8 GHz (GigaHertz) PC could be purchased for around $1,600, about half the price of an IBM PC/XT in 1983; however, the Dell machine was a staggering 1 million times faster than its predecessor.

The second advance saw the rapid commercialization of software into integrated suites of standard applications supporting basic business functions, such as accounts payable, payroll, and general ledger. Data processing no longer requires the development of custom applications to execute core business transactions or transform transaction data into usable information. Package software provides proven functionality at much lower risk with a lower overall cost of ownership than custom-developed software. The final piece of the technology puzzle has been the emergence of low-cost, ubiquitous, and easy-to-use mechanisms for communication, collaboration, and commerce. E-mail, the Internet, and wireless and broadband communications offer multiple ways for people to share information and communicate in both synchronous and asynchronous ways. By 2005, it was estimated that there were 120 million U.S. broadband subscribers, an increase of 36 percent in a little over a year.[8]

The convergence of powerful computers, sophisticated software, and ubiquitous high-speed communications has provided the catalyst for much of the advances

Exhibit 1.5 Moore's Law

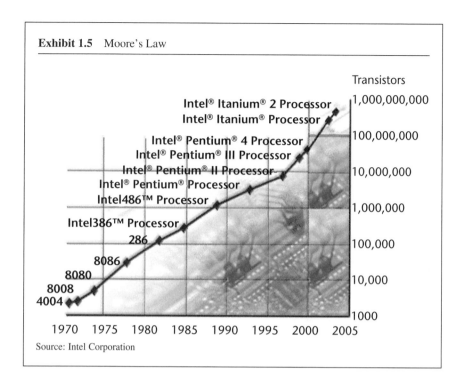

Source: Intel Corporation

seen during the last 20 years. Alan Greenspan, chairman of the Federal Reserve, described the phenomena in a speech in June 2001:

> The inexorably rising share of the nation's output that is conceptual appears to have accelerated following World War II with the insights that led to the development of the transistor, microprocessor, laser, and fiber optic technologies. By the 1990s, these and other critical innovations had fostered an enormous new capacity to capture, analyze, and disseminate information and had begun to alter significantly how we do business and create economic value, often in ways that were not foreseeable even a decade ago. Indeed, it is the proliferation of information technology throughout the economy that makes the current period so special.[9]

The continuous advances in technology create new opportunities that offer enormous potential benefits while also creating new risks. Applications that only a few years ago were science fiction are now everyday reality. Buying a soda using your cell phone, printing tickets for a concert on your home printer, purchasing a book at 3 A.M., or sending a photograph of the kids to their grandparents seconds after it was taken were all far-fetched notions that are now commonplace. Unfortunately, so are viruses that destroy users' computers, hackers who crash users' systems, and thieves who steal people's identities. Despite the risks, organizations feel under tremendous pressure to implement every new innovation. Fear of being at a competitive disadvantage drives a pace of adoption that allows little margin for error and is unlikely to slacken. Periodic breathers, such as that induced in the post–dot-com era, will occur, but the relentless pace of technological innovation and adoption is inexorable, and business performance management is moving into the eye of the storm. While much work remains to clean up the inefficiencies that remain in the core operational processes, many organizations are shifting their focus. They want to move beyond simple transaction processing and reporting; they want to use the information they now have to make better decisions, faster. Nimble, flexible planning processes and rich, targeted reporting are two important elements in enhancing an organization's decision-making ability.

NEED FOR A BURNING PLATFORM

Even though all the ingredients were in place, progress toward the development and adoption of best practices for performance management was relatively slow. Although manufacturing, supply chain, and accounting processes underwent significant change throughout the 1990s, most companies muddled along with slow, bureaucratic, detailed budgeting processes that created plans that were largely obsolete the day they were created. In essence, many managers were flying blind and didn't really care.

However, it was rare for the pain to be sufficient to trigger a fundamental redesign of the performance management processes. For most of the 1990s, business was good; sales and profits were growing. Some commentators even went so far as to predict the death of the normal economic cycle of alternating periods of growth and recession. In such an environment, imperfections were an irritant but not a major problem. However, that was all about to change.

Beginning in March 2000, a series of events dramatically changed the business climate and brought the problems inherent in the planning and reporting processes sharply into focus. On March 10, 2000, the Nasdaq Market Index reached a new high of 5,048. It then began a decline that saw the index fall to less than 1,400 by the summer of 2002, over a 70 percent decline. Aside from wiping out billions of dollars of paper wealth, the decline precipitated a massive shakeout in the nascent dot-com segment. More important, it ushered in a new era of realism. The speed of the slowdown was so rapid that few companies had any forewarning. Annual budgets set only weeks earlier were suddenly obsolete. The much-vaunted visibility offered by integrated sales and supply-chain forecasting systems failed to materialize in the time of greatest need.

The effects of the shakeout in the technology industry started to ripple through the economy. The broader U.S. stock market indices began to decline in the third quarter of 2000. The Standard and Poor's (S&P) 500 peaked at a little over 1,500 before starting its decline to less than 900 by the summer of 2002. While it fell less than the technology-heavy Nasdaq, the S&P 500 still declined by 40 percent.

Starting in the fourth quarter of 2000, company after company was forced to admit that it had little or no visibility into its future business prospects. The number of public companies forced to make negative earnings preannouncements doubled from just a year earlier—a damning indictment given the amount of effort expended on planning, budgeting, and forecasting. Throughout the rest of 2000, a steady stream of high-technology business failures rocked investor confidence and the first signs of a mainstream economic slowdown appeared with the usual round of layoffs and expense reductions.

The dawn of 2001 offered no respite from the bad news. In May, Cisco, one of the acknowledged leaders in developing a highly integrated e-business and much admired for its flexibility and responsiveness, announced a $2.25 billion inventory write-down. In July, Webvan, one of the most heavily financed and lauded Internet-based businesses, closed its doors after spending $830 million of investors' money without ever turning a profit. As if this stream of bad news was not enough, then came the terrorist attacks of September 11, 2001.

The economic impact was immediate as fear and uncertainty resulted in slashed spending plans and a deepening of the economic crisis. Adding further fuel to the fire on December 2, 2001, Enron Corporation—ranked fifth on that year's Fortune 500 list—filed for bankruptcy protection amid accusations of fraud, deception, and false accounting. Additional bankruptcy filings from Kmart, WorldCom, and Global Crossing, and the collapse of Arthur Andersen, one of the oldest and largest accounting firms, added to the general uncertainty.

The passage of the Sarbanes-Oxley Act in 2002 ushered in a new era for corporate managers; integrity in reporting and accuracy in forecasting were no longer optional. The cumulative effect of all these events served to highlight the shortcomings of the typical planning and performance management process. No CEO likes to admit to having no insight into the future performance of the business, let alone being seen as anything less than ethical in his or her stewardship. Improving the quality, accuracy, and efficiency of all aspects of planning and reporting moved rapidly to the top of the management agenda. Investors began demanding greater assurance that reported numbers were based on sound business and accounting principles. Future plans and other forward-looking statements were placed under intense scrutiny.

The effects of corporate failures and new regulations initiated a significant economic restructuring that continues apace. At the time of writing, the automotive and airline industries continue to struggle despite sales recovering to record levels after the post 9/11 decline. Merger activity in financial services, retail, telecommunications, and many other industries is at new record levels. The velocity of change has only been multiplied by the effects of the War on Terror, $70-per-barrel oil prices, Hurricanes Katrina and Rita, the Asian tsunami, and other one-time events that have battered many parts of the world.

The need for best practices for effectively managing in today's increasingly volatile and uncertain world has never been greater.

NOTES

1. Mintel International Group, March 8, 2006.
2. Digest of Education Statistics 2004, National Center for Education Statistics, Table 278.

3. John S. McClenahen, "Where Will Boeing Land?" *Industry Week*, May 5, 2001.

4. Larry Bossidy and Ram Charan, *Execution* (New York: Crown Business, 2002), p. 2.

5. George Stalk and Thomas Hout, *Competing Against Time: How Time-Based Competition Is Reshaping Global Markets* (New York: Free Press, 1990).

6. Peter Lyman and Hal R. Varian, *How Much Information* (Berkeley: School of Information Management & Systems, University of California, 2000).

7. Jack Welch with John A. Byrne, *Jack—Straight from the Gut* (New York: Warner Books, 2001), pp. 93–94.

8. Nielsen/NetRatings, October 2005.

9. Alan Greenspan, "The Growing Need for Skills in the 21st Century," speech before the U.S. Department of Labor 21st Century Workforce Summit, Washington, D.C., June 20, 2001.

Chapter 2

Performance Management Defined

The budgeting process at most companies has to be the most ineffective practice in management.

—Jack Welch, *Winning*

Jack Welch's comment refers to only one aspect of the performance management process, but its implications are significant since most companies still make the budget the cornerstone of their performance management process. Budgets: define the targeted level of performance for the business; are the basis for communication of expectations to investors, managers, and employees; define how resources will be allocated; and typically form the basis on which rewards are calculated. Few executives cite the budget as their most valued management tool, although it should be.

The effects of changing market boundaries, redefined supply chains, increased merger and acquisition (M&A) activity, better-informed customers, changing regulations, and shrinking cycle times discussed in Chapter 1 are placing tremendous pressure on planners to accommodate complexity and change into what have been largely static processes. In the face of such challenges, many managers are questioning whether their management processes are appropriately focused, fast, and integrated to accomplish their objectives. Best practice companies are rising to the challenge and taking a radical look at how they plan and manage. The need to be more agile, more responsive, and more tolerant of uncertainty demands that best practice compliance becomes a basic operating principle. Organizations are being forced to radically rethink their performance management processes. They are looking for tools that help them simplify the challenge. Best practices are just such a tool. They offer proven, commonsense approaches to dealing with many of the complexities managers face today.

Organizations need to adapt constantly if they are to achieve sustained success. An organization's performance management processes are the principal mechanism for assessing the impact of change and tuning the business in order to survive and prosper.

DEFINING BUSINESS PERFORMANCE MANAGEMENT AND BEST PRACTICES

Before embarking on a discussion of the value of implementing best practices, it is appropriate to provide definitions of business performance management and of best practices.

Business Performance Management

As with almost all business terms, no single accepted term or definition describes business performance management or as Gartner Research defined it in 2001— corporate performance management. For the purposes of this book, I will use this definition:

> Business performance management encompasses all the processes, information, and systems used by managers to set strategy, develop plans, monitor execution, forecast performance, and report results with a view to achieving sustainable success no matter how success maybe defined.

This simple definition is intentionally broad in scope and is not limited to organizations that have a for-profit motive, because many best practices are equally applicable to not-for-profit organizations. Given this overall definition, let's look at working definitions for the most common subprocesses that comprise a performance management process.

Strategic Planning

Strategic planning is the process of developing approaches to reach a defined objective. Simply put, strategy comprises the definition of a goal or objective and then describes the approaches an organization is going to take to achieve the goal. Strategic planning takes a broader and generally longer-term view than tactical planning, which describes the specific activities in which an organization is going to engage. Strategic planning seeks to define: an organization's purpose; the basis of its competitive differentiation; the markets in which it will participate and the position it will take in those markets; and how it will adapt to external changes in markets to take advantage of attractive opportunities or mitigate threats. Strategic planning also includes the definition of milestones or targets that track the organization's progress towards its goals and objectives. These targets serve as the primary input to the tactical planning process.

Tactical Planning

Tactical planning is the process of defining the tactics, initiatives, and allocation of resources required to meet agreed-on targets and overall business objectives and strategies that have been defined during the strategic planning and target-setting processes. Tactical planning includes: the development of tactics and initiatives to

sustain and improve current business operations and the evaluation and prioritization of new initiatives and projects at all levels of the organization to assess their
ability to contribute to the overall objectives and targets. This evaluation will include the definition of activities that should be continued, changed, commenced,
or stopped and the impact on resource requirements. Tactical planning begins after
management has completed the strategic planning process and established near-
term performance targets to guide more detailed planning. The tactical plan provides a road map for the organization. It identifies a destination, plots a course,
defines intermediate checkpoints on the journey, and estimates the resources required to complete the journey. An effective plan also provides insight into alternative routes that may be taken as obstacles or opportunities emerge during the
journey.

Financial Planning

Financial planning is the process of establishing financial plans and targets that describe the expected financial results from executing on the agreed portfolio of tactics designed to meet agreed performance targets and overall business objectives
and strategies. Financial planning includes: preparation and consolidation of plan/
target schedules; establishment of basic business and economic assumptions, guidelines, and timing requirements; development of budgets for operating expenses and
the use of capital; consolidation of plans for all major activities (e.g., sales, production, marketing, etc.); and the analysis, review, approval and commitment of all
plans by management and the board.

The tactical planning and financial planning processes are iterative as potential
tactics are evaluated in terms of their ability to contribute to meeting the organization's strategic objectives and achieving the targeted financial performance.

Management Reporting

Management reporting comprises all activities associated with the reporting of
performance measures, events, analysis, news, and other information to support
decision making. It includes, but is not necessarily limited to: reporting the results
of the current and prior period and forecasts of future periods; comparisons to
plans or to relevant external measures; calculation and reporting of all relevant performance measurements, both financial and nonfinancial; preparation of various
variance analyses comparing actual results to any comparison basis (e.g., to plan,
forecast, or market); preparation of various analyses around customer, product, and
organizational performance; fulfillment of ad hoc reporting requirements; consolidation; development, analysis, and presentation of business results; maintenance
of performance scorecards, and other reporting tools and systems. The information
reported to management comprises financial and nonfinancial, internal and external, predictive and historic data. Reporting requirements are a function of the roles
and responsibilities of the recipient, the goals and plans of the organization, and the
actual results achieved in executing those plans.

Forecasting

Forecasting is the process of periodically updating the current view of future business performance to reflect new or changing information. Forecasting includes: the preparation and consolidation of interim forecasts of various dimensions of performance, typically including external market factors such as market size and market share, sales, capital spending, production, operating expenses, and other key business measures; the preparation of variance analysis explaining the changes to the previous forecast or plan; reviews with management; and the discussion of any changes that should be made in light of the updated forecast. The difference between forecasting and tactical/financial planning can be described in this way: tactical/ financial planning is about defining action plans and targets for a fixed, typically annual period, while forecasting involves updating action plans periodically and revising near-term targets in response to actual or expected events.

Business Risk Management

Business risk management is the process of identifying, measuring, and assessing the potential impact on business performance of different risks and then developing strategies to manage the risk effectively. These strategies can include transferring the risk to another party, avoiding the risk, reducing the negative effect of the risk, accepting some or all of the consequences of a particular risk, or taking advantage of the risk if the return is adequate to compensate for the risk incurred. Business risk management can encompass many different types of risk from traditional financial risks, such as credit, interest rate, exchange rate, and market price risks, to risks such as product obsolescence, business continuity, reputation, and regulatory. The components of the risk management process are fivefold: (1) identification, (2) quantification of materiality, (3) estimation of probability, (4) agreement of need to manage, and (5) the development of appropriate risk management and mitigation techniques.

BEST PRACTICES DEFINED

Throughout this book we will use a definition of best practice that establishes a clear set of criteria that must be met. There are too many "better practices" out there masquerading as "best practices." Simply put, a best practice must:

- Effect a measurable change in performance
- Apply to a broad spectrum of organizations
- Be proven in practice
- Exploit proven technologies
- Ensure an acceptable level of control and risk management
- Match the skills and capabilities of the organization

Effect a Measurable Change in Performance

No organization consciously changes something without expecting benefits to accrue; unfortunately, all too often implementation does not translate into a measurable improvement in cost, quality, or service. A best practice allows an organization to achieve its maximum potential level of performance in the area to which it is applied and for that level of performance to be measured. This is the standard to which all best practice implementations must be held.

Apply to a Broad Spectrum of Organizations

For a best practice to have value, it must be applicable to a broad range of organizations; wide applicability distinguishes a best practice from a distinctive capability. A distinctive capability reflects a level of performance a company can achieve that is a function of a company's unique skills or abilities in an area. Examples of unique capabilities are those that result from internal innovation, proprietary knowledge, or some other driver of competitive advantage. In contrast, a best practice should be capable of being adopted by a wide range of organizations, given reasonable resources and commitment. This does not mean that all best practices can, or should, be applicable to all companies. Many best practices cannot, and in many cases should not, be adopted by all organizations. For example, the automotive industry has been a major driver of best practice design and deployment in the area of collaborative design and development. Automobile manufacturers and their suppliers have linked their design and engineering teams. When a new car is designed, the risks of quality and integration problems are minimized as the suppliers are participating directly in the design process. This works well in the automotive industry; however, for many companies, collaborative design is not either applicable or necessary. To merit consideration, a best practice should be applicable to more than one industry and more than one company; however, few best practices in performance management are broadly applicable to all companies. Typically the suitability of any particular best practice is a function of its match to a company's:

- Culture
- Strategy
- Level of maturity
- Internal structure
- Execution capability

In addition, use of a specific best practice may be best suited to organizations that share one or more common attributes. For example, best practices can be:

- *Industry-specific.* These are restricted to a small group of industries but still are capable of being leveraged by many participants in the industry, as in the case of collaborative design in the automotive industry.

- *Scale-driven.* Such best practices require a certain size or scale to effectively implement. Typically this applies to practices that require significant investment or that require a certain level of business activity to be economically justified. Until relatively recently, many software-enabled best practices required a significant investment in large, complex enterprise resource planning (ERP) systems. The introduction of lower-cost options, including Web-based services, has brought such best practices within reach of all but the very smallest businesses.

- *Regulatory.* There are legal barriers to implementation. For example, in some countries, companies have to provide the option for employees to be paid in cash or by check instead of mandating direct deposit, which is a best practice.

- *Business model–specific.* These types of best practice are applicable to companies that share a similar business strategy, practice, or model. For example, clearly defined best practices for companies that conduct business over the Internet or seek to target the affluent are not broadly applicable to companies that do not share that focus.

Be Proven in Practice

Perhaps the most important criterion is that a best practice must work. This sounds obvious, but many purported best practices that exist in the laboratory, business school, or a consultant's PowerPoint presentation have not been proven in practice. Although the ideas may be compelling and the logic incontrovertible, best practices exist only if they have been applied successfully. Given that best practices have to be proven to work, they have a lower risk profile and deliver results that are much more certain than those resulting from innovation or experimentation. Organizations run the risk that an experiment, masquerading as a best practice, may not be subjected to the same rigorous evaluation and management. This can significantly increase the risk of failure. Proof that a best practice really works should be demonstrable through both observation of the practice in operation and measurement of the results.

Exploit Proven Technologies

This is the most poorly applied criterion for defining a best practice. Since the advent of the computer, creative marketing and sales types have touted the almost limitless potential of technology to revolutionize the world. No self-respecting technology company would dare launch a new product that was not revolutionary, groundbreaking, or transformational. However, the gap between technology promise and delivery has proven dishearteningly wide. Jim Stent, who was a client of mine in the 1980s when he was senior vice president of the Bank of Thailand, eloquently expressed this point: "Our ability to create wondrous new technologies greatly outstrips our ability to use them effectively." He was right then and remains so today. Each new wave, from client-server, relational databases, data warehousing, decision support systems, knowledge management systems, to Web portals, has promised to redefine business best practices. While all these innovations have had some positive impact, often they have fallen short of the initial expectation or hype. For users to have confidence in a proposed best practice, it is essential for it to be based on proven technology, not vaporware.

Ensure an Acceptable Level of Control and Risk Management

Simply put, best practices are synonymous with a well-controlled and managed process. Clearly, a best practice that results in an unacceptable increase in risk is not really a best practice. Usually the problem lies in the way in which the best practice has been implemented. Simply eliminating approvals without implementing the other elements weakens the controls and increases the risk to an unacceptable level.

At a minimum, best practices must maintain the existing level of control. In many cases, they increase the level of control and reduce overall risk. The visibility of best practices has even reached the White House. In the fallout from the collapse of Enron, the *Washington Post* reported in March 2002 that the White House was proposing that "[a]uditors . . . would be required to gauge a firm's accounting systems by measuring against 'best practices,' not simply against minimum standards."[1]

Match the Skills and Capabilities of the Organization

Implementing a best practice without ensuring that the skills are in place to leverage the practice fully is a common mistake. It does not make sense to try to implement the best practice unless the required capabilities are available or there is an explicit plan to acquire or develop them. For example, a large financial institution decided that the balanced scorecard would be an effective management tool. It embarked on an initial deployment and communicated the value of using scorecards across the organization. Less than two years later, the company found that there were over 10,000 scorecards in operation and that it was costing over $25 million a year to maintain them. More damaging was that there was little or no consistency or linkage between the scorecards; many areas had scorecards that reported excellent performance while overall company performance was stagnant. Another company pursued the design of an executive information system to report key performance metrics to senior management. One of the highest-priority measures was the ability to report daily sales by product. As design progressed, it became apparent that this was going to be nearly impossible because of constraints in the order processing system. Only 70 percent of sales locations captured order information on a daily basis; the rest entered order information once a week. Thus an accurate daily figure was impossible to ascertain. An additional problem that in the end took even longer to address was that the 70 percent of locations that could enter sales directly into the order entry system used 15 different product-numbering schemes and over 14,000 different product and packaging combinations. An apparently simple request proved to be well beyond the capability of the organization without significant additional effort.

TYPES OF BEST PRACTICE

Best practices come in many shapes and sizes. There are best practices around policy, process, information, organization, people, and technology. Taken together, best practices provide a comprehensive framework for designing, implementing, and operating at the optimal level of performance.

Policy best practices establish the standards and rules that govern the operation of the overall process. Effective policies are logical, practical, and ensure consistency and compliance without limiting flexibility. Process best practices describe the method by which an activity or task is accomplished. Processes are the building blocks around which any organization is based. For example, a recipe takes a set of ingredients and lays out a process that, the cook hopes, transforms them into a delectable dish. In the same way, a strategic plan takes an idea and translates it into an action plan; a budget takes the action plan and translates it into a financial representation of how resources will be allocated.

Information best practices describe the information needed to initiate the process, track progress, and verify completion. Information infuses all aspects of a process; it encompasses specific measures of the process as well as contextual information that help managers understand the continuing value of the process. It can be as simple as checking the larder to see if all the ingredients are there to make the recipe or as complex as years of research to identify exactly the right combination of chemicals to create a new blockbuster drug.

Technology best practices embrace the integration of mechanical, computer, and communications technologies in support of a process. For the chef, technology includes mixers, ovens, and pans. For the planner, it includes management information systems, e-mail, and simulation models.

Organizational best practices describe how all the ingredients should be deployed and managed. Included are all the key human factors, such as motivation, incentives, skills, experience, education, training, loyalty, and commitment. Organization should not be confused with bureaucracy. Bureaucracy represents the dark side of organization and tends to be an impediment to fast, effective execution. As General Electric stated in its 2001 annual report:

> We cultivate the hatred of bureaucracy in our Company and never for a moment hesitate to use that awful word "hate." Bureaucrats must be ridiculed and removed. They multiply in organizational layers and behind functional walls—which means that every day must be a battle to demolish this structure and keep the organization open, ventilated and free. Even if bureaucracy is largely exterminated, as it has been at GE, people need to be vigilant—even paranoid—because the allure of bureaucracy is part of human nature and hard to resist, and it can return in the blink of an eye. Bureau-

cracy frustrates people, distorts their priorities, limits their dreams and turns the face of the entire enterprise inward.

People best practices are the most crucial ingredient in the recipe and the hardest to get right. After all, a great meal that the diner does not like is not a great meal to him or her. The results of a best practice program will stand or fall on the motivation, preparation, and performance of the individuals associated with the processes being addressed.

APPLYING BEST PRACTICES

Best practices can be applied in a wide range of situations with reasonable confidence that successful implementation and operation will allow an organization to realize the potential benefits. So how do you apply best practices?

An effective program follows a logical four-step process of measurement, prioritization, investigation, and application. This process needs to be continuous if an organization is not to fall behind, since best practices are continuously being updated and refined.

> *Step 1: Identify an opportunity for improvement.* This can be accomplished in a number of ways, from informal observation that a problem or improvement opportunity exists, to a continuous and systematic process of measuring performance against internal or external benchmarks.

> *Step 2: Determine whether the opportunity is sufficiently attractive to pursue.* For many organizations this step represents a weakness. Prioritization is not conducted in a rigorous manner, and appropriate resources are not assigned; the results are the failure to realize the benefits and a waste of resources.

> *Step 3: Internally investigate the causes of a shortfall in performance, and identify appropriate best practices that can be applied.* Techniques such as process mapping and analysis, primary research, benchmark visits, the engagement of subject matter experts, and other forms of knowledge gathering can be used to assemble a body of knowledge that provides insight into best practices that can be applied. During the investigation, it is important to distinguish between the symptoms and the root causes of the problem. A common mistake is to assume that the problem can be fixed by implementing a new computer system. One of the most dangerous phrases to look out for is "We need a new system to [insert the solution to any business problem]." Automatically assuming that a new system will solve all problems is a common and very expensive mistake. Often the real problem is not the lack of an effective system but the quality of the

data or inputs, as in the garbage-in, garbage-out syndrome, or a failure to train people adequately to use the current system. Neither problem will be resolved by implementing a new system; in fact, the problem is more likely to be magnified as bad data travel faster or people have to cope with a more complex system.

Step 4: Implement the change. Here the best practices identified during the investigation process are translated into practical applications within the business. Sometimes the best practices can be implemented in vanilla form; more often they require some adaptation or customization. Part III of this book discusses the practical aspects of best practice implementation.

Following these steps in a systematic and rigorous manner is the most effective way to implement best practices. The process is analogous to the medical diagnostic process, which can provide a useful reference point. Take the example of someone who is a little overweight. Typically, the process starts with the identification of some symptoms that may indicate a problem or an opportunity for improvement. Symptoms can be identified by a change in performance, such as finding it harder to climb the stairs, or through measurement, such as standing on the scales. In each case, a comparison is made to a relevant benchmark: Here it is past performance and an external measure, such as target weight relative to height.

Based on the results of the initial measurement, a decision on whether to take action is made. The litany of broken New Year's resolutions is testimony to the difficulty many people encounter at this stage. Unfortunately, all too often we make the mistake of prioritizing the need for change—"I must get fit"—but fail to allocate adequate resources—"I do not have time to exercise." Of course, the result is no improvement in performance.

However, assuming the commitment to act is matched with an appropriate allocation of resources, the next stage is the diagnosis phase. The objective is to identify the causes for relatively poor performance and seek out possible options for improvement. In our example, the root causes may be diagnosed as a combination of poor diet, lack of exercise, and perhaps a metabolic problem. With the diagnosis complete, it is then possible to identify and select possible treatments based on what has worked for other people with similar problems—in other words, identify candidate best practices. In our example, the prescription may be to cut out the beer and pizza (diet), swap the La-Z-Boy for the Stairmaster (exercise), and complete a course of prescribed drugs. The desired result is to restore the patient to full fitness and, preferably, to improve the patient's overall quality of life. Following completion of the treatment program, the crucial final step is to ensure the benefits of improved performance are sustained or even enhanced over time. A continuous program comprising a balanced diet and exercise will help sustain the improved level of performance. Throw in the odd half-marathon, and the overall level of fitness may improve still further. Ongoing measurement helps ensure that the results remain what were expected and can provide an early warning of new potential improvement opportunities.

BEST PRACTICE ADOPTION IS NOW A NECESSITY

Today no organization can afford the luxury of failing to leverage acknowledged best practices. The cumulative effects of a sustained period of economic growth for most of the developed world; deregulation in key sectors, such as U.S. telecommunications and utilities, and within markets, such as the North American Free Trade Agreement (NAFTA) and European Community; and increasing globalization all fueled by technology have redefined the economics of business. Although technology has created phenomenal potential, it also has raised the competitive stakes in all markets. Inefficiency can no longer hide behind annual price increases, limited competition, and high barriers to market entry. Market leaders are not solely defined by their ability to produce the best product; they must combine great products and services with competitive prices and operational excellence to meet the expectations of their customers and earn the right to their business. The use of benchmarking to ensure the minimization of inefficiency and waste is a powerful argument for developing a best practice–driven culture.

Applying a best practice found in one business or process to a different business or process can allow an organization to achieve a distinct advantage. It is possible to redefine the standard of excellence and thereby set a new best practice standard. Benchmarking pioneer Xerox applied warehousing and distribution best practices learned from L.L. Bean to its own processes; Chrysler's finance department adapted best practices found in its manufacturing operations to its accounts payable process; The Mayo Clinic adapted the use of bar code technology to track medical equipment as it moves around the hospital; and Merck applied techniques developed in the financial services industry to the drug development process to identify those drugs with the greatest potential of being successful.

Best practice adoption can drive competitive advantage in three situations:

1. Applying a best practice from one industry to another industry, as Merck did
2. Applying a best practice from one process to another process, as Chrysler did
3. Applying a best practice from the same industry and process but gaining an advantage through superior execution, as the Japanese automobile manufacturers accomplished

More often than not, the use of best practices is a competitive necessity. Using a best practices approach makes a lot of sense in areas where competitive advantage is not needed or offers no value. It is unlikely that a company is going to conquer the world simply because it can close its books or process benefits enrollments better than any other company. Companies are far better saving their innovative talent and resources for those product and service differentiators that can really make a difference. Giving competitors a significant advantage in any area places an unnecessary handicap on your business if clear best practices have been defined. Think of a bank without ATMs, a gas station without card payment at the pump, or a retail Web site that does not allow customers to order online.

Eliminating unnecessary work, reducing error rates, and simplifying core business processes all drive productivity improvements and are sound business practice. Using best practices as a vehicle for improving performance has allowed companies to implement significant changes much more quickly and at lower risk than if they had attempted to redesign the current process from scratch. Another advantage of using a best practice–driven improvement process is that it provides a counterpoint to an organization's existing process. For all the hype that has surrounded reengineering and the belief that "starting with a blank sheet of paper" and "thinking out of the box" will somehow result in a radical breakthrough, the reality is somewhat different. Generally people find it very difficult to adopt a radical new point of view without some outside stimulation since their only frame of reference is the current process. Occasionally a breakthrough will result; however, more often the outcome is simply a modified version of the current process. Adopting a best practice approach can stimulate a much more productive thought process. Instead of starting with nothing but individual experiences, one starts with a well-documented best practice process that has delivered measurable results. Doing this allows you to challenge the group tasked with the redesign to do two things:

1. Prove why the best practice is better than the current process.
2. Make it better.

Early in my career, a mentor told me something very simple that conveyed the essence of why a best practice–inspired process is effective: "It's a lot easier to edit than create." Not only is it easier, it is also less risky and quicker—all attributes that appeal to managers.

Best practices are most effective in situations where these criteria are met:

- A clearly defined improvement opportunity has been identified.
- The opportunity is not unique to the company.
- Credible best practices can be identified.
- The organization has the skills necessary and motivation to support implementation.
- Managing a portfolio of management tools is itself a best practice. One of management's primary tasks is to select the right tool or tools for the situation at hand and ensure that the organization possesses the necessary skills to use each tool effectively.

Best practices are attractive when a company lags so far behind that seeking to achieve a leadership position is not a realistic objective. The first step has to be to reach a level of competitive parity through best practice application. When best practice standards are attained, users can evaluate whether seeking true differentiation makes sense.

Typically the search for best practices has been about cutting costs. There is nothing wrong with adopting a cost-cutting focus—any waste of resources is unproductive. However, a singular focus on cost cutting misses the other benefits to be realized. In addition to achieving immediate absolute cost reductions, best practices can deliver more valuable, longer-term benefits. Applying best practices combines a number of powerful drivers of efficiency, from simplification through technology leverage. One effect is to create more scalable processes so that increases in the level of activity do not always require commensurate increases in the resources required. A good example is a credit card, which has two primary features:

1. It provides a financing vehicle by offering a means of purchasing goods and services and, for a price, delaying payment for those items.
2. It provides a transaction-processing feature by allowing multiple purchases to be settled with a single payment. Instead of writing a check or handing over cash for every purchase, all purchases are consolidated on a single statement, and payment can be made with one transaction. This is very scalable since the incremental transaction cost of making one more purchase on your credit card is nil. By using a credit card, the marginal cost of processing incremental transactions is greatly reduced. Many best practices provide the same benefits of not only reducing current costs but also reducing future costs.

Exhibit 2.1 shows the effect of implementing a best practice and reducing current costs through a step change (A) but also lowering the cost of future activity (B).

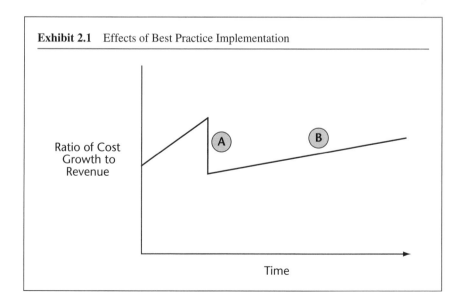

Exhibit 2.1   Effects of Best Practice Implementation

In addition to changing the overall cost structure, it is increasingly clear that best practice application is synonymous with a well-managed and controlled business. Companies that adopt best practices make fewer mistakes, get the right information at the right time, and make better decisions faster.

NOTE

1. Glenn Kessler, "New Accountability for Accounting," *Washington Post,* March 7, 2002.

Chapter 3

Sizing the Opportunities

Knowledge comes, but wisdom lingers.

—Calvin Coolidge

Since the first edition of this book was written in 2002, the amount of information available to companies seeking to improve their performance management processes has grown exponentially. The availability of rich metrics and best practice content has changed the way in which companies should approach the change effort.

The Value of Benchmarking

Quantitative benchmarking exercises of performance management processes are of marginal value.

Benchmarking with other organizations can help you understand how to approach the change management effort

---

BEYOND BENCHMARKING

It is time for organizations to move beyond benchmarking for three reasons.

1. Many companies have expended significant time and money on comprehensive benchmarking exercises yet failed to move beyond simply measuring the size of the gap. They are willing to pay to get on the scales but never make it to the gym!
2. Unlike best practices for routine processes, such as accounts payable or payroll, there is no "one size fits all" in terms of best practices for performance management. Simply because a set of practices works really well at one company, even a company that looks like your own, is no guarantee that the same practices will work or are even appropriate for your organization.
3. The completion of a benchmark used to be the only means available to access process metrics and best practices. Much of that information is now in the public domain.

DEFINING THE RIGHT METRICS

Improvements in transaction processes can be measured in terms of lower cost, higher productivity, or reduced error rates. The results are tangible and incontrovertible. Measuring the value of planning and performance management best practices is more subjective. How do you place a value on good information or a better decision? Many diagnostic tools have been developed to help organizations identify and size the improvement opportunities. The three-step diagnostic that follows comprises three elements which progressively allow an organization to:

- Identify the magnitude of pain inflicted by a defective performance management process.
- Isolate the underlying causes.
- Understand the metrics that help define a best practice performance management process.

Step One: How Broken Is Your Performance Management Process?

Having completed over 300 benchmarks of performance management processes over the last 20 years, I have looked at an awful lot of data—way too much, in fact. Isolating pain within a performance management process does not need an exhaustive analysis of the current process. Fifteen simple statements can allow any organization to determine whether a case for change can be made.

How many of the following statements do you agree with?

1. The planning and budgeting process is viewed as one of the most valuable management processes.
2. Senior management has confidence in the outputs of both the planning and forecasting processes.
3. It takes less than 60 days to complete the planning process from issuance of corporate targets/guidelines to management approval
4. Plans specifically identify tactics, resource requirements, and expected results in each of these areas:
   o Attracting new customers
   o Retaining existing customers
   o Attracting and retaining talented associates
   o Developing innovative new products or services
5. Plans clearly identify the expected impact on key measures of all major initiatives that are included in the plan.
6. Sandbagging of plans and forecasts is virtually nonexistent.
7. Incentive compensation is not directly tied to meeting plan or budget.
8. Technology has been fully leveraged to improve both the efficiency and the value of the planning and performance management processes.
9. Analysts spend less than one-third of their time assembling data, developing and maintaining spreadsheet models, and creating reports.
10. Business risks are clearly identified, and appropriate contingency plans developed.
11. A new forecast can be developed on demand within 24 hours.

12. Managers rarely complain that they are unable to get the information they need to make important business decisions.
13. Management reports contain a balance of leading and lagging information and clearly show the linkage between key business drivers and financial results.
14. Analysts are able to analyze the impact of alternative decisions on future performance without the need to create new models or spreadsheets
15. Analytical support costs have been reduced by at least 10 percent a year (relative to business growth) for each of the last three years while the level of internal customer satisfaction has simultaneously increased. (Answer "No" if you do not even measure these two things!)

How do you rate? Add up the total number of "No" or "Do not agree" answers and compare your score with the table in Exhibit 3.1.

So why are so many organizations still wrestling with such fundamental problems?

Step Two: Understanding the Causes of Dissatisfaction

Digging further into the underlying causes of the failure of traditional performance management processes, it is apparent that many of the problems are deep-rooted but soluble. It is not necessary to rely on conjecture, perception, and anecdotes to make the case for change—the data are compelling. Most performance management reporting processes not only fall far short of best practice but are broken. By every measure, the gap between actual and desired performance is significant.

Research data reveal a common theme that challenges the basic foundation on which traditional processes for planning, forecasting, and management reporting have been built. The data show that most organizations are trying to manage increasingly volatile and complex processes with management practices that are

Exhibit 3.1   Assessment

Number of "No" Answers	Assessment	Approximate Percentage of Organizations that Fall in This Category
Less than 3	Read no further. You can write the next edition of this book.	5%
4–7	On the right track/close to the standard of today's best companies.	20%
8–11	A good foundation on which to build; lots of potential to deliver more value.	30%
More than 11	Keep reading and start selling the need for change.	45%

more than half a century old. Detailed five-year strategic plans, static annual budgets, calendar-driven reporting, and mind-numbingly detailed financial forecasts are largely ineffective tools for managing change, uncertainty, and complexity, yet for many organizations they remain the foundation of the management process. So what are the drivers of such inadequacy?

About the Sonax Group Research

All the data referenced in this chapter were derived from research conducted by the Sonax Group from mid-2005 through mid-2006. Over 1,000 finance executives from North America, Europe, and Asia participated in surveys or working sessions focused on describing the current state of the art with respect to business performance management. Companies from all major industry groups were represented. Approximately 25 percent of the companies have annual revenues of less than $500 million, 55 percent are between $500 million and $5 billion, and 20 percent have revenues in excess of $5 billion.

Planning and Reporting the Wrong Stuff   Perhaps the most damaging attribute of many performance management processes is that they focus on the wrong things. Tactical plans fail to describe the major initiatives that will be undertaken; financial plans do not show the expected costs and benefits of each initiative nor do they identify the total investment being made in critical areas of the business. These sound obvious but the reality is that many organizations plan and report the things they can rather than the things they need. Consider the items listed in Exhibit 3.2. How many plans, budgets or reports have you seen that provide information on the items in the left-hand column compared to those in the right-hand column? Now ask yourself which column is more important.

Barely 60 percent of all companies develop plans that describe the tactics and investments to be made in key areas, such as attracting new customers or retaining existing customers; only 20 percent consider the retention of talented employees to merit specific focus in their plans (see Exhibit 3.3).

Exhibit 3.2   What's Budgeted Versus What's Important

What's Typically Budgeted	What's Really Important
◆ Salaries and wages	◆ Acquiring customers
◆ Rent	◆ Retaining customers
◆ Telecommunications	◆ Retaining talent
◆ Travel and entertainment	◆ Fostering innovation
◆ Depreciation	◆ Managing projects

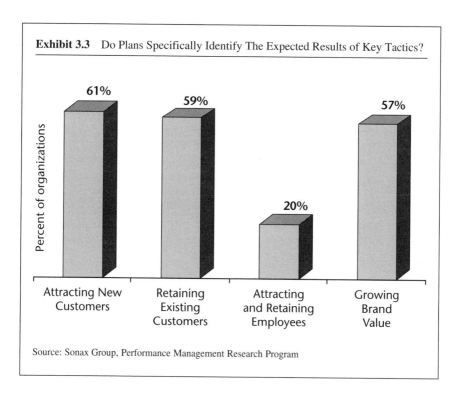

Exhibit 3.3 Do Plans Specifically Identify The Expected Results of Key Tactics?

Percent of organizations

| Attracting New Customers | Retaining Existing Customers | Attracting and Retaining Employees | Growing Brand Value |
| 61% | 59% | 20% | 57% |

Source: Sonax Group, Performance Management Research Program

Poor Ownership and Accountability   Unclear ownership and accountability is the root of many performance problems. Often the two elements are mismatched so that the individual or organization being held accountable has little or no ownership. This can be a problem, but it is nowhere near as damaging as the reverse situation. Any situation where ownership of an activity, asset, or resource is not matched by some clear accountability for performance is a recipe for creating performance shortfalls. For many organizations, defining appropriate ownership and accountability is the single most important factor in driving successful execution of strategy. A number of leading indicators should raise the red flag that potential ownership and accountability issues may exist:

- Highly complex organizations characterized by matrix structures
- Shared ownership of activities, assets, or resources
- Numerous allocation or internal transfer pricing mechanisms required to create business unit, functional, or departmental financial statements
- Redundant management of common processes, such as procurement, human resources, or information technology.

Tying Plan Achievement to Compensation   Everyone agrees that how people are rewarded influences how they behave. The basis on which an individual is rewarded is a critical component of an effective management process. Given the overtly financial focus of most business plans, it is not surprising that for one-third of all companies, incentives are completely tied to performance relative to the annual financial plan (see Exhibit 3.4). At a further 45 percent of companies, plan achievement is a major determinant of bonuses.

Although it seems very logical, this linkage can cause a number of unintended side effects. The primary purpose of developing plans is to decide on tactics and allocate resources in an optimal manner to achieve the agreed-on objectives. If compensation is tied directly to meeting the numbers in the financial plan, there will be an inevitable tendency to be conservative—some call it sandbagging—to maximize the chance of achieving the plan. Instead of motivating exceptional performance, the results may be the exact opposite as people seek to maximize the chance of earning the incentives. The data clearly support this assertion; 86 percent of companies struggle with some degree of sandbagging in their plans and budgets (see Exhibit 3.5).

Given the frequent disconnect between strategic plans and financial plans identified earlier, linking compensation to financial plans can induce a very short-term focus at the expense of strategy and long-term value creation.

Overall, the lack of alignment and integration between strategy and tactics leaves many organizations dangerously exposed when things do not turn out exactly as

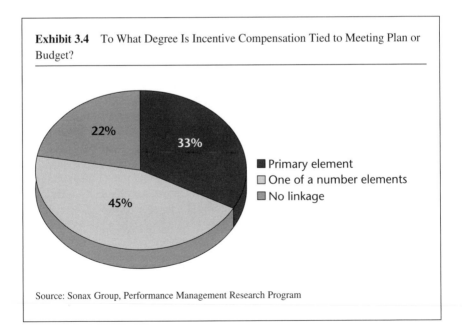

Exhibit 3.4   To What Degree Is Incentive Compensation Tied to Meeting Plan or Budget?

- Primary element
- One of a number elements
- No linkage

Source: Sonax Group, Performance Management Research Program

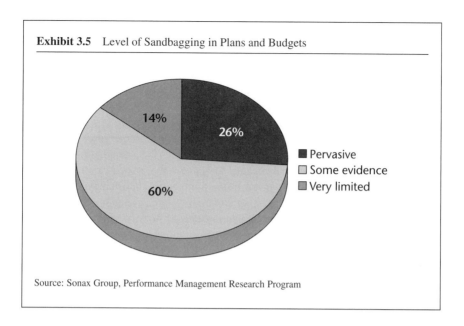

Exhibit 3.5 Level of Sandbagging in Plans and Budgets

14%

26%

60%

- Pervasive
- Some evidence
- Very limited

Source: Sonax Group, Performance Management Research Program

projected—which is most of the time. Without a clear understanding of the cause-and-effect relationships between tactics and objectives, you can have little confidence that today's actions will produce tomorrow's desired results. Best practice organizations do not necessarily develop better predictions or plans; however, they are far better equipped to quickly identify changes or problems, diagnose the root causes, and take corrective action.

Incomplete Strategy Definition Strategies are very good at describing what an organization wants to do; however, few strategic plans define those things a company will *not* do. In many respects, defining what will not form a part of the strategy can be more important than defining what will be included. If the strategic plan clearly states areas that are not part of the strategy, the choices to be made are greatly simplified, particularly when considering possible new ventures or acquisitions. One of the great success stories in the troubled automotive industry in recent years has been BMW. While its erstwhile competitor, Mercedes, has been distracted by trying to integrate its acquisition of Chrysler, BMW has stayed focused on its core, which is the premium sector of the market. This has not prevented the company from expanding, as its acquisition and refocusing of the Rolls-Royce and Mini brands show. The results have been impressive with sales and profits growing steadily and BMW passing Mercedes in total sales for the first time in 2005. Focus has clearly helped; BMW describes this in unambiguous terms: "The BMW Group has its sights firmly on the premium sector of the international automobile market."

Inadequate Risk Recognition   Effective performance management requires that managers explicitly address risk and uncertainty in order to make rational decisions. In addition to formal scenario planning, a number of internal and external risk factors need to be considered in developing plans. We will explore these more fully in Chapter 9; however, 89 percent of companies pay no more than rudimentary attention to risk in their plans (see Exhibit 3.6)—a truly frightening statistic.

Few companies follow a rigorous risk assessment process. Most disturbing is the fact that less than one in five organizations systematically addresses major external risk factors related to reputational risk, labor relations, special interest groups, or community impact. The failure of the planned acquisition of Honeywell by General Electric in 2001 thwarted by regulatory concerns, the Chapter 11 filing by United Airlines in 2002, and the negative publicity associated with the use of child labor by several multinational companies all illustrate the potential magnitude of such issues.

Poor Communication   "Strategic alignment" is a favorite phrase used to indicate that everyone is on the same page. All people and activities in an organization share a common purpose and are focused on the same goals and objectives. In many instances strategic alignment is handicapped by the simple fact that strategic plans are not widely communicated or understood. It is tough to ensure strategic alignment when the strategy is secret! Communication is not just about broadcasting the strategy. The acid test for determining whether a strategy has been com-

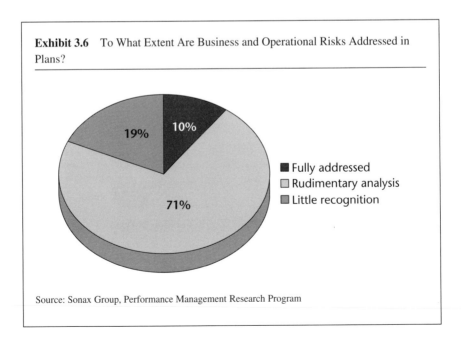

Exhibit 3.6   To What Extent Are Business and Operational Risks Addressed in Plans?

19%   10%

71%

■ Fully addressed
☐ Rudimentary analysis
■ Little recognition

Source: Sonax Group, Performance Management Research Program

municated effectively is that each individual within an organization can describe how their contributions directly contribute to the fulfillment of the strategy.

Weak Integration Alignment between all elements of the performance management process is critical. After all, the whole objective of the process is to translate strategies into results. Unfortunately, less than a third of all companies have tightly integrated performance management processes. The degree of integration can be evaluated across a number of dimensions. For example:

- Are the metrics that are reported to management directly linked to the major strategies contained in the strategic plan?
- Is it possible to review the financial plan or budget and identify the total investment being made in each element of the strategy or in each initiative defined in the tactical plan?
- Can each manager explain how his or her department directly contributes to the overall mission and strategy of the organization?

For a performance management process to be effective, it is logical to expect a clear line of sight from the business strategy, through the operational and financial plans, to what is then reported and forecast. Organizations struggle with disconnects between each step. For example, often it is impossible to discern anything about the strategic priorities of an organization by reviewing its financial plan.

Information Overload An additional consequence of glorying in detail is that much of the information provided to managers is of questionable value. The first bar in Exhibit 3.7 shows the balance between operational and financial information.

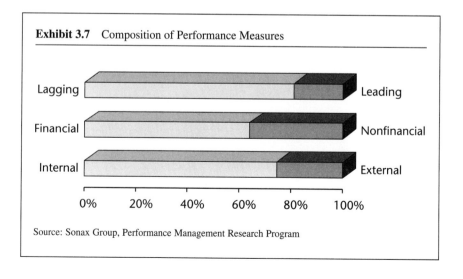

Exhibit 3.7 Composition of Performance Measures

Lagging | Leading
Financial | Nonfinancial
Internal | External

0% 20% 40% 60% 80% 100%

Source: Sonax Group, Performance Management Research Program

Operational measures tend to track specific values associated with the activities of the business, such as volumes, cycle times, productivity, quality or defect rates, on-time percentage, and service levels. Financial measures translate operational measures into financial values, such as sales, cost of sales, margin, expenses, and profit. The second dimension looks at the balance between leading and lagging measures. Leading measures address expected future values or results for operational or financial measures. Lagging measures report actual results for a prior time period. The third dimension looks at the balance between internal and external measures. Internal measures relate to things within the boundaries of the organization; external measures are taken from outside the organization and can include competitor pricing, customer satisfaction, supplier inventory, and market demand.

At the average organization, management reporting is biased toward internal, historic financial measures. This is the exact reverse of the information most managers value when making decisions. They are seeking useful predictive information about customer and competitor actions that offers insight into how the organization can respond most profitably. A bias in favor of internal financial information fails to recognize that the financial impact of a business event is the last step in the process. By the time a credit is issued to a customer, it is usually too late to fix the problem. More than three-quarters of the information reported to management is historic and internally focused; less than a quarter is predictive of the future or focused on the marketplace. Most organizations face significant challenges in delivering the right information to the right people at the right time. The focus is wrong, cycle times are too long, detail is overwhelming, and analytical tools are weak.

Mistaking Detail for Accuracy   There must be something in the DNA of finance professionals that creates an insatiable thirst for detail. Starting with the earliest experiments in scientific management in the 1920s, the volume of data generated within organizations has grown at a phenomenal rate. Widespread deployment of computers has only added fuel to the explosion of data. As the volume has increased so has the potential to plan, budget, and report at ever increasing levels of detail. Unfortunately, many companies have taken advantage of this fact and created performance management processes of such detail that the really important items become obscured. It is not unusual for a company to develop a budget item for spending on office supplies in the third quarter of the next year but have little or no idea how much business it expects to generate with its 20 best customers.

There is no evidence that developing more detail in the financial plan results in either a more accurate plan or, more important, better performance. Organizations that insist on excruciating detail often fail to appreciate the consequences.

- People will have less time to plan each line item. To get the job done, they are more likely simply to plug in a number than develop a rational basis and set of tactics to support each line item.
- Given that plans by definition deal with the future, there is no guarantee that more detail will result in greater accuracy. In fact, the reverse is more likely to be true.

- The more detail contained in a plan, the more complex and time consuming the processes for tracking performance against plan, reporting and analyzing variances, developing forecasts, and restating plans to reflect the impact of major business events.

The net effect is to slow down decision making, precisely the opposite of the effect most companies are seeking. Not only does excessive detail hamper the planning process, it also tends to translate into very detailed management reporting. We have all seen or had to use management reports that were more suitable as doorstops than insightful decision support tools. Inundating managers with metrics in an unstructured manner actually can make their job harder. Managing performance against a multitude of measures not only creates a complex equation that cannot easily be solved, but it also increases the risk that a material trend in one key measure may be overlooked.

Overtly Financially Focused   Almost two-thirds of companies view the planning process as a primarily financial exercise that is completed annually. In effect, the budget is a plan with little detail on the specific tactics to be employed but lots of detail on the expected financial results.

The financial focus of plans is not surprising. Until recently, little operational data were readily available, and accounting systems usually were the only source of any reliable data. Financial plans and forecasts are very good at quantifying expected results; they are very bad at defining the activities and tasks that produce the results. For example, a plan or forecast may predict a 10 percent growth in sales during the next quarter. This figure provides a clear estimate of the result expected but provides no insight into how the sales growth will be achieved. For example, how much will come from finding new customers or selling more to existing customers, from new products versus increased sales of existing products?

All too often, plans provide little or no insight into these important questions. The consequences are twofold.

1. Financial plans or budgets cannot be linked directly to the strategies they support.
2. As the inevitable variances to plan occur during execution, management will immediately start to ask questions about the causes of the variances. The financial plan will be of little assistance. Analysts will be forced to complete significant additional analysis to identify the root causes and suggest possible corrective actions.

Lack of Process and Project Orientation   The *Oxford English Dictionary* defines a process as "a series of actions or operations used in making or manufacturing or achieving something." Organizations are the sum of their processes. The relative efficiency and effectiveness of an organization's processes largely determines its overall performance. The objective is to develop a series of performance management processes that provide rapid access to real-time information and sophisticated planning and modeling that produces fast, confident decision making. The reality is often more akin to what Larry Bossidy describes finding on becoming chief executive officer of Allied-Signal in 1991:

> The processes were empty rituals, almost abstractions. People did a lot of work on them, but very little of it was useful. The business unit strategic plans, for example, were six-inch-thick books full of data about products, but the data had little to do with strategy. The operating plan was strictly a numbers exercise, with little attention paid to action plans for growth, markets, productivity, or quality.[1]

I was able to observe firsthand the speed with which Bossidy and his management team brought a laserlike focus on process efficiency. The results were impressive. Over the next decade, many of the company's processes reached first-quartile performance levels, operating margins tripled, and shareholders benefited from a ninefold return on their investment. Unfortunately, the benchmark data show that 15 years after Bossidy began his revolution, most companies still resemble the Allied-Signal he took over in 1991.

Allied with poor process discipline is the fact that most companies fail to organize their plans around the tactics, projects, or initiatives they intend to pursue in order to meet their goals. Narrative plan documents go to great lengths to talk about the new products that will be launched, the innovative marketing campaigns and the new computer systems that will drive performance improvements; however, a cursory glance at most financial plans will reveal a chilling absence of information showing the resources that will be committed to each initiative and, more important, the results that are expected to accrue. Companies will know precisely how much they plan to spend on rent next year but have little or no insight into the total investment being made in acquiring new customers or developing new products. Fewer than 3 out of 10 companies develop plans that clearly identify the expected results of major projects or initiatives (see Exhibit 3.8).

TIP

Estimate the total amount of time finance staff members spend supporting the strategic planning, tactical planning, management reporting, and forecasting processes and multiply by 8 to get a rough estimate of the total time the organization spends on these processes. Are you getting a return on your investment?

Calendar Driven   Numerous companies tout flexibility as a key characteristic of their organization. Words such as "agile," "responsive," and "nimble" have become staples in the vocabulary of corporate public relations. In many instances, the adjectives are appropriate. Dell's ability to configure and ship a PC to your personal specifications and the Four Seasons' much-vaunted level of personalized service both require a significant organizational commitment for such flexibility to appear

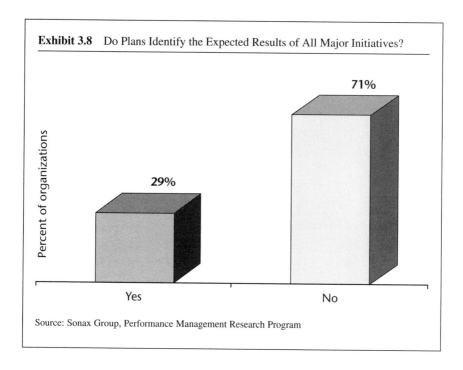

Exhibit 3.8 Do Plans Identify the Expected Results of All Major Initiatives?

Source: Sonax Group, Performance Management Research Program

routine. However, flexibility rarely extends to the performance management processes. A good indicator of flexibility is the ability of an organization to get the right information at the right time in order to make timely decisions. Unfortunately, management reporting is typically available only on a predetermined calendar basis. Reliance on the calendar also impacts the forecast process.

Most organizations treat forecasting as a purely fiscal exercise tied to the current financial year. A small but growing group has recognized the potential of the forecast to be a powerful forward-looking tool for business planning. Instead of a static view of the business that looks only at the current financial year, these companies have adopted a rolling time horizon that provides visibility into the future. A more detailed review of the pros and cons of a rolling forecast process is presented in Chapter 7.

Extended Cycle Times Not only is performance management expensive, it is also time-consuming. In an era of cycle time compression in nearly every other aspect of business, the performance management process has been left behind. Exhibit 3.9 shows that the average lapsed time to develop a tactical plan is 89 days.

Compounding the overall inefficiency is the fact that much of the time dedicated to the performance management process is wasted. At the average company, 81 percent of professional staff time is spent collecting and validating data rather than analyzing and planning (see Exhibit 3.10).

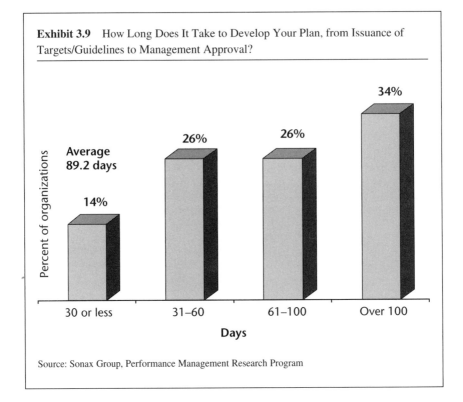

Exhibit 3.9 How Long Does It Take to Develop Your Plan, from Issuance of Targets/Guidelines to Management Approval?

Source: Sonax Group, Performance Management Research Program

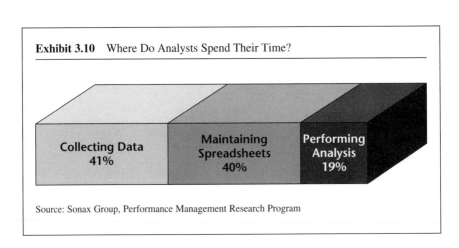

Exhibit 3.10 Where Do Analysts Spend Their Time?

Source: Sonax Group, Performance Management Research Program

Productive use of expensive and scarce talent is a key differentiator between best practice companies and the rest.

Poor Staff Leverage Benchmarks have for many years highlighted the cost-reduction opportunities that companies can realize in different business processes. However, as companies have successfully taken cost out of many of these processes, finance function costs have declined by two-thirds relative to revenue in the last 15 years, the focus has shifted to achieving further cost reduction while simultaneously increasing the value-added contribution to the business. Few real measures exist to help companies achieve this hugely attractive goal.

The staff leverage ratio (SLR) measures the ratio of productive, high-value work undertaken by professional staff versus lower-value data manipulation and reporting activities. In short, it measures where the organization is allowing its people to be successful. Examples of high- and low-value activities are shown in Exhibit 3.11. The SLR can be calculated for any group of manager and professional staff and is particularly useful in areas such as finance, marketing, pricing, and human resources.

Sonax Group research shows that the average SLR for most U.S. industries is 0.2 to 0.3. This means that only 20 to 30 percent of a professional's time is devoted to high-value work. With average fully loaded compensation for these positions typically in the range of $80,000 to $100,000 per year, the waste is clear. Two examples will illustrate this.

The Power of Leverage

Example A: Large Telecommunications Service Provider

Current SLR = 0.25

Total planning and analysis staff = 760 full-time equivalents (FTEs)

Average compensation = $86,000.

Achieving a target SLR of just 50 percent allowed this company to increase high-value work by 50 percent, or 95 FTEs, while reducing costs by $15.2 million (190 FTEs @ $86,000).

Example B: Medium-size Regional Grocery Chain

Current SLR = 0.4

Total planning and analysis staff = 50 FTEs

Average compensation = $66,000

Achieving a target SLR of 70 percent would allows this company to increase high-value work by 40 percent, or 8 FTEs, while reducing costs by $800,000 (10 FTEs @ $80,000).

Exhibit 3.11   High Value vs. Low Value

High Value	Low Value
• Direct dialogue with decision makers	• Data sourcing
• Development of business analyses	• Data validation
• Evaluation of risk and variability	• Report creation
• Team-based analytical reviews	• Spreadsheet model maintenance

Increasing the SLR increases the analytical horsepower that is focused on delivering insight and hence supporting better decision making however this needs to be married with the right skill sets. Analysts have broad business and operating experience; they cannot just be number crunchers. This broader knowledge enables analysts to collaborate much more effectively with operating management throughout the planning, forecasting, and reporting processes. Not surprisingly, analysts working for best practice organizations are held in higher regard by operating management with over 90 percent being considered business partners. Achieving the right balance between financial and operational knowledge can be facilitated by implementing an effective program for rotating analysts into operational roles as part of their career development; this process has the added benefit of increasing retention rates by up to 20 percent, allowing organizations to keep their most talented managers and professionals.

Successfully achieving and sustaining best practice performance levels does not come for free. The need to continuously invest in people through career development programs is essential. Training represents the most visible investment in people; again, in this area, best practice companies score well, investing up to one-third more per head on training than the average. Again, a high SLR helps since given their lower overall staffing levels, best practice companies can deliver more value while spending 30 percent less in total than the average company.

Automating Inefficiency   Contributing to management's frustration has been the comparative failure of the vast investments made in technology in recent years to provide the much-promised improvements in visibility, control, and information. Many bought the promise of technology, and now they felt cheated. Far from liberating management from the dearth of timely, useful information, computers have, if anything, exacerbated the problem. Organizations wrestle with long, tortuous accounting close cycles, which Sarbanes-Oxley has in many cases served to extend still further. Last-minute year-end events invalidate budgets prepared in excruciating detail over many months. Basic questions, such as "How much do we sell to our biggest customers?" still trigger days, sometimes weeks, of frenzied activity. Managers and analysts had become slaves to their PC-based spreadsheets. Technology was supposed to solve these problems; however, despite massive investments in data warehousing, executive information systems, and other reporting and decision support tools, most organizations are frustrated at the lack of progress.

The reason is not a lack of investment but rather poor implementation. Organizations have failed to leverage their investments in enterprise resource planning (ERP), data warehousing, and online analytical processing (OLAP) systems. Exhibit 3.12 shows that only 2 percent of companies believe they have fully leveraged technology in their performance management processes. Six out of 10 companies believe they have barely scratched the surface.

Management by Spreadsheet The gaps created by partially deployed systems typically are filled with spreadsheets, Almost two-thirds of all companies rely on spreadsheets as their primary plan and budget development tool. Since the early days of VisiCalc and Lotus 1-2-3, the spreadsheet has been the workhorse of finance professionals and analysts everywhere. Unfortunately, the spreadsheet's greatest strengths are also its greatest weaknesses. The ability to develop models and analyses provides great independence and flexibility for the user. In many cases, spreadsheets serve as the system of record for critical plan, forecast, and reporting information. This is a risky and potentially expensive proposition. Most spreadsheet models exist outside an organization's normal data management environment.

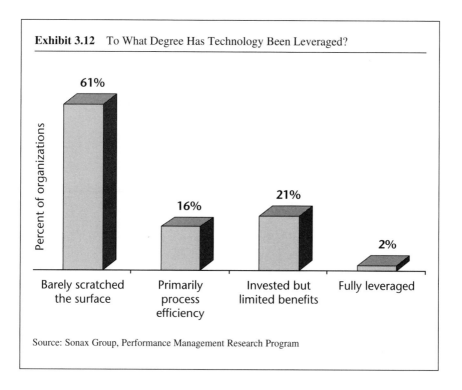

Exhibit 3.12 To What Degree Has Technology Been Leveraged?

Source: Sonax Group, Performance Management Research Program

Basic quality assurance and control processes that ensure data integrity, the accuracy of calculation routines, security, and backup often are circumvented when a key planning model is maintained by a single analyst on a laptop computer. Besides the obvious data integrity risks, the care and feeding of a multitude of independently developed and maintained spreadsheets is time consuming. In some organizations, analysts have become slaves to their spreadsheets. They spend much of their time gathering data from multiple sources to support their spreadsheet habit.

Ironically, one of the major reasons analysts resort to using stand-alone spreadsheets is the difficulty organizations have had in fully deploying the more advanced analytical tools that streamline access to information and integrate the analytical tools. By failing to deploy expensive systems fully, many of the expected benefits have been forsaken. The picture is slowly changing: 20 percent of companies now utilize an integrated performance management system (see Exhibit 3.13), up from less than 10 percent just five years ago.

Understanding the relative impact of each of these symptoms on your current performance management processes lays a sound foundation for identifying those best practices that:

- Are most applicable to your organization
- Will have the biggest beneficial impact

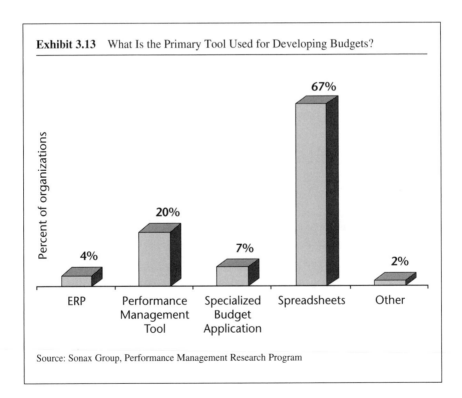

Exhibit 3.13   What Is the Primary Tool Used for Developing Budgets?

Source: Sonax Group, Performance Management Research Program

There are two ways to know if you have a world-class performance process:

1. You will have fewer than five "Nos" on the test earlier in this chapter.
2. You will be able to match your process against the seven metrics described next.

Step Three: Best Practice Metrics

One of the consequences of the explosion in the amount of data companies can now access combined with the increasing availability of competing benchmarks is that it is very easy to suffer from metric overload. The risk of having too many metrics is that it becomes increasingly difficult to identify those that really matter. Exhibit 3.14 shows seven metrics that provide a quick snapshot of the relative health of your performance management processes.

CONCLUSION

It is rare that a company is shocked by the results of an evaluation of its performance management process. Managers generally know if their management processes are cumbersome, inaccurate, and of limited value. The key is to get beyond identifying

---

Exhibit 3.14   Best Practice Process Metrics

Metric	Acceptable	Best Practice Standard
Plan achievement[1]	Within 5% of target range	Within target range
Forecast accuracy[2]	+/- 3%	+/- 1%
Staff leverage ratio[3]	0.5	0.75
Value-added ratio[4]	1:1	1:1.5
Forecast completion time[5]	< 3 days	< 1 day
Annual plan completion time[6]	8–12 weeks	< 8 weeks
Management satisfaction[7]	50% "top 2 box" score	75% "top 2 box" score

Metric Definitions

[1]Achievement of revenue and net income goals assuming a target range is defined. Ranges should not exceed 5 percent of the midpoint.

[2]Achievement of revenue and net income forecasts for the next quarter.

[3]Ratio of professional staff time spent on value-added tasks versus lower-value tasks.

[4]Ratio of managerial and professional finance staff engaged in transaction processing as opposed to business risk management and decision support.

[5]From request or trigger of a forecast activity to executive management approval.

[6]From the issuance of targets to board approval.

[7]Percentage of managers rating the performance management process a "9" or "10" on a 10-point scale.

the problems to fixing them by instituting more effective processes. Spend less time sizing up the problem; spend more time architecting and selling the solution. In summary, best practice companies:

- Have simpler, faster, more focused processes
- Deliver information that is tailored to the needs of the individual
- Spend twice as much time planning and analyzing as they do collecting and validating data
- Spend less money supporting more effective performance management processes
- Attract, retain, and leverage more talented staff

Notwithstanding the considerable gap that exists between the best and the rest, today's best organizations still have considerable room for improvement, most notably in two areas:

1. Further reducing the effort expended on lower-value transaction processing activities by managers and professionals; few companies have an SLR above 0.75
2. Fully leveraging their technology investments

As best practice companies seize these opportunities, it is quite likely that the gap between the best and the rest will widen before it begins to narrow. Moving beyond the cold, hard facts, managers everywhere feel constrained by their relative inability to get the right information to make better decisions. The level of frustration is such that many executives openly question whether the massive investments in technology made over the last few years have come anywhere close to delivering the payoff originally expected. Compelling quantitative evidence and basic human insecurity are combining to bring the issues into sharp focus.

In summary, the effective deployment of performance management best practices can enable an organization to deliver significantly more value-added planning and analytical support at lower overall cost. Given the relative scarcity and high cost of top-flight analytical resources, best practices can deliver not only economic value but also competitive advantage. Part II explores the best practices that allow top-performing companies to differentiate themselves.

NOTE

1. Larry Bossidy and Ram Charan, *Execution: The Discipline of Getting Things Done* (New York: Crown Business, 2002), p. 2.

Part Two

Best Practices

Chapter 4

Using Best Practices to Drive Change

Plan ahead: It wasn't raining when Noah built the ark.

—Richard Cushing

A BRIEF HISTORY

Seeking out and copying the best products, methods, or tools has been a routine part of life ever since the earliest humans copied and refined the skills of the best hunters, tool makers, and warriors. A continuous cycle of innovation, adaptation, and enhancement underpins the creation of knowledge and wealth throughout history (see Exhibit 4.1).

The breakthrough event in any innovation cycle is the invention of a radically new product, method, or application. From the invention of the wheel (ca. 3,200 B.C.), through paper (ca. A.D. 105), to the telephone (1876) and the Internet (1973), each new breakthrough creates something that demonstrably has value and is a clear best practice relative to the other alternatives available at the time. Once a best practice is recognized and communicated, adoption rates tend to accelerate dramatically as imitators seek to realize the same benefits. Increasing adoption inevitably leads some imitators to enhance or adapt the breakthrough to new applications, thereby improving on the original. Such is the process by which best practices are created, deployed, and enhanced.

Any individual, product, or activity that succeeds in distinguishing itself becomes a target for imitation. You do not have to be a student of economics to observe this phenomenon. For example, in the entertainment world, the first James Bond film, *Dr. No*, released in 1962, ushered in a whole cadre of imitators (*The Avengers*, *The Man from U.N.C.L.E.*, *The Ipcress File*, etc.) as well as numerous sequels as market participants' sensed demand for more and more product. More recently, the television show *Survivor* brought reality television to the fore of programming schedules. Nowhere is imitation more prevalent than in the world of fashion. Almost before the models leave the catwalk, replicas of the latest designer creations are making their way to the mall.

Numerous examples can be found of innovations that rapidly established themselves as best practices (see Exhibit 4.2).

The phrase "to learn from a master" describes the essence of applying best practices. An explosion of interest in best practices occurred during the 1980s, although the process of improving operations by observing and copying the behavior

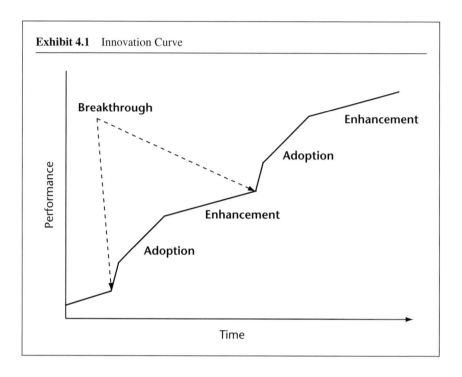

Exhibit 4.1 Innovation Curve

of market leaders goes back much further. Christopher Bogan and Michael English, in the book *Benchmarking for Best Practices: Winning Through Innovative Adaptation*, trace the early origins.[1] Thomas Lowell, a nineteenth-century New England industrialist, initiated one of the earliest examples of best practice knowledge transfer in the industrial age. Lowell visited England to observe the manufacturing techniques of English mill factories that were acknowledged to be the most productive in the world. After touring a number of factories in the north of England, he returned to Massachusetts and set out to apply what he had learned by building a new mill incorporating the best practices he had observed. So successful was his experiment

Exhibit 4.2 Inventions That Became Best Practices

Invention	Inventor	Adopters and Enhancers
Double-entry bookkeeping	Benedictine monks (15th century)	All businesses
Plastic	Alexander Parkes (1862)	Too numerous to list
Moving assembly line	Henry Ford	All manufacturing companies
Electronic spreadsheet	Visicalc/Dan Bricklin (1979)	Lotus, Microsoft

that the area where he built the factory was subsequently renamed Lowell, Massachusetts, and by 1840 it had become the second largest city in America. Such success was a powerful testament to the value of copying and adapting ideas and helps explain why benchmarking has since become an increasingly popular tool for improving performance. Lowell also provided an early example of another trait that characterizes the most effective practitioners of best practice benchmarking: He went beyond simply copying what he had seen in England by incorporating many improvements of his own. He observed the best practices in operation in England, adapted them for use in the United States, and enhanced them to achieve a level of performance that set a new benchmark standard. Through comparing the practices of the acknowledged industry leaders and then improving on those practices, Lowell was able to establish a clear leadership position for his business.

Unfortunately, not all instances of imitation reflect the adoption of best practices; the numerous pet supply Web sites that sprang up during the Internet bubble testify to this truism. The secret is to discern those practices that truly merit imitation and application as demonstrated by tangible results and sustainability.

More and more companies see value in copying business processes used in making a product, delivering a service, or completing an activity if they are shown to be more efficient or more effective than current methods. The ability to translate the successful experiences of one organization for the benefit of another represents a core element of operating philosophies of many companies including General Electric, Microsoft, and Alcoa. This trend is not restricted to North America; many Asian and European companies, including Sony, Toyota, Philips Electronics, and Renault, integrate best practices into their operating philosophies.

FROM BATTLEFIELD TO BOARDROOM

It all began with Adam and Eve assessing the implications of removing the apple from the tree in the Garden of Eden. Prehistoric man planned out the hunt and reported the results: "Bagged two woolly mammoths, a third got away. Still, not a bad day's work." The discipline of setting objectives, developing plans, measuring progress, and making adjustments based on actual results is fundamental to all human activity.

This chapter describes a framework for identifying those best practices that are most appropriate for an organization, discusses some of the overall guiding principles for implementation, and lays to rest a few sacred cows that perpetuate inefficiency in many organizations.

The fundamentals of planning and hence business performance management were honed on the battlefield and in military colleges. Only in the last century did the disciplines of strategy, planning, forecasting, risk management, and reporting move to the boardroom. Until recently, the leading thinkers on strategy and its application were almost exclusively military men. Sun Tzu, Hannibal, Frederick the Great, Machiavelli, and Clausewitz all made major contributions to the body of knowledge.

B. H. Liddell Hart's *Strategy* provides a comprehensive discussion of the evolution of strategy from early Greek and Roman conflicts through World War II.[2] While military strategy tends to focus on vanquishing a single foe to achieve an agreed-on objective, the application of military thinking to business is both appropriate and pervasive.

The expansion of thinking from the battlefield to the boardroom can be traced to two events. The first was the promotion of Alfred P. Sloan, Jr. to the presidency of General Motors in May 1923; the second was the publication of Peter F. Drucker's *Practice of Management* in 1954.[3]

Sloan, the first professional manager of a large corporation, guided GM from being a weak competitor to the legendary Henry Ford to seizing market leadership from Ford. During his tenure as chief executive officer (CEO) from 1926 to 1946, Sloan codified and implemented many of the management principles that became standard operating procedure for businesses everywhere. Drucker, who was a close friend of Sloan's and wrote the foreword for Sloan's account of his time at GM, *My Years with General Motors*, is widely recognized as the first true management guru.[4] His first major work on management, 1954's *The Practice of Management*, remains an essential component of the library of any student of business.

After Sloan's and Drucker's groundbreaking work, the recognition that business management was a distinct profession gathered speed. A whole publishing and public speaking industry has grown up around the subject.

The emergence of best practices as a viable branch of management research was initiated by the 1982 publication of *In Search of Excellence* by Tom Peters and his coauthor, Robert Waterman, the first best-selling business book that sought to identify the common characteristics of high-performing organizations.[5] As the book's subtitle, *Lessons from America's Best-Run Companies*, explained, Peters and Waterman sought to define the best practices that underpin superior performance so that others could benefit.

Since the publication of *In Search of Excellence*, the body of knowledge surrounding best practices has grown steadily. However, as the benchmarks discussed in Chapter 3 show, most organizations still have tremendous room for improvement. Not only are most planning and reporting processes slow, unfocused, and expensive, they also fall far short of adapting to the needs of today's businesses. By applying best practices, an organization can focus its people on value-creating activities, confident in the knowledge that the performance management processes are appropriately focused on the organization's objectives. Of course, a best practice performance management process does not guarantee business success—only great products and great service can do that—but it certainly will not do any harm.

COMPONENTS OF A BEST PRACTICE FRAMEWORK

Best practices are about operational excellence. As one chief executive said to me, "If we reach best practice in everything we do, we will have effectively isolated management stupidity as the only possible cause of failure!"

By implementing proven practices, an organization eliminates waste, reduces risk, and frees up resources to focus on those tasks that can truly differentiate the organization in the marketplace.

For a best practice–driven approach to work, all the component parts must come together to achieve the maximum level of performance in much the same way in a high-performing team where all members works together to sustain superior performance. Applying best practices to the strategic planning process without addressing the tactical planning, financial planning, management reporting, and forecasting processes will not deliver optimal results.

BEST PRACTICE RECIPE

Best practices are a recipe in which the right mix of ingredients combined with the right preparation is the key to realizing the latent value.

As Bill Gates puts it, the payoff from technology is "the accuracy, immediacy, and richness of the information it brings to knowledge workers and the insight and collaboration made possible by the information."[6]

SELECTING THE RIGHT BEST PRACTICES

The early research into performance management best practices tended to follow the same approach as those defined for more operational processes; that is, "one size fits all," where each best practice is seen as being applicable to a broad range of organizations. Everyone should use balanced scorecards, rolling forecasts, business performance management systems, scenario planning, and the like. Although this is true for some performance management best practices—particularly those related to the use of technology—it is not true for all of them. In order to identify those practices that are most appropriate for an organization, it is necessary to look at two dimensions:

1. The maturity level of the organization
2. The organizational risk profile

The overall objective of a best practice performance management process is to enable an organization to translate ideas into results. All organizations, no matter how small, follow the same basic process although the degree of formalization evolves over time.

In small or start-up businesses, the need for structure is not great, so many of the principles do not need to be formalized. Entrepreneurial leadership can drive the business forward. However, the basics of setting goals, developing plans, measuring progress, adjusting tactics, and forecasting results still manifest themselves throughout the business. As companies grow, it becomes increasingly difficult for them to survive without more structure and discipline (see Exhibit 4.3).

Exhibit 4.3   Typical Business Life Cycle Stages

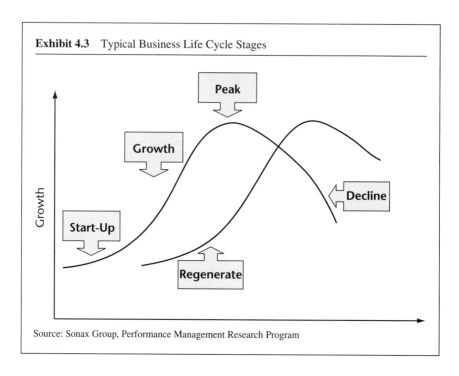

Source: Sonax Group, Performance Management Research Program

The ability to manage this transition often determines the future viability of the business. One of three things can happen:

1. The transition works and the company continues on to further success. Home Depot, Microsoft, Nike, Oracle, Southwest Airlines, and Wal-Mart are all good examples of companies that have negotiated this change successfully.
2. The transition does not work fully, and the company struggles to move to the next level as it becomes strangled by bureaucracy or is unable to move beyond the products that drove its initial success. The result is either a slow decline or the loss of independence. Polaroid, Lotus, Digital Equipment, and Laura Ashley all fall into this category.
3. Businesses simply choose not to make the transition and accept a limit to their future growth. These companies can be very successful but rarely dominate their markets. Think of those successful local companies that deliver great service, inspire strong customer loyalty but have no desire to expand nationally or globally.

The best practices described in this book have been gleaned from many different organizations. One of the advances made in the last few years is that the process of determining the practices that are best suited to a specific organization is becoming much more sophisticated. From our research at the Sonax Group, we have learned that defining the right solution for a specific organization is a function of understanding two elements, the:

1. External environment in which the organization operates
2. Internal structure, maturity, and management style of the organization

The first factor is the external or market environment in which an organization has chosen to participate. The performance management processes that an oil company needs to adopt will be different in important ways from those used by a world-class consumer electronics company. The dynamics of the two businesses are very different and will influence not only the content of plans, forecasts, and reports but also other dimensions, such as the planning time horizon, the value of using certain tools (e.g., scenario planning or real options), and the application of the different risk assessment techniques.

The second variable is the internal business mechanics. This is made up of three elements:

1. Structure and process
2. Maturity
3. Management style

A company that has adopted a highly centralized management model will utilize different processes from one with a decentralized model. A command and control model typically will dictate much more uniformity and standardization across the organization with ownership and accountability resting with a few senior executives. Conversely, a decentralized model with permit greater variability and devolve accountability to the outer limits of the organization.

Likewise, a company's use of best practices will evolve as the business develops. For example, eBay, Yahoo, and Goggle are all evolving their management practices from those of those of a disruptive innovator in start-up mode to those of a maturing industry leader. Exhibits 4.4 show how an organizations focus can evolve as it matures.

Notwithstanding these situational complexities, it is essential that performance management processes do not become impediments to execution. Business is about identifying a need that someone values and meeting that need at a price that the customer is willing to pay. Performance management processes are simply tools to help people navigate through the management process. In a perfect world, the process would be fast and frictionless. Best practices seek to lubricate decision making by removing impediments, such as unnecessary work steps, or detail, and allowing managers to focus on the highest-value tasks by ensuring they have the right information at the right time to make good decisions. Keeping this simple objective in mind can help ensure against developing overly bureaucratic processes.

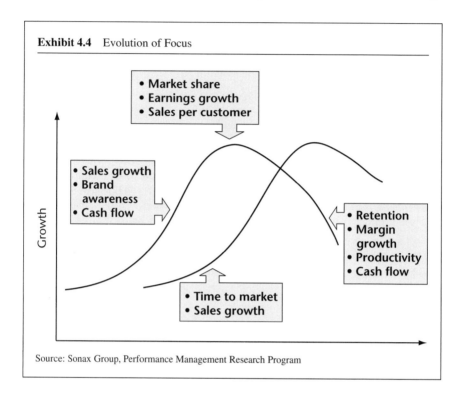

Exhibit 4.4 Evolution of Focus

Source: Sonax Group, Performance Management Research Program

GOLDEN RULE OF BEST PRACTICE APPLICATION

Part II of this book describes best practices in the areas of strategic planning, tactical and financial planning, reporting, forecasting, and technology. For those pressed for time who are looking for a single silver bullet, Peter Drucker defined it long ago: "There is nothing so useless as doing efficiently that which should not be done at all."[7]

The essence of Drucker's comment is at the heart of all best practices. The guiding principle of a best practice program is first to eliminate all unnecessary work, then to standardize and simplify all work that remains, and only then to seek to apply technology to achieve superior performance.

GOLDEN RULE

There is nothing so useless as doing efficiently that which should not be done at all.

—Peter Drucker

There is absolutely no value to be gained from simplifying or automating activities that should not exist. The more steps or moving parts there are in a process, the greater the risks of an error or process failure. Simple processes are easier to manage, more productive, and cheaper. The start point for improving any business process is to ask: "Is it needed?" Eliminating as many low-value tasks as possible greatly simplifies the redesign challenge. Typical candidates for elimination are redundant or ineffective control processes, most reconciliation processes (it is much better to get it right the first time), excessive detail, almost all standard reports, and for-information-only copies of any document. It is not unusual for up to one-third of all work steps to be eliminated from the average process.

After having eliminated all the unnecessary activities, the next step is to make those that remain as standard and simple as possible. Simplification tends to focus on ensuring that all the information, skills, and knowledge to execute a particular task are available at the point of execution. Actions that can simplify processes include standardizing policies and terms, centralizing homogeneous activities to realize scale economies, replacing detective controls with preventive controls, and defining a single point of accountability for each task.

The net effect of eliminating unnecessary work and simplifying all the tasks that remain is to make the deployment of technology much easier and cheaper. The less complex a process, the less likelihood there is that significant customization will be required to the systems that are needed to support the process. Today many organizations get it the wrong way around. They insist that all new systems are implemented "vanilla" or "out of the box." The intent is to minimize the level of customization that is carried out—a practice that has been shown to drive much of the technical complexity and high costs that organizations suffer from today. In many cases, the requirement to customize in the first place was driven by an unwillingness to eliminate and simplify the underlying processes.

TIME TO SACRIFICE A FEW SACRED COWS

At most companies, planning and performance management has changed little since the days of Alfred P. Sloan. His disciplined and structured approach to management based on very strong financial planning and control processes became the norm for all businesses. As Sloan explained in *My Years at General Motors*, GM's objective was to "deliver a long-term rate of return consistent with the sound growth of the business."[8]

This objective led GM to institute clearly defined processes that made a major contribution to the company's rise to become the largest corporation in the world (by sales), a position it ceded only in 2000. The methods of professional management that defined GM's success became the standard for business. Unfortunately, not all practitioners were as skilled as Sloan in their application, and a number of flaws became institutionalized. Today many companies find themselves struggling with planning processes that seem overly complex and time consuming while delivering mediocre results at best. It is time to challenge some accepted norms that infuse much of the planning and reporting that, far from improving the process, actually appear to drive many of the problems.

Slavish Adherence to the Calendar

Planning and reporting always has been a calendar-driven activity. Typically, most planning occurs annually, and most reporting is monthly or quarterly. From an accounting standpoint, it is convenient to divide business into logical time blocks. However, doing this misses the reality of the way most businesses operate in the twenty-first century. Business is a continuous activity—it does not conveniently stop according to the calendar.

Factories operate three shift systems; some stores open 24 hours a day; most are open seven days a week; supply chains hum 24/7; securities are traded globally around the clock; Amazon.com sells books continuously; CNN reports the news nonstop. Even computers have moved from batch processing to always-on real-time processing. Perhaps most shockingly, the archaic licensing laws in my homeland were finally changed in 2005 to allow pubs to be open 24 hours a day if they so desire. Although the use of discrete time periods will continue to support the needs of the accountant, it does not meet the needs of the business manager. There is no such thing as "Closed" in today's world.

Decoupling your internal management processes from the calendar by implementing a set of processes that utilize continuous processing and monitoring of activity not only recognizes today's reality but can equip managers with vital information, allowing them to react to both opportunities and threats in a timely fashion. The passage of time becomes just one of many criteria for triggering the reporting of information or the initiation of plan or forecast activities.

Preeminence of the Annual Budget

For most people, the annual budget process induces emotions akin to tooth extraction without Novocain. Budgeting takes too long, is too detailed, and delivers little of lasting value. At most companies, the budget is obsolete the day it is created despite the many thousands of hours and excruciating detail that go into its development. Traditional budget processes need to be obliterated and rebuilt from the ground up. The irony is that budgeting ought to be one of the most valuable and stimulating processes an organization can engage in. It is unlikely that most people have heard a budget described by either of these adjectives.

Chapter 6 explains how simplifying and integrating the budget into the overall planning, forecasting, and reporting processes can deliver much more value with much less effort.

Internal Transfer Pricing

Transfer pricing, much like budgeting, is a business process that started out with the best of intentions; however, somewhere along the way it all went horribly wrong. Debates over allocations or transfer pricing mechanisms can dominate management time as managers seek to reduce their share of the allocated cost under some misguided assumption that performance miraculously will improve.

The basic premise behind transfer pricing is sound. A transfer price is a means of allocating fixed or shared costs among the different operations of a company with the aim of providing a realistic view of the relative performance of each entity. Managers can be held accountable for the profit or contribution their unit makes and can see their total share of costs; doing this encourages them to make rational decisions. The process sounds fine in theory, and in some cases it works in practice; however, all too often the allocation or transfer pricing mechanism paralyzes the planning process and obstructs clear thinking. I have yet to see a Wall Street analyst cite the quality of a company's internal transfer pricing mechanism as a basis for recommending its stock. The bottom line is that the debates add little or no value.

Singular Focus on Financials

Business is all about money. Everything a business does ultimately has a financial value assigned to it. If it does not have a dollar, euro, or yuan sign in front of it, then it is not real. The focus on financial results is not a bad thing unless it becomes the only focus. There is a tendency to assume that financial information can explain everything that goes on within a company. This assumption is dangerous; financial information reflects the results of business actions, often well after the actual event took place.

For example, by the time a refund is issued to a customer and the credit is recorded in the accounting books, it is too late to correct the problem. Management can seek to prevent the same problem from recurring, but it cannot influence the outcome of this transaction. As many commentators have noted, managing by financial information alone is akin to driving a car by only looking in the rearview mirror.

Leveraging Professional Staffs

The rise of the knowledge worker has been one of the great changes in the workplace over the last 30 years. The combination of increasing automation and the rise of the service economy has reduced the number of workers actually engaged in manufacturing and increased the number of workers who make information rather than things. As technology continues to generate more and more data, there are more and more things to be analyzed. Companies seem to be adding more and more knowledge workers. Exhibit 4.5 describes the dual effect most organizations have sought from their process reengineering, restructuring, and automation efforts and contrasts that with what best practice companies strive to achieve.

The first effect (A) is a reduction in total cost primarily accomplished by dramatically reducing operational or transactional costs through the application of best practices and the automation of routine activities. The second effect (B) is a reallocation of resources from lower–value-adding operational tasks to higher–value-adding decision support or knowledge worker tasks. There is nothing wrong with the first objective of lowering total costs; however, the second effect, although logical, displays a failure to understand the nature of the work actually being undertaken by most knowledge workers. As discussed in Chapter 3, it is not atypical for

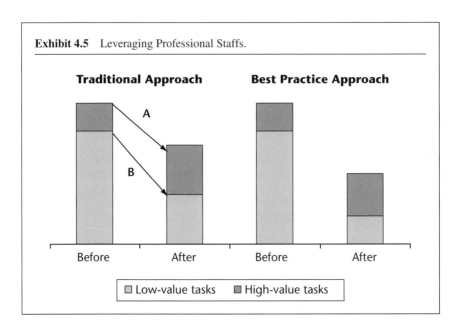

Exhibit 4.5   Leveraging Professional Staffs.

the average knowledge worker to spend less than one-fifth of his or her time focused on the so-called higher-value analytical and decision support tasks.

Basic tasks, such as assembling and validating the data needed for higher-value tasks, consume most of the average knowledge worker's time. These are the very tasks that information technology was supposed to automate. For many reasons, easy access to data remains a myth for many. The correct application of best practices eliminates the need for more knowledge workers by increasing the productivity of existing knowledge workers by two to three times.

NO SILVER BULLETS

Any discussion of best practices in planning and performance management should be prefaced by a severe warning. Simply implementing best practices is no guarantee of superior performance. There are simply too many other variables involved in creating value. Having a great performance management process will never compensate for building poor-quality products that people do not want to buy.

The next six chapters describe and demystify the best practices observed in leading organizations. The aim is to describe the best practices in each of the major processes that comprise an organization's typical performance management activities. Each chapter addresses a separate group of best practices, starting with strategic planning and moving on through tactical and financial planning, management reporting, forecasting, business risk management, and technology. I have chosen to dedicate a separate chapter to the use of technology for two reasons:

1. Technology is now so pervasive in business that the interaction of people and technology is the single most important driver of process excellence.
2. The benefits realized from technology have not yet matched the promise. Many executives have become cynical and somewhat jaded by the hype surrounding each new technology. There is a need to instill greater confidence that the potential returns can be realized.

NOTES

1. Christopher Bogan and Michael English, *Benchmarking for Best Practices: Winning Through Innovative Adaptation* (New York: McGraw-Hill, 1994).
2. Basil H. Liddell Hart, *Strategy*, 2nd rev. ed. (London: Meridian Books, 1991).
3. Peter F. Drucker, *The Practice of Management* (New York: Harper & Row, 1954).
4. Alfred P. Sloan, Jr., *My Years with General Motors* (New York: Doubleday, 1963).
5. Thomas J. Peters and Robert H. Waterman, *In Search of Excellence* (New York: Harper & Row, 1982).
6. Bill Gates, *Business @ the Speed of Thought* (New York: Warner Books, 1999), p. xviii.
7. Peter F. Drucker, *Managing in a Time of Great Change* (E.P. Dutton/Truman Talley Books, 1995).
8. Sloan, *My Years with General Motors*, p. 141.

Chapter 5

Strategic Planning:
The Ideas That Drive Results

By failing to prepare, you are preparing to fail.

—Benjamin Franklin

Planning in general and strategic planning in particular have, at various times, been seen as the single most critical tasks in business; at other times, they have been ridiculed as an impediment to innovation and a constraint on execution. Formalized business planning reached its zenith in the two decades following World War II. The power of large-scale, formal planning processes was demonstrated by the spectacular success of the Allied invasion of Normandy on June 6, 1944. This event, coupled with the remarkable transformation the U.S. economy was able to make in mobilizing for war in 1942 and then reverting back to peacetime operation in 1945 to 1946, brought planning to the forefront of management.

The experience of General Motors illustrates the scale of this transformation. GM's commercial vehicle production dropped from 2.3 million units in 1941 to just over 300,000 units in 1942—an 87 percent reduction in just 12 months. In fact, GM did not produce a single passenger vehicle between March 1942 and September 1945. At the same time, orders for defense-related products totaled over $8 billion in 1942 alone, almost four times the total orders for military equipment the company had received in its entire history to that point. As chief executive officer (CEO) Alfred P. Sloan, Jr. commented with a touch of understatement:

Fortunately, we had done some advance planning which enabled us to take on this vast problem systematically.[1]

By the end of the 1960s, strategic planning was ingrained in the culture of business. Planners were seen as the elite of the corporate staff, and a career path through the corporate planning function was an essential step on the road to the corner office. However, the accepted wisdom of formalized strategic planning was about to come under attack. As organizations started to move away from a centralized model to a more decentralized approach, the concept of the strategic business unit (SBU) took hold, and planning was no longer solely the domain of statisticians and corporate planning groups. New thinking argued that large businesses should be managed as series of smaller businesses, each with its own management team whose members would be held accountable for the results of their individual unit. The rationale was based on providing a combination of increased accountability, speed, and responsiveness. Jack Welch at General Electric, Larry Bossidy at Allied-Signal (renamed Honeywell), Bill Gates at Microsoft, and Herb Kelleher at Southwest Airlines all challenged the value of large centralized planning staffs by building very successful companies without large corporate planning departments. When Robert Iger became CEO of Disney in late 2005, one of his first moves was to shrink Disney's central planning unit, giving the business units more authority. The effect was to accelerate decision making and reduce bureaucracy. A deal to offer downloads of hit Disney shows *Desperate Housewives* and *Lost* on Apple's iPod was cemented in just three days. Apple CEO Steve Jobs openly praised Iger, in stark contrast to Jobs's frosty relations with Iger's predecessor, Michael Eisner. It is reasonable to assume that this paid a part in Jobs's agreement to sell his other company, Pixar, to Disney just a few weeks later. Decision-making flexibility and agility go hand in hand with good strategy.

Iger's moves simply reaffirmed a trend that has been picking up pace for the last 20 years. Mechanized formal planning was all but obsolete as a "Just Do It" mentality took hold. Speed, innovation, and ideas have become the hard currency of business. Sometimes this can be taken too far when it is accomplished at the expense of logic, process, and preparation, as happened during the dot-com era—a surreal period at the end of the 1990s when basic business logic seemed to be forgotten. The story of Boo.com, a well-funded but ultimately flawed Internet retailer, illustrates how reality was temporarily suspended. In his excellent account of Boo's rapid rise and fall, cofounder Ernst Malmstein describes the timeline the founders and their advisors, including such bluebloods as J. P. Morgan, saw for the business:

> Boo would launch in May 1999. Our IPO [initial public offering] would come six to nine months later, once revenues hit $5 million on an annualized basis.[2]

No mention of profits or a proven track record. Despite such shortcomings, Boo was still expected to garner a market valuation of around $400 million even with minuscule revenues and large losses—many other companies already had proven the model. Unfortunately, Boo was a little late to the party. By May 2000, after burning through $120 million of investors' money, Boo collapsed—one of the first but by no means the last high-profile start-up that set out to change the world but served only to burn through a large amount of its investors' money while offering no return.

Notwithstanding the temporary suspension of economic reality, the signs were there that effective planning could be combined with speed, agility, and innovation. Technology became a key catalyst for the change. New supply chain systems, enterprise resource planning (ERP) systems, customer relationship management systems, data warehousing and data mining tools all found broad commercial application. The effect was to infuse planning in general and strategic planning in particular with a new energy. The foundation was being built for many of the best practices described in this book.

DEFINING STRATEGY

"Strategy" is one of the most overused and least understood terms in modern business. Strategy is sexy—everyone wants to be seen as a strategic thinker. People talk of strategies for everything from product development, to recruiting, to managing stationery inventories. The effect of indiscriminately using the term "strategy" to describe many things that are patently not strategic in nature clouds rather than clarifies the word's true meaning. Referring to the military origins of strategy helps clarify the true purpose. As Liddell Hart explained, "Strategy depends for success . . . on a sound calculation and co-ordination of the end and the means."[3]

At a minimum, an effective strategic plan contains three elements:

1. A clear definition of the business and how it will operate
2. A plan that lays out the major goals, objectives, and the means for achieving them
3. A set of targets that guide operational execution and allow progress to be tracked against the overall goals and objectives

Above all, strategic planning is a leadership tool. It helps leaders set direction, communicate intent, describe desired behaviors, and guide implementation. To be effective, a strategy needs to describe both a framework for the organization (see point 1 in the list) and offer specific guidance on execution (points 2 and 3). To this end, strategic planning has two sides: a soft side and a hard side (see Exhibit 5.1). The soft side of strategy helps define the culture of the organization; the hard side provides concrete direction and targets to guide detailed planning and execution. Strategic planning, whether performed formally or informally, provides the basis for all subsequent planning, reporting, and forecasting activities.

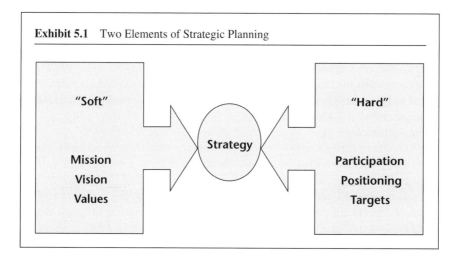

Exhibit 5.1   Two Elements of Strategic Planning

TYPICAL PROCESS

All too often, strategic planning takes on a life of its own. Fascination with the process can lead to strategic planning becoming an annual ritual that seeks to define the long-term future in excruciating detail. A 1990 article in *Fortune* magazine described the malaise:

> At too many companies, strategic planning has become overly bureaucratic, absurdly quantitative, and largely irrelevant. In executive suites across America, countless five-year plans, updated annually and solemnly clad in three-ring binders are gathering dust—their impossibly specific prognostications about costs, process, and market share long forgotten.[4]

Many organizations follow what they think is a rigorous, formal strategic planning process. In reality, they spend most of their time developing very detailed long-term operating plans and budgets. The essential attributes of a strategy—defining a unique market position and making tough choices and trade-offs on how to get there—are lost in the minutiae of 10-year production forecasts and 3-year expense budgets. The strategic planning process becomes a preprogrammed, annual exercise that proceeds at a leisurely pace throughout the spring and summer. Ostensibly this allows the results to feed into the year-end operational and financial planning processes. Coincidentally it also coincides with the golf season across most of Europe and North America. Thus the strategic planning process can begin with an executive management off-site meeting, often termed a retreat, at a top resort in the springtime. In the United States, Arizona, Florida, and California are popular destinations; Europeans head for Spain, Italy, or a Mediterranean island. The output of this first meeting is a series of ideas, often termed strategic planning assumptions, that management deems to be worthy of further evaluation. The second session typically is scheduled for June or July. As it is now too hot to return the original venues, the second retreat migrates north to locations such as the Broadmoor in Colorado, the Greenbrier in West Virginia, or Gleneagles in Scotland. The results of the detailed analyses developed in preparation for the meeting are reviewed in a series of two- to three-hour morning meetings. Debate is vigorous and curtailed only by the arrival of a boxed lunch signaling that the first tee time is imminent. The output is usually an agreed-on set of priorities together with some initial targets to guide operational and financial planning.

Formal target setting around goals, critical success factors, and drivers of the business is not done in a consistent manner; nevertheless, the updated plan and targets are agreed on by management and reviewed with the board of directors. The board approves the plan but changes the first-year targets to make them a little more ambitious. The strategy is updated for the agreed-on changes, and all the managers place their own personal copy of the new strategy on a shelf next to its older siblings, never to be opened again.

Following approval by the board, each executive communicates selected elements of the plan and the relevant targets to his or her organization to initiate the operational and financial planning process. Many weeks later, after much effort, the individual financial plans are consolidated, and management finds that the results fail to come close to the targets agreed on in the strategic plan. On seeing the shortfall, management convenes a third strategy session. The CEO opens the meeting by asking everyone to "roll up his or her sleeves" and "work as a team" to "get the plan back on track." After a few days of meetings, budgets are cut and projects are reprioritized so that the detailed plans now meet the targets. The numbers work but the disconnect between strategic intent and operational tactics is complete. Management laments the lost opportunities and commiserates about the painful process to "get the numbers to work." Commitments are made to improve the process—next year!

Untypical? Unfortunately not. In an interview, one executive expressed his frustration to me in this way:

> We spend a few days brainstorming exciting ideas and strategies for changing the world only to find that we can't make the numbers work so we regress to updating last year's plan and moving on with the process. The net result is that our strategic planning process becomes a numbers exercise that requires us to develop immense detail in order to come up with precisely the wrong answer.

Challenge of Sustaining Success

There is no mystery to success. Simply combine a continuous stream of great ideas with a clear vision, effective mobilization, superior execution, outstanding customer loyalty, consistent profitable growth, and continuous regeneration. Companies such as General Electric, Microsoft, Southwest Airlines, Sony, Toyota, and Wal-Mart share these characteristics and have sustained strong performance over many years. They all also realize that past success is no guarantee that it will be sustained in the future.

Tom Peters and Robert Waterman, in their seminal business book *In Search of Excellence*, first published in 1982, listed six measures that defined the financial results of excellent performance:[5]

1. Compound asset growth
2. Compound equity growth
3. Ratio of market value to book value
4. Average return on capital
5. Average return on equity
6. Average return on sales

To qualify as a top performer, a company had to have been in the top half of its industry in at least four of the six measures from 1961 to 1980. Thirty-six companies made the cut. Twenty years after Peters and Waterman's analysis, it is illustrative to look back at the fate of each of the players. Of the original 36 companies, 7 (19 percent) of those on the list no longer exist as independent entities: Amdahl, Cheseborough-Ponds, Data General, Digital Equipment, Raychem, and Wang Labs. Another company, Revlon, was acquired in 1986 and only reemerged as a public company in 1996. Kmart filed for Chapter 11 bankruptcy protection in January 2002 and then merged with Sears in 2005. Delta Airlines filed for Chapter 11 in September 2005. Many others, including Avon, Boeing, Caterpillar, Disney, Dupont, Eastman Kodak, Hewlett-Packard, IBM, Levi Strauss, McDonald's and Merck, have found the intervening 25 years to be anything but a smooth ride. Of the original 36 companies, not one rated in the top in terms of 10-year shareholder returns on the 2005 Fortune 500. This is not to suggest that Peters and Waterman's analysis was in any way flawed; all 36 companies had logged 20 years of excellent performance at the time of the study. It simply illustrates how difficult it is to sustain performance over the long term.

STRATEGIC PLANNING BEST PRACTICES

A simple search for books on the subject of strategic planning at Amazon.com yielded 7,649 results (an increase of 42 percent since 2002); suffice to say that the subject is well covered. This chapter seeks to describe the attributes of a best practice strategic planning process. It is not intended to define a methodology or approach to strategic planning.

Soft Side of Strategy

The soft side of strategy is often ridiculed and its importance underestimated. For example, Scott Adams, through his comic strip creation Dilbert, defined a mission statement as "a long awkward sentence that demonstrates management's inability to think clearly."[6] Despite the cynicism, any study of high-performing organizations will identify the pervasive presence of softer strategic elements. Southwest Airlines, GE, Microsoft, Nordstrom, and Toyota all have distinctive styles, cultures, and values that are at the heart of much of what they do. The ability to create a framework that motivates the types of individual behavior that maximize the probability of achieving strategic objectives is a consistent feature of best practice organizations. Conversely, the development of mission and vision statements, values, and cultural norms that exist only on paper is an excellent leading indicator of an organization that will struggle in times of great opportunity or threat.

Nurture the Culture

Culture is one of the most ambiguous aspects of any organization, yet many companies cite their culture as the most critical element in their success—more important even than any product or service. When asked what keeps him awake at night, Herb Kelleher, former chairman and CEO of Southwest Airlines, replied:

> My biggest concern is that somehow, through maladroitness, through inattention, through misunderstanding, we lose the esprit de corps, the culture, the spirit. If we ever do lose that, we will have lost our most valuable competitive asset.[7]

Strong, distinctive cultures can be found at the heart of many great companies. For decades, Hewlett-Packard lived the HP Way as defined by founders Walter Hewlett and David Packard. Software company SAS has defined a very distinctive culture that centers on the employee (see www.SAS.com). All companies espouse the importance of their employees; few make it a reality.

SAS's overall mission is not particularly unique:

> At SAS, our mission is to empower organizations around the world with superior software, solutions and services that give them the power to know. We want to be the most valued competitive weapon in business decision making.

However, the company goes further to define a specific cultural objective:

> If you treat employees as if they make a difference to the company, they will make a difference to the company.

SAS backs up its words with actions. The company has created a culture dedicated to achieving a reasonable work/life balance based on the premise just set out. No one is pressured to work through the night or on weekends; if someone is ill, there is no pressure to be back at work in five days or less; and the company values time spent with the family. As a result, the company has appeared eight consecutive times in the top 20 of Fortune's "100 Best Companies to Work for in America."

Culture is the sum of all the principles, behaviors, and values that guide the everyday actions of people within an organization. Although an organization's culture cannot be created by words alone, the development of vision, mission, and value statements helps to describe the type of culture an organization is seeking to develop. W.L. Gore & Associates, a billion-dollar polymer company perhaps most famous for its Gore-Tex fabric, has made its corporate culture the centerpiece of its overall operating philosophy. Exhibit 5.2 shows that W.L. Gore seeks to describe its culture as the governing mechanism for every individual within the organization.

Proof of its effectiveness is that Gore, like SAS, has been named one of the "100 Best Companies to Work for in America" on eight separate occasions.

Define a Purpose

Beyond culture, every organization needs a reason for being or a purpose. An organization's business purpose is not just a description of what it does—often that can be very mundane. It would be easy to simply describe Federal Express's purpose as "delivering packages." This is not terribly exciting and is unlikely to serve

---

Exhibit 5.2   Culture at W.L. Gore

How we work sets us apart. At Gore, we don't tax creativity with conventional hierarchy. We encourage hands-on innovation and discourage bureaucracy, involving those closest to a project in decision-making. Teams organize around opportunities and leaders emerge. Instead of a pyramid of bosses and managers, Bill Gore created a flat lattice organization. There are no chains of command, no predetermined channels of communication. Instead, we communicate directly with each other and are accountable to fellow members of our multidisciplined teams. How does all this happen? Associates (not employees) are hired for general work areas. With the guidance of their sponsors (not bosses) and a growing understanding of opportunities and team objectives, associates commit to projects that match their skills and interests. Everyone can quickly earn the credibility to define and drive their own projects. Sponsors help associates chart a course in the organization that will offer personal fulfillment while maximizing their contribution to the enterprise. Leaders (defined by followership) emerge naturally by demonstrating special knowledge, skill, or experience that advances a business objective.

Source: W.L. Gore

as a basis for inspiring employees or investors. FedEx agrees and chooses to describe itself in this way (see www.FedEx.com):

> FedEx will produce superior financial returns for shareowners by providing high value-added supply chain, transportation, business and related information services through focused operating companies. Customer requirements will be met in the highest quality manner appropriate to each market segment served. FedEx will strive to develop mutually rewarding relationships with its employees, partners and suppliers. Safety will be the first consideration in all operations. Corporate activities will be conducted to the highest ethical and professional standards.

Many terms are used to describe an organization's business purpose. Typically there are three common elements:

1. Vision
2. Mission
3. Values

A number of commentators and scholars have tried to explain the difference between a vision and a mission statement. Here is William Drohan's attempt in an article published in 1999 by the American Society of Association Professionals: "A vision statement pushes the association toward some future goal or achievement, while a mission statement guides current, critical, strategic decision making."[8]

Despite Drohan's attempts to define each term, there is no commonly accepted distinction between a mission and a vision, and the terms are often used interchangeably. This semantic ambiguity is distracting but does not alter the need for a simple statement of aspiration that can guide and motivate the organization.

If the difference between a mission and vision is unclear, values are a lot easier to define. An organization's values establish the guiding principles that govern the organization's thinking, behavior, and operation. My own contribution to the definitional debate is that, taken together, the vision, mission, and values should answer three simple questions:

1. What is our primary objective or reason for being? (vision)
2. What do we do in order to reach our vision? (mission)
3. How will we behave? (values)

A 2002 study by the American Management Association illustrated the crucial role values play in many organizations.[9] The study found that 86 percent of companies have clearly defined values and that 64 percent include some element of value alignment in performance evaluations and compensation. The top five values were in order:

1. Customer satisfaction: 77 percent
2. Ethics/integrity: 76 percent
3. Accountability: 61 percent

4. Respect for others: 59 percent
5. Open communication: 51 percent

Interestingly, the three lowest occurring values were empowerment (32 percent), employee job satisfaction (31 percent), and "have fun" (24 percent), which raises the question as to how effective companies that cite customer satisfaction as a key value will be when their employees are not empowered, satisfied, or happy. Perhaps the most disturbing finding is that fully 49 percent of employees were uncertain as to how the company's values translate into job performance and the bottom line; this fact points to the challenge many organizations face in making their value systems work.

Visions Should Inspire The debate over the value of a vision or mission has raged for many years. John F. Kennedy's exhortation to go to the moon and Martin Luther King Jr.'s "I have a dream" speech are both great examples of vision statements that changed the world. Kennedy's challenge to America, made in a special address to Congress in 1961, provides a powerful example of visionary goal setting: "I believe this nation should commit itself to achieving the goal, before this decade is out, of landing a man on the moon and returning him safely to earth."

In 29 words, the president described a very clear objective, "landing a man on the moon"; set a deadline for accomplishing the objective, "before this decade is out"; and established a key measure of successful completion, "returning him safely to earth." As a statement of strategic intent, it is crisp, clear, and concise, attributes that many corporate vision statements would do well to replicate.

A mission statement clarifies why an organization exists. It helps set direction and prevent confusion. Mission statements do not concern themselves with the details of how the mission will be accomplished; that is the task of the broader planning process. Failure to clearly articulate an organization's mission can make subsequent elements of strategic planning very difficult indeed. As the Cheshire Cat so eloquently comments in Lewis Carroll's *Alice's Adventures in Wonderland*, "If you don't know where you are going, it doesn't matter which way you go."

Leading management thinkers Tom Peters and Warren Bennis see a vision as an essential trait for a high-performing company and its leaders. Not everyone always agrees. On becoming chairman of IBM in 1993, Lou Gerstner commented that "the last thing IBM needs right now is a vision."[10]

Many interpreted Gerstner's comments as a repudiation of the value of mission statements. It was not; his point referred to the fact that at the time he took over the corner office, he believed that IBM's problems were much more basic. A year later Gerstner was ready to embrace the need for a mission, which he defined during a speech in Barcelona, Spain, in March 1994:

> IBM's mission is to be the world's most successful and important information technology company. Successful—in helping our customers apply technology to solve their problems. And successful in introducing this extraordinary technology to new customers. Important—because we will continue to be the basic resource of much of what is invented in this industry.

By 2006 the company's mission had further evolved (see www.IBM.com):

At IBM we strive to lead in the creation, development and manufacture of the industry's most advanced information technologies including computer systems, software, networking systems, storage technologies and microelectronics.

We translate these advanced technologies into value for our customers through our professional solutions and services businesses worldwide.

This is an interesting mission statement since it is much more specific than many. It clearly states the businesses that IBM is in and by omission those that it is not in. It defines the company's scope as embracing both products and services on a global basis. Although it is a little dry, it offers clear guidance as to what to expect from IBM.

The perceived absence of vision can have a damaging effect on even the most powerful people. George H. W. Bush's presidency was dogged by his perceived lack of vision. When challenged in 1987 to refocus on long-term issues rather than short-term campaign objectives, he famously responded by saying "Oh, the vision thing." Although he went on to win the presidency, the "vision thing" dogged his term. A well-crafted vision or mission statement is a powerful motivating force provided it is brought to life in the everyday actions of the organization and particularly its leaders.

Mission and vision statements should be short, inspirational, and easily understood. Alcoa, for example, aspires "to be the best company in the world—in the eyes of our customers, shareholders, communities and people."

Starbucks has been a phenomenon since its founding in 1971, persuading millions of people that $4 is not too expensive for a cup of coffee; however, Starbucks has also made a name for itself through its commitment to the environment and its unique culture. The company's mission and values help illustrate this (see www.Starbucks.com):

Establish Starbucks as the premier purveyor of the finest coffee in the world while maintaining our uncompromising principles while we grow.

The following six guiding principles will help us measure the appropriateness of our decisions:

1. Provide a great work environment and treat each other with respect and dignity.
2. Embrace diversity as an essential component in the way we do business.
3. Apply the highest standards of excellence to the purchasing, roasting and fresh delivery of our coffee.
4. Develop enthusiastically satisfied customers all of the time.
5. Contribute positively to our communities and our environment.
6. Recognize that profitability is essential to our future success.

Pharmaceutical company Glaxo Smith Kline's mission illustrates how a for-profit business can express its reason for being in terms of the organization's ability to improve the quality of life. Its mission is "to improve the quality of human life by enabling people to do more, feel better, and live longer." (See www.gsk.com.)

Although mission statements are an integral part of the strategic framework of most commercial organizations, some of the most perceptive mission and vision statements can be found in the public or not-for-profit sectors. One of the major reasons for this is that both groups depend on continuous support from their patrons—taxpayers and donors respectively—to survive. Two examples (see Exhibit 5.3) from the U.S. Forest Service and the charity Save the Children illustrate the ability of well-crafted mission and vision statements to succinctly define an organization.

An organization's mission, vision, and values help define its behavior and hence contribute to its ethical standing—an increasingly important consideration in the light of the increasing scrutiny of corporate integrity. The next few years will see regulators, investors, and customers paying much more attention to an organization's business practices. Some companies, such as the cosmetics retailer The Body Shop and the Canadian mutual fund company Ethical Funds, have developed successful business models predicated on missions and visions that espouse social responsibility.

Vision and mission statements serve as a crisp focal point for communicating the essence of what an organization stands for to multiple audiences. My own personal favorite is not drawn from any corporation but meets all the best practice criteria. In the immortal words of the organization's CEO, Captain James T. Kirk:

> Space, the final frontier. These are the voyages of the *Starship Enterprise*—its five-year mission to explore strange new worlds, to seek out new life and new civilizations, to boldly go where no man has gone before.

Exhibit 5.3   Mission and Vision Statements

U.S. Forest Service

The U.S. Forest Service describes its mission as "caring for the land and serving the people . . . the mission is to achieve quality land management under the sustainable multiple-use management concept to meet the diverse needs of people." Its vision is to be "recognized nationally and internationaly as a leader in caring for the land and serving people."

Save the Children

Save the Children, the world's largest independent charity serving children, describes its mission as "leading the fight towards making a reality of a world which respects and values each child; which listens to children and learns; and where all children have hope and opportunity."

Sources: U.S. Forest Service and Save the Children

Walk the Talk

Much of the criticism of vision and mission statements stems from the view that they represent meaningless, empty words. The scenario goes something like this: New management is seeking to energize the organization. It determines that a compelling vision can serve as a foundation for changing the culture and driving major improvements in performance. Consultants are hired, numerous interviews and workshops take place, and senior management spends many hours debating the merits of every single word of the proposed mission statement. With much fanfare, the new mission is rolled out. The CEO makes sincere presentations, handy laminated cards are given to employees, and colorful posters appear on every notice board. A few weeks later the first layoffs occur and it is back to business as usual—nothing changes. Mission and vision statements have value only if they are translated into everyday behaviors across the organization.

Best practice organizations inculcate their vision into everything they do. Management constantly asks, "How does this move us closer to achieving our vision?"

The true test of an organization's culture does not come when things are going well. Organizations that really walk the talk of their mission, visions, and values are those that can stay true to them when times are tough. At the height of the dot-com boom, the culture of the fast-growing Internet start-up became synonymous with a new world of work. Bring your dog to work, play foosball during cappuccino breaks, and be a CEO at 25 defined success in the supposed new world. Within weeks of the Nasdaq peaking in March 2000, the party was over. The foosball table and cappuccino machine were for sale on eBay, an irony in itself, and the CEO had moved back in with his or her parents. In contrast, a strong culture coupled with excellent financial performance allowed Southwest Airlines to maintain profitability and keep its entire staff employed after the terrorist attacks on September 11, 2001, while many of its competitors were forced to make drastic staff cuts.

Missions Change   Leaders need to continually assess whether the organization's vision remains relevant. For example, for many years Microsoft chairman Bill Gates described his company's vision thus: "Our vision is very simple. It's a computer on every desk and in every home, running Microsoft software" (Interview, All Things Considered, NPR 9/19/05).

When Microsoft was formed in 1975, this was a very ambitious vision. The personal computer industry was largely restricted to garages in southern California, and Microsoft software was far from the industry standard it was to become. Less than 20 years later, the concept of a computer on every desk and in every home running Microsoft software was no longer a stretch of the imagination. The company had come very close to realizing its original vision; it needed a new one. Microsoft recognized that its original vision was now a limiting factor for the company. In June 2002 Microsoft's CEO, Steve Ballmer, communicated the company's updated vision: "Empowering people through great software—any time, any place and on any device." This moved the company away from the computer in the home or office and cast Microsoft as ubiquitous when it comes to software. By February 2005 the mission had evolved still further and read:

> At Microsoft, we work to help people and business throughout the world realize their full potential. This is our mission. Everything we do reflects the mission and the values that make it possible.

Now the mission becomes even more inclusive—now it's not just people, it's businesses as well, reflecting Microsoft's aggressive push into the world of corporate computing. In addition, Microsoft explicitly states the global coverage of its business. If the effort that companies spend in developing mission, vision, and values statements is to be worthwhile, they must remain relevant.

Recognize the Value of Values   The third element in defining the cultural framework of an organization is the set of values that guide behavior. The mission and vision statements define an organization's objectives and reason for being; values describe the types of behaviors the organization believes are essential in working toward achieving its objectives. In some organizations, values are unwritten rules that guide behavior. Simply working together can be very effective when an organization is small; however, as organizations grow and become more complex, many find the need to document their values to promote consistent communication and acceptance. A well-crafted set of values can sustain an organization for many years and be a powerful mechanism for driving performance.

Three widely admired organizations, Johnson & Johnson (J&J), General Electric (GE), and Google, illustrate the importance of values as part of an organization's overall strategy.

Johnson & Johnson's values illustrate the sustainability of a well-crafted set of values over a long period of time. Its Credo (see Exhibit 5.4) has its origins in a pamphlet titled "TRY REALITY," written by General Robert Wood Johnson in 1935. Johnson not only guided J&J from a small, family-owned business to a worldwide enterprise but also developed a clear view of his company's responsibilities beyond the simple manufacturing and marketing of products. Johnson defined these as the corporation's responsibility to customers, employees, the community, and stockholders. Eight years after he wrote the initial pamphlet, these thoughts were crystallized into the J&J Credo. Johnson urged his management to apply it as part of their everyday business philosophy. At the time, the Credo, with its emphasis on putting customers first, was farsighted, foreshadowing the customer-centric movement in business by almost half a century. Johnson believed that by putting the customer first, the business would be well served. Management credits the Credo for continuously guiding their decision making in both good times and bad.

An excellent example was the company's handling of the Tylenol scares of 1982 and 1986. One of the company's most successful products, Tylenol was intentionally contaminated with cyanide, killing seven people in 1982 and spawning a series of copycat attacks over the next few years. With the company's reputation

---

Exhibit 5.4 Johnson & Johnson Credo

We believe our first responsibility is to the doctors, nurses and patients, to mothers and fathers and all others who use our products and services. In meeting their needs everything we do must be of high quality. We must constantly strive to reduce our costs in order to maintain reasonable prices. Customers' orders must be services promptly and accurately. Our suppliers and distributors must have an opportunity to make a fair profit.

We are responsible to our employees, the men and women who work with us throughout the world. Everyone must be considered as an individual. We must respect their dignity and recognize their merit. They must have a sense of security in their jobs. Compensation must be fair and adequate, and working conditions clean, orderly and safe We must be mindful of ways to help our employees fulfill their family responsibilities. Employees must feel free to make suggestions and complaints. There must be equal opportunity for employment, development and advancement for those qualified. We must provide competent management, and their actions must be just and ethical.

We are responsible to the communities in which we live and work and to the world community as well. We must be good citizens—support good works and charities and bear our fair share of taxes. We must encourage civic improvement and better health and education. We must maintain in good order the property we are privileged to use, protecting the environment and natural resources.

Our final responsibility is to our stockholders. Business must make a sound profit. We must experiment with new ideas. Research must be carried on, innovative programs developed and mistakes paid for. New equipment must be purchased, new facilities provided and new products launched. Reserves must be created to provide for adverse times. When we operate according to these principles, the stockholders should realize a fair return.

Source: Johnson & Johnson

---

at stake, management made countless decisions using the Credo as their guide. The company's reputation was preserved, and the Tylenol business survived and grew stronger. The company's handling of this potentially damaging situation has become a case study in crisis management. More than 60 years after it was first conceived, the Credo continues to guide the actions of this $50 billion corporation.

By contrast, GE's values seem to be more a reflection of the leadership style of the current chief executive. Looking back at the 20-year reign of Jack Welch as CEO, the company's high-performance culture shines through in the use of words such as "unyielding," "intolerant," "energize," and "edge" (see Exhibit 5.5). Almost evangelical in tone, you can hear Jack Welch driving the point home as he pounds on the table.

Welch retired from GE in 2001 and was replaced by Jeffrey Immelt. The transition in leadership is reflected in the shift in the way the company describes its values. Instead of the bombastic, almost confrontational, tone of the Welch era, Immelt's GE describes its values thus:

Exhibit 5.5   General Electric Values, May 2001

All of us . . . always with unyielding integrity . . .

Are passionately focused on driving customer success

Live Six Sigma Quality . . . ensure that the customer is always its first beneficiary . . . and use it to accelerate growth

Insist on excellence and are intolerant of bureaucracy

Act in a boundaryless fashion . . . always search for and apply the best ideas regardless of their source

Prize global intellectual capital and the people that provide it . . . build diverse teams to maximize it

See change for the growth opportunities it brings . . . e.g., "e-Business"

Create a clear, simple, customer-centered vision . . . and continually renew and refresh its execution

Create an environment of "stretch," excitement, informality and trust . . . reward improvements . . . and celebrate results

Demonstrate . . . always with infectious enthusiasm for the customer . . . the "4-E's" of GE leadership: the personal Energy to welcome and deal with the speed of change . . . the ability to create an atmosphere that Energizes others . . . the Edge to make difficult decisions . . . and the ability to consistently Execute

---

Source: General Electric Annual Report, 2000

Imagine, solve, build and lead—four bold verbs that express what it is to be part of GE. Their action-oriented nature says something about who we are—and should serve to energize ourselves and our teams around leading change and driving performance. (See www.GE.com.)

The tone is more pragmatic and reflects the style Immelt has brought to GE. His public profile is more subdued than that of his predecessor, although his actions during his first few years in charge have been no less bold—embarking on a major restructuring of the business and continuing to buy and sell businesses at a rapid rate.

It is interesting to contrast the approaches of J&J and GE, the two companies that have the longest records of sustained commercial success in U.S. industry. Both have been extraordinarily successful yet one is guided by a 70-year-old set of values while the other constantly adapts to the changing environment. Both approaches work; it all depends on execution—walking the talk.

Turning from two stalwarts of American commerce to the poster child of the new economy, Google reflects a very different style. Since its founding in 1998, Google has blazed a trail that few companies have ever matched. Its name has become a common noun and following its initial public offering in August 2004, its stock soared to a high of $475 and sported a market capitalization of $117 billion even after a pull-back to under $400 in February 2006; that is eight times the market cap of GM, and almost double that of both Yahoo and eBay. According to its Web site, Google's mission is, as you would expect, ambitious: "To organize the world's information and make it universally accessible and useful." This leaves plenty of scope for growth. Google's culture and values can be better understood when reviewing a piece written in 2002 entitled "Ten Things Google Has Found to Be True." (See http://www.google.com/intl/en/corporate/tenthings.html.)

1. Focus on the user and all else will follow.
2. It's best to do one thing really, really well.
3. Fast is better than slow.
4. Democracy on the web works.
5. You don't need to be at your desk to need an answer.
6. You can make money without doing evil.
7. There's always more information out there.
8. The need for information crosses all borders.
9. You can be serious without a suit.
10. Great just isn't good enough.

Sounds like a pretty cool but challenging place to work, doesn't it? Of all the statements of values I have reviewed, this one offers perhaps the best insight into the real culture of an organization. That is not to say that all companies should use the same style; you want the words and their phrasing to reflect the true values and culture you want your organization embrace; nothing else will suffice.

Despite being written in very different styles, there is a high degree of consistency in the values expressed by all of three companies. The same two constituencies—customers and people—resonate throughout, as do the core values—integrity, innovation, and excellence. Each set of values reflects the organization it represents. Perhaps more accurately, each of these organizations is a reflection of its values. The organizations will not always be successful, but in each case the organization adheres to both the substance and the style of its values. The most crucial aspect of defining a set of values is the degree to which an organization's leaders live by the values and succeed in getting the rest of the organization to commit to them. To illustrate that values in action are infinitely more important than words on paper, consider these statements from Enron's 2000 annual report:

> We have an obligation to communicate. Here, we take the time to talk with one another . . . and to listen. We believe that information is meant to move and that information moves people . . . . We treat others as we would like to be treated ourselves . . . . We work with customers and prospects openly, honestly and sincerely. When we say we will do something, we will do it; when we say we cannot or will not do something, then we won't do it.

Enron's former shareholders and many of its former employees must be wondering if the company's values were given any more than lip service during its spectacular rise and fall.

The lesson to be learned is that visions, missions, and values are effective only if they are shared, supported, and followed.

Visions, missions, and values are valuable tools for setting an organization's direction. As such, they are powerful inputs to the strategic planning process. Collectively they help guide behavior, create a common language and communication process, and serve as a basis for testing alternative strategies that are surfaced during the planning process.

Practically speaking, these tools help an organization define a set of behaviors that can accelerate decision making and execution through the creation of a strong internal culture based on a set of shared objectives and values that drive everyday performance.

COMMUNICATE, COMMUNICATE, COMMUNICATE

Strategies are only as good as the ability of an organization to implement them successfully. Scott McNealy, former chief executive of Sun Microsystems, emphasizes the importance of communication:

> Communication is a core competency of any business. It starts with the CEO.[11]

Implementation requires that the strategy be communicated effectively to all the individuals and groups that must contribute to its execution, including all the people within the organization and increasingly extending into the organization's suppliers and other business partners. At one large service company, senior management had developed a new strategy centered on the customer. A key assumption of the strategy was that by paying closer attention to each and every customer, the company had a far greater likelihood of retaining each customer and cross-selling additional products and services. It was a very sound strategy; however, the communication process left a lot to be desired. Staff members in the company's three customer service centers were still being directed to minimize the length of time spent with each customer to maintain productivity and minimize costs. The effect was exactly the opposite of that intended by the strategy. A failure to communicate and align performance objectives can render the most effective strategies worthless.

Communication is a prerequisite for execution. An excellent example of the willingness to communicate can be found at Berkshire Hathaway, the company created by legendary investor Warren Buffett. Buffett's annual chairman's letter has become standard reading for many investors. Each year he sets out his thoughts on Berkshire Hathaway's business, the company's strategy, and the economy in general. Besides the annual letter to shareholders, Berkshire Hathaway also has produced a booklet called "An Owner's Manual," targeted at shareowners, which provides a clear description of the broad principles of operation that govern the business.[12] Written in plain English, the manual details 13 business principles that Buffett and his vice chairman, Charlie Munger, use to lead the company. Included among the principles are specific statements regarding such key items as the most appropriate measures of business performance, the use of debt, objectivity in management reporting, and discipline in decision making. Effective leaders take every opportunity to extol the value of their organization's strategy.

STRATEGIC PLANNING IS A COLLABORATIVE PROCESS

Running any organization successfully is a collaborative process. Nowhere is this collaboration more crucial than in planning. Unfortunately, for many organizations, the individual steps in the planning process are often completed in isolation from each other. This isolation may explain the lack of creativity in many strategic plans. The smartest executives are those who are able to identify and nurture a great idea; rarely are they the source of the idea. The PC, the personal digital assistant, the Web browser, 24-hour news channels, the drive-through window, everyday low prices, and the Egg McMuffin were not created in the executive suite. Breakthrough strategic thinking requires a broad solicitation of ideas from a diverse group of people. Best practice companies invest time and effort in nurturing innovative thinking; they create forums by which senior managers are exposed to new thinking both from within and from outside the organization. The strategic planning process should encourage the development of innovative ideas and provide a mechanism to ensure the potential value is not lost. Xerox is a classic example of a company that was successful in fostering innovation but failed to capitalize on the potential of many of its internally developed innovations. The company invented some of the most significant components of the PC, including the mouse and the graphical user interface, yet conspicuously failed to exploit any of them for its own commercial advantage. Not only does a lack of collaboration hinder innovation; it also limits the perspectives that can be brought to bear during the strategic planning process. The best time to challenge or test any strategy is during the planning process. Seeking a broad range of inputs can provide senior management with a balanced perspective of the risks and opportunities associated with pursuing a particular strategy.

CEO AS CHIEF STRATEGIST

Strategic planning is the management process that is most impacted by the personality and style of the CEO. Leaders such as Jack Welch at GE, Robert Goizuetta at Coca-Cola, and Larry Bossidy at Honeywell all made dramatic shifts in the planning processes during their tenure. Bill Gates went so far as to cede the CEO title at Microsoft to Steve Ballmer and take on a new role as chief software architect. Gates described his new role as allowing him "to dedicate myself full time to my passion—building great software and strategizing on the future and nurturing and collaborating with the core team helping Steve [Ballmer] run the company."[13]

Strategy is not a process that can be delegated. John Reed, former chairman of Citigroup, often commented that "a CEO has just two jobs, deciding what to do and making it happen." This does not mean that CEOs must develop the strategy; it does mean that they must lead the process. Leadership styles and organizations vary greatly, and the strategic planning process needs to adapt rather than constrain the ability of leaders to lead. Effective CEOs nurture the strategic planning process. They are open to new ideas and not vested in the present. This attitude requires considerable self-confidence. The ability to accept challenges to the conventional wisdom within their organizations is a refreshing hallmark of enlightened CEOs. Leading the strategic planning process does not mean that CEOs dictate the content of the strategy—far from it. It means that they ensure that rich debate results in clear direction. Chief executives must strike the right balance between open debate and decision making. They are always seeking to crystallize the thinking that emerges during the debate into a coherent strategy.

HARD SIDE OF STRATEGY

Strategic planning is about making choices—often very hard ones that require an organization to place large bets on inherently uncertain outcomes. The soft side of strategy creates the environment for successful execution by encouraging an open, creative, and high-performing culture; however, without a clear focus, direction, and set of objectives, an organization lacks purpose. The hard side of strategy defines exactly what an organization will do and the major strategies it will employ, and quantifies objectives and targets.

Clearly Define the Business

What business are you in? This is one of the first questions consultants ask a client. Initially it sounds facetious—after all, it is pretty clear that McDonald's is in the fast food business and that Dell is in the computer business. As someone who has asked the question numerous times, I must emphasize that it remains a great source of insight into a company and its strategy. I asked this question of the top 10 executives at one of America's largest financial institutions, and I got 10 very different answers. Some simply described their business as financial services, banking, or insurance, depending on their organizational focus. Some went further to describe the aspects of providing savers with a safe haven for their money; others focused on the lending side—all offered very reasonable descriptions of the business. Finally I met with the chairman and asked him the same question. He responded, "We are in the business of helping make people's dreams come true—buying a home, taking a great vacation, putting their children through college, or retiring comfortably." Such a range of responses to a seemingly straightforward question is not unusual; however, it does illustrate the challenges many organizations face in ensuring complete alignment and consistent understanding of their purpose and objectives.

Two elements are involved in defining the business purpose:

1. The markets in which the organization will participate—sometimes called participation strategy

2. The positioning it will take within those markets—sometimes called positioning strategy

Participation strategy typically involves a description of the broad industry or service classification. For example, Coca-Cola participates in the beverage market, General Motors in the automotive market, and Citigroup in the financial services market.

Positioning strategy defines an organization's competitive positioning within its chosen markets. For example, Fiat and Ferrari both participate in the automotive market and are part of the same corporation; however, they have defined radically different positions within the market. Positioning can be defined in a number of ways: by product, as in the Fiat/Ferrari example; by customer segment, as in Home and Garden Television (HGTV) and Lifetime; or by delivery channel, as in Progressive Insurance's direct approach and State Farm's agent-based model. The key for a successful strategy is for the positioning to be distinct. Southwest Airlines has a very distinct positioning in the airline business; similarly Wal-Mart, Kohls, Wendy's, Starbucks, Dell, and Harley-Davidson have all based much of their success on defining a distinct and differentiated position in their respective markets.

Define What You Are Not Going to Do

Strategic plans are very good at defining an organization's goals and objectives and describing the strategies for how they are to be accomplished. Beyond stating what will be done, a good strategic plan also clearly states what an organization will not do: the markets it will not enter, the types of product or service it will not offer, and the types of customer it will not serve. As Larry Bossidy of Honeywell commented about the need for clarity about what an organization will and will not do: "Honeywell is an industrial company; consumer products won't play well in this arena, no matter how exciting they may be."[14]

Describing areas that a business will not venture into simplifies planning since it immediately takes certain items off the table. Management then can focus on those opportunities that are consistent with the business purpose and strategic objectives of the organization.

Strategies Set Targets

A strategy that does not provide clear direction for the operational and financial planning processes is incomplete. Setting targets is crucial because they translate overall strategic goals and stakeholder expectations into quantifiable objectives that guide detailed planning.

The target-setting process is a mechanism for senior management to communicate expectations to operating divisions and service providers, such as finance, human resources, and information technology. Operating divisions and service providers then develop plans and budgets based on capabilities to meet or exceed the agreed-on targets.

Targets are set around a few key metrics. Targets should balance external expectations, market pressures, and internal capabilities. When setting targets, senior management considers a number of factors, including the overall business strategy; any adjustments that need to be made to reflect new opportunities, threats, or changes in basic assumptions; past performance relative to agreed-on plans and targets; stakeholder expectations, including those of owners and, if publicly traded, analysts; likely impact of any major initiatives that are contemplated; and the results of the most recent forecasts.

The overall objective during target setting is to balance external expectations and internal capabilities in a realistic way (see Exhibit 5.6).

Once the overall targets have been established, they are cascaded and communicated throughout the organization. The cascading of targets involves the allocation of targets to individual businesses and the translation of a high-level target into lower-level targets to guide the development of tactical plans. For example, senior management may set an overall profitability target for a business. The management team then works to translate the overall profitability target into its component parts. The target-setting process establishes who has responsibility and accountability for each aspect of performance and therefore forms the basis for developing individual reward and compensation mechanisms.

Targets Are Not a Substitute for Strategy

Although targets are essential outputs of the strategic planning process, they are not the only output. Over the last few years, many executives have sought to define

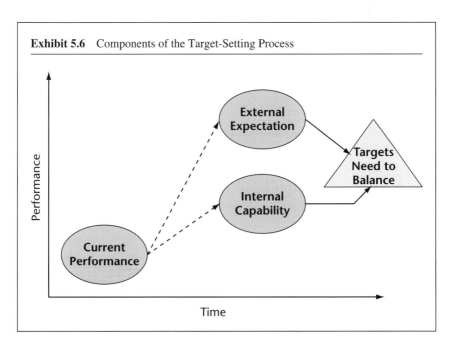

Exhibit 5.6   Components of the Target-Setting Process

their business vision in terms of a sensational goal or target. Called BHAGs, for big hairy audacious goals, by Collins and Poras, they serve as the focal point for execution.[15] In some cases they represent a bet-the-business play, as with Boeing's commitment to the 747 or IBM's development of the 360 mainframe computer. BHAGs can be powerful motivating tools to rally people around a stretch goal that all can recognize as revolutionary for the organization.

While they can serve as powerful motivational tools, ambitious goals or BHAGs are no substitute for a strategy. Goals establish destinations but provide little insight into the journey. Management needs to ensure that the strategy addresses not just the overall objectives but also the major plans by which they will be accomplished.

Effective strategy defines more than a target or objective. Strategy involves a discussion not just of objectives but also of actions to achieve those objectives.

Decisions Are More Important than Plans

Strategic planning almost always produces a document that memorializes the results of the process. Best practice organizations understand that although the plan document itself has value, the real value of the strategic planning process is threefold.

1. Strategic planning is about management making decisions, choices, and trade-offs about the objectives and goals of the organization and the major strategies for achieving them. This includes decisions about markets, products, organization structure, and resource allocations.
2. The strategic planning process provides a potent forum for soliciting input and securing commitment to a common strategy that then can be promulgated throughout the organization.
3. The strategic planning process provides a risk-free opportunity to debate radical questions, ideas, and assumptions that, while they eventually may be discounted, can serve to increase management's confidence in the agreed-on direction.

It is all too easy to lose focus on the purpose of the strategic plan. Herb Kelleher of Southwest Airlines described his approach to avoiding this problem in this way:

> One way we avoid complacency—and this may just be because I don't have a long attention span—is that we reject the idea of long-range planning. We say, do strategic planning, define what you are, and then get back together soon to define whether you need to change that. And have the alacrity of a puma. Because this plan about what we're going to do ten years from now will almost certainly be invalidated in the next six months.[16]

Focus is critical in the strategic planning process, both in terms of managing the process itself and also in terms of what is contained within the strategy. Strategic planning processes tend to become leisurely strolls that lack a clear direction.

Although debate and dialogue are essential components of the process, the purpose of strategic planning is to make decisions—decisions about the scope of the business, the major initiatives to be pursued, and the level of performance to be targeted. A strategic planning process that does not reach any conclusions is ineffective. Companies that stray beyond their core capabilities can lose their way. The retail industry offers a good example of the pitfalls of dilution.

From 1985 to 1994, about $163 billion of stock market value was created in the retail industry. Of the total, Wal-Mart accounted for $42 billion and Home Depot for $20 billion, while industry leader Sears captured less than $1 billion of the growth. Competitors used new business designs based on stand-alone megastores outside shopping malls, with low prices, quality merchandise, and broad selection to attack Sears' heartland. Home Depot, Wal-Mart, and others like Target, Best Buy, and Bed Bath and Beyond all stole leadership positions in market segments that Sears used to own. At the precise time that its core business was under assault, much of Sears' management time was consumed in managing a series of diverse businesses, including Discover Card, Dean Witter Reynolds, and Allstate Insurance, businesses that had, at best, tangential relevance to the core franchise. Sears ultimately ended up divesting itself of all these businesses and sought to refocus on its core business. Unfortunately, much of the damage had already been done and in March 2005, Sears was acquired by Kmart, itself only just emerging from Chapter 11 bankruptcy protection.

Loss of focus is not restricted to the retail industry. In 2000 the French utility company Vivendi embarked on an interesting diversification into movies with its purchase of Seagram and Universal Studios. Less than two years later, the architect of the diversification, CEO Jean-Marie Messier, was ousted amid massive debt and declining overall performance. In fact, the movie industry has proven a somewhat fatal attraction for businesses. Seagram itself had attempted a similar diversification away from its core liquor businesses with its own acquisition of Universal. Earlier both Coca-Cola (1982) and Sony (1989) owned Columbia Pictures with mixed results. MGM passed through the hands of both Pathé Communications and Credit Lyonnaise. Pathé went bankrupt and Credit Lyonnaise ended up selling the studio back to former owner Kirk Kerkorian. At the time of Vivendi's purchase of Seagram which included Universal Studios, British analyst Terry Smith commented, "The economics of the movie industry seems to represent the ultimate triumph of hope over experience."[17]

Of course, there are examples of companies successfully combining very different businesses, such as General Electric, which manages to profitably combine light bulbs, jet engines, television stations, and consumer loans, and Berkshire Hathaway, with shoes, furniture, insurance, fractional jet ownership, and underwear; however, such firms are few in number.

Almost every study of successful companies—from Peters and Waterman's *In Search of Excellence* in 1982 through Jim Collins's *Good to Great* in 2002—have found that most companies that met their criteria for excellence and greatness respectively maintained a very clear strategic focus.

Balance Creativity and Rigor

Thomas Edison once said, "Genius is one percent inspiration and 99 percent perspiration." The same could well be said of strategy development. Strategic planning is a creative, event-driven process focused on setting future direction.

Inputs to strategic planning are broad and can include analyses of past performance, forecasts of future performance, internal research, results achieved relative to previously defined objectives, likely changes in markets, customers, the political environment, technology, and global competition, internally generated ideas, and externally commissioned research or expert counsel. Collecting all these data and synthesizing them effectively requires a systematic methodology. Strategic planning needs to balance creativity with rigor combining unstructured and structured activity. Achieving this balance is what makes a good strategy so hard to define; refining innovative thinking into an executable plans requires a continuous flip-flop between the creative and the analytic.

Many business success stories start with a "eureka" moment of blinding insight or plain luck. Translating great ideas into commercial success requires a lot of hard work. Many innovative companies failed to build on a great original concept and visionary leadership. Lotus dominated the spreadsheet market in the mid-1980s but lost its leadership position to Microsoft and ended up as part of IBM. Digital Equipment dominated the minicomputer market and boasted of its plans to overtake IBM as the largest computer company in the world. Less than a decade later, Digital had been acquired by Compaq, which in turn merged with Hewlett-Packard.

Maintaining the right balance between creativity and rigor requires constant attention. Some experts have gone as far as to define strategic thinking and strategic planning as two discrete activities. They recommend that distinct time be set aside for each element during the strategic planning process. Doing so can be helpful in aligning the management team. Strategic thinking draws on skills and tools such as brainstorming, unstructured what-if analysis, debate, and free association. It is not designed to be completely rational, logical, or practical. The objective is to stimulate discussion and promote creative thinking. "Out-of-the-box thinking" is a favorite phrase in American business to describe creative or innovative thinking.

Many organizations have found that maintaining a clear distinction between strategic thinking and strategic planning promotes a richer discussion and a more inventive overall strategy.

Embrace Innovation

One of the enduring debates in business is whether formal, structured planning processes serve as an impediment to innovation. One body of thought believes that the discipline of planning and the creativity of innovation are somehow incompatible with each other. The track records of renowned innovators, such as 3M, IBM, and Johnson & Johnson, would appear to dispel this notion. Clayton Christensen, in his book *The Innovator's Dilemma*, defined two types of innovation.[18] The first and more prevalent type is what he terms "sustaining innovations," which primarily improve existing products. The second and more dangerous type for established companies is the emergence of disruptive innovations that change the rules of the game. Examples of disruptive innovations include the impact of discount retailers, such as Wal-Mart and Target, on traditional department stores, including Sears and J.C. Penney, and the impact of fast, high-quality Japanese motorcycles from Honda, Kawasaki, and Suzuki on the large, touring bikes of Harley-Davidson and BMW.

Sustaining innovations are very compatible with a structured planning process. As Christensen comments:

> [C]ompanies must not throw out the capabilities, organizational structures, and decision making processes that have made them successful in their mainstream markets just because they don't work in the face of disruptive technological change. The vast majority of innovation challenges they will face are sustaining in character . . . [M]anagers . . . simply need to recognize that these capabilities, cultures, and practices are valuable only in certain conditions.[19]

The key is to match the right planning approach to the situation at any given time. The objective is to identify the appropriate organizational and planning model to cultivate different types of innovation. A one-size-fits-all model is not the answer.

Explicitly Address Uncertainty

The only certainty about the future is that it is uncertain. Renowned economist John Kenneth Galbraith cautioned against placing too much reliance on future plans when he said: "Very specific and personal misfortune awaits those who presume to believe that the future is revealed to them."[20]

Planning is not about developing a singular view of the future; one of the most valuable elements of any planning activity is the ability to factor in the impact of risk on the assumptions, initiatives, and targeted results. The potential impact of unpredictable or unforeseen events can be devastating. In the early hours of December 3, 1984, gas leaked from a tank of methyl isocyanate at a plant in Bhopal, India, owned and operated by Union Carbide India Limited. Nearly 4,000 people died and over 2,600 suffered permanent disability of some sort. On March 24, 1989, the *Exxon Valdez* ran aground in the Prince William Sound, spilling 10.8 million gallons of oil and causing significant environmental damage. In each case, the impact on the companies linked to the tragedy—Union Carbide and Exxon respectively—was significant.

Although it is unreasonable and impractical to expect a planning process to consider all possible events that may impact a business, plans must explicitly deal with uncertainty. For long-term strategic planning, the development of a range of alternative scenarios can provide management with a basis for assessing the reasonableness of the strategies that are being developed. As planning becomes more detailed, sensitivity and what-if analyses can help further assess the impact of uncertainty.

At most organizations, scenario planning, if performed at all, is generally informal and inconsistently applied. While adoption rates have increased in recent years, few companies systematically integrate scenario planning into the planning process. There appear to be three major reasons for this reluctance:

1. *Simple fear of the unknown.* Peter Schwartz, author of *The Art Of The Long View* explained the fear thus: "To act with confidence, one must be willing to look ahead and consider uncertainties: 'What challenges could the world present me? How might others respond to my actions?' Rather than asking such questions, too many people react to uncertainty with denial. They take an unconsciously deterministic view of events."[21]
2. *Lack of time.* Most organizations are working up to the last minute simply to complete a single plan of action. There is no time left to evaluate alternative scenarios.
3. *Lack of adequate training in the development of effective scenario plans.*

The application of rigorous analytical techniques to inherently uncertain future situations is a difficult concept. To apply such techniques and then confidently make decisions based on the resulting analysis requires both education and experimentation.

Scenario planning can help organizations contemplate the unthinkable. Taking time out during the strategic planning process to contemplate nightmare scenarios can be useful preparation when major changes occur that threaten the health of individual companies or whole industries. The U.K. textile industry, the U.S. consumer electronics industry, and companies such as Wang, Polaroid, and Digital Equipment all went from market domination to near obliteration in less than a generation. Developing scenario plans that help define the leading indicators of such seismic changes can buy management that most precious commodity of all: time.

Sometimes It's Better to Be Provocative than Right

The perfect time to be a contrarian is during the planning process. One of the most effective roles to play is that of devil's advocate. By challenging the basic assumptions an organization makes during the strategic planning process, you can force management to clearly articulate why its assumptions and strategies are valid. Instead of simply accepting them, management must develop coherent and compelling arguments in support of its beliefs and assumptions. Doing so not only tests the validity of management's thinking but also equips it to communicate strategy much more effectively to people both inside and outside the company. Sometimes it makes sense to argue a contrarian point of view even though you are in complete agreement with the management team; by doing this you force its members to hone their arguments and revalidate their assumptions. If you happen to be both provocative and right, you have provided an even more valuable service.

Strategic Planning Is a Continuous Process

One of the most significant trends in recent years has been for management to recognize that aspects of strategic planning are not once-a-year events but a continuous process. The pace at which markets, customers, and products change is so great that management needs to monitor the strategic implications of new developments on a continuous basis. Very few of the material events of the last few years were timed to fit nicely into the traditional calendar-based planning cycle. Best practice companies develop a mechanism that allows them to initiate elements of the strategic planning process outside of the normal planning calendar. For example, the passage of the Telecommunications Act in 1996, which sought to liberalize competition in many markets, triggered an immediate strategic reassessment at Sprint to ensure that the implications and opportunities presented by the act were fully understood and factored into the firm's future strategy. Similarly, the events of September 11, 2001, forced the airline industry to radically reassess the strategic implications on the industry. The impact was not only on short-term travel plans and profitability but also on the implications for capacity, scheduling, and even airport design for many years to come. Being flexible enough to reevaluate long-held strategies in response to new information or events is a hallmark of an agile organization. These events do not necessarily change the basic strategy in terms of market choices and positioning, but they can change the assumptions and approaches of organizations in pursuit of those objectives.

At Bank of America, chairman and CEO Ken Lewis frequently explains that his expectation of the core businesses that make up the bank is to provide the company with the means (capital and cash) to take advantage of attractive opportunities as and when they present themselves. This core strategy of agility was clearly demonstrated when the deal to acquire FleetBoston was announced in October 2003, less than two weeks after FleetBoston approached the bank. The scenario was repeated less than two years later when the bank announced its acquisition of MBNA just over a week after MBNA approached it after talks with the bank's crosstown rival Wachovia broke down. Developing a clearly defined strategy is perfectly consistent with agile and fast decision making; in fact, in today's volatile and uncertain world, it is essential.

Minimize the Level of Detail

Defining the appropriate level of detail is a recurring theme throughout this book. Simply put, the more detailed any aspect of planning or forecasting becomes, the greater the odds of the plan being wrong. Nowhere is this more dangerous than in the strategic plan. If a strategic plan sets out in precise detail exactly what will happen, how it will happen, and what the results will be, the organization will spend all its time explaining variances. A strategic plan sets a direction or, as Bossidy says, "provides a road map lightly filled in."[22] It is essential that the strategy provide flexibility. The impossibility of predicting the future accurately demands that management has room to react as events unfold.

Taking Bossidy's analogy further, the strategy will define the major milestones on the journey to the agreed-on destination or goal. For example, when planning a road trip, people often lay out the major cities or attractions that they wish to visit and maybe define overnight stops; however, people are unlikely to go so far as to plan out every rest room or refueling stop along the way. It is highly unlikely that those who attempt to do so will follow their plan as intended, particularly if they are traveling with children.

An effective strategic plan narrows the focus on a range of objectives and actions but does not seek to prescribe everything. People need the flexibility to respond to events. An effective strategy provides them with a framework for making choices and trade-offs as events arise. The objective is to provide effective guidance to support execution, not to create a set of detailed, predefined targets and action plans that have little hope of being implemented or achieved.

Remember: A detailed five-year budget is *not* a strategic plan.

Why Bother with Strategy?

Many people question the value of strategic planning, and, in fact, many successful companies and leaders deny putting any effort into developing strategy. Is a strategy a prerequisite for success? Some organizations have replaced true strategic planning with long-term operational planning; others have given up on strategy altogether. In a March 2001 interview with *Fast Company* magazine, Michael Porter, one of the foremost strategic thinkers, commented, "It's been a bad decade for strategic planning. Companies have bought into an extraordinary number of flawed or simplistic ideas about competition—what I call 'intellectual potholes.' As a result, many have abandoned strategy almost completely."[23]

Some organizations argued that the pace of change made strategic planning obsolete. These firms missed the point. It would be more accurate to say that the pace of change had made the long-term tactical plans that masqueraded as strategic plans obsolete. Is a formal strategy necessary for everyone? The answer is no; a formal strategy, as most people understand the term, is not a prerequisite for success. It is doubtful that William Hewlett and David Packard or Steve Wozniak and Steve Jobs had a clear strategy in their minds as they toiled away in their garages sowing the seeds of what would become Hewlett-Packard and Apple. Perhaps one of the best examples of the absence of strategy not impeding great success was Christopher Columbus. He left Portugal with no idea of where he was going, had no idea of what he had found when he reached the New World, and had no idea of where he had been when he got back. When he found the West Indies, he thought he was in India—hence their name. Despite all that, he successfully made the journey across the Atlantic on three separate occasions and achieved immortality in the process.

Although Columbus lacked a clear strategy, there were distinctive elements of strategic thought in his actions. He was looking to discover answers to questions that in themselves would give him a purpose. Many organizations have no clear understanding of strategy; as a consequence, they do not address formal strategy development at all. Strategy is not essential, but it is highly desirable, if only as a communication vehicle. As General H. Norman Schwarzkopf has commented, "Leadership is a potent combination of strategy and character. But if you must be without one, be without the strategy."[24]

ACID TEST

The overall message of this chapter can be summarized succinctly. The four attributes of a best practice strategic planning process are:

1. Simplicity
2. Focus
3. Clarity
4. Ownership

The strategic plan must be easily understood and communicated if it is to be quickly translated into practical actions and deliver sustainable results. Finally, a strategy that is not bought into by people within the organization has little chance of success.

BEST PRACTICE SUMMARY

- The organization's mission, vision, and values are shared by all.
- Visions are inspirational, crisp, concise, and easily understood.
- Mission statements describe a highly desirable objective.
- Senior management consistently leads by example in the application of the organization's values.
- All members of the senior management team describe the organization's vision and strategy in a consistent manner.
- Communication is constant and consistent.
- The business purpose clearly defines both the participation strategy and the positioning strategy.
- Senior management understands the importance of and difference between strategic thinking and strategic planning.
- Creative ideas and thinking are nurtured within the organization, and their commercial potential is constantly evaluated.
- Management leverages its outside directors as a sounding board for testing the quality of the strategic thinking and resulting plans.
- Big hairy audacious goals (BHAGs) are not used as substitutes for strategic plans.
- Detail is balanced with predictive ability so as not to unnecessarily limit management's ability to make effective decisions.
- All major project proposals are tested for strategic "fit" as well as returns on investment.

- The process clearly defines the likely reasons a particular strategy may fail and establishes the criteria for abandonment.
- Uncertainty and risk are explicitly addressed, and appropriate scenarios and contingencies are considered.
- The strategic plan clearly defines the goals that are to be accomplished (destination), the major steps and actions to be taken (direction), and the time frame for execution (speed).
- The strategy explicitly defines not just what the organization is seeking to do but also what it will not do.
- The strategic plan is developed and owned by the management team with the most senior executive as acting as chief strategist.
- Specific targets are produced that guide operational and financial planning.
- Incentives are tied directly to meeting the goals set out in the strategic plan.
- Targets, operational plans, financial plans, and management reports all clearly link back to the strategy.

NOTES

1. Alfred P. Sloan, Jr., *My Years with General Motors* (New York: Doubleday, 1990), p. 378.
2. Ernst Malmstein, Erik Portanger, and Charles Drazin, *boo hoo* (New York: Random House, 2001).pp. 50
3. Basil H. Liddell Hart, *Strategy* (London: Penguin Books, 1991), p. 322.
4. *Fortune.* (May 1990).
5. Tom Peters and Robert Waterman, *In Search of Excellence* (New York: Harper & Row, 1982), pp. 19–26.
6. Scott Adams, *The Dilbert Principle* (New York: HarperCollins, 1996), p. 36.
7. John Huey and Geoffrey Colvin, "The Jack and Herb Show," *Fortune*, January 1, 1999.
8. William Drohan, "Writing a Mi=ssion Statement," *Association Management* 51 (1999): 117.
9. American Management Association, Corporate Values Survey, New York 2002
10. Lou Gerstner, speech at Stanford Business School, 1993.
11. Scott McNealy Speech at the Gartner IT Expo, Orlando, FL, October 2000.
12. Warren E. Buffett, "An Owner's Manual," 1996: www.Berkshire Hathaway.com, 1996.
13. Press release from Microsoft Corporation, Redmond, WA, January 13, 2000.
14. Larry Bossidy and Ram Charan, *Execution* (New York: Crown Business, 2002), p. 183.
15. James C. Collins and Jerry I. Poras, *Built to Last* (New York: Harper Business, 1994).
16. John Huey and Geoffrey Colvin, "The Jack and Herb Show," *Fortune,* January 1, 1999.
17. Collins Steward, Inc., Research Report, June 2000.
18. Clayton M. Christensen, *The Innovator's Dilemma* (New York: Harper Business, 2000).
19. Ibid., p. 225.
20. *The Forbes Book of Business Quotations* (New York: Black Dog & Leventhal,1997), p. 318.
21. Peter Schwartz, *The Art of the Long View* (New York: Bantam Doubleday Dell, 1991).
22. Bossidy and Charan, *Execution*, p. 185.
23. Keith H. Hammonds, "Michael Porter's Big Ideas," *Fast Company* (March 2001) p. 150.
24. "Schwarzkopf on Leadership," *Inc* Magazine 1/92.

Chapter 6

Tactical and Financial Planning: Translating Ideas into Action

The will to win is useless, if you do not have the will to prepare.

—Thane Yost

The tactical plan and the financial plan constitute the organization's operating plan and serve as the primary mechanism for translating strategic objectives into tactical actions.

DEFINING TACTICAL AND FINANCIAL PLANNING

Defining tactical and financial planning is as simple as asking two questions: What tactics will be pursued to meet the performance targets emanating from the strategic plan? What are the expected financial results of executing the tactics?

The financial plan includes two elements: the operating budget and the capital budget. The operating budget defines the revenues and expenses that are projected from executing the operating plan, and the capital budget defines capital investments required to support execution. The need for two financial plans is driven largely by the different accounting treatment of capital and operating expenses. This differentiation was brought into sharp focus in the summer of 2002, when the second largest U.S. long-distance telephone company, WorldCom, admitted that it had deliberately classified $3.8 billion of operating expenses as capital expenses to inflate earnings.

TIP

Planning has no reason to exist as a function within a company other than to enable resource reallocation. If I can get our speed of reaction to increase, we gain competitive advantage.[1]

Greg Myers, former CFO, Symantec Corporation

TYPICAL PROCESS

The tactical and financial planning process starts with the communication of some preliminary targets by senior management. These targets typically include sales and profit growth numbers plus a few other key measures. On receipt of the targets, departments immediately dust off last year's budget and start updating it to try to make the numbers work by applying a series of arbitrary net change factors to the prior plan. Estimates are rarely based on a true understanding of the likely drivers of performance in the period being planned. In effect, the tactical plan is really an updated budget. True tactical planning is limited to the development of a series of independent project plans and proposals. These proposals follow no standard format, and the calculation of return on investment (ROI) is inconsistent from project to project. The level of detail varies widely in different parts of the plan. Budgets are developed in excruciating detail while action plans are limited to a few bullet points on a PowerPoint slide listing the major initiatives for the year.

The level of detail in the budget is the same for all periods. Little notice is taken of the fact that predictive ability declines the farther out you look. The sheer volume of detail leaves little time for scenario planning or sensitivity analysis to address variability or develop contingencies.

Each department manager diligently seeks to develop a plan that comes close to meeting or in very rare cases exceeding the given target. Hours of data collection, modeling, and negotiation are expended, culminating in the submission of the completed plan to senior management. During the ensuing consolidation and review process, further compromises and changes are made, but the consolidated plan still falls short of the target. After a month or so of negotiation, horse-trading, and even blackmail, the gap has been closed but not eliminated. By now it is getting perilously close to the time when the plan must be submitted to the board of directors for approval. In desperation, the chief executive officer (CEO) instructs the chief financial officer (CFO) to make whatever changes are needed to make the plan meet the targets. A top-down mandate calls for everyone to reduce expenses by a fixed percent while holding revenue constant. Managers respond by cutting budgets, canceling projects, and adjusting resource levels. Everyone scrambles to adjust his or her spreadsheet models to reflect the cuts, the consolidation is rerun, and, miraculously, the new consolidated budget meets the target. Everyone breathes a huge sigh of relief, and the budget is ready for presentation to the board. Unfortunately, many of the changes invalidate all the detailed work completed earlier in the process. The top-down adjustments destroy any ownership and commitment to the budget.

Overall integration among operating plans, financial plans, project plans, and capital plans varies widely. There is no direct link between the results of specific projects and items in the financial plan. The plan development process is characterized by a lot of bargaining and negotiation to ensure individual projects get approved or to get the numbers to work. The bargaining is rarely fact-based and results in plan commitments that cannot be met realistically, particularly for allocations and transfer pricing between internal units. The numerous iterations, excessive detail, and financial orientation serve only to reduce business managers' ownership of the resulting plans. Those managers cede ownership of the process to the finance organization.

The whole process takes four to five months as the organization prepares multiple iterations of the plan. The tactical and financial planning processes are viewed as a necessary evil rather than a valued management tool. Often the results are obsolete soon after they are created as actual events change basic assumptions.

At the end of the process, morale is poor and commitment variable at best. Most adopt the attitude of "Thank God that's over for another year"—not exactly a glowing recommendation for one of the most critical management processes.

TACTICAL PLANNING BEST PRACTICES

The goal of tactical planning is to translate the targets and strategic objectives of the organization into a practical plan that defines the tactics and actions to be taken, the resources required, and the results expected for some future time period, typically but not always a year. Tactical plans drive financial plans. Getting the basics right establishes a sound platform for developing and implementing the right tactics in pursuit of the agreed-on targets.

Components of the Tactical Plan

Tactical plans typically address three different activities (see Exhibit 6.1):

1. Sustaining current operations
2. Improving current operations
3. Embarking on new ventures or initiatives

Sustaining current operations defines the actions required to continue operating in the current way and the areas where no material change in performance or behavior is required. Improving current operations defines those actions or projects that seek to improve the level of performance of an existing part of the organization. It could encompass a process change, an organizational change, a change of supplier, or a new marketing program. New ventures or initiatives break new ground for the organization. Perhaps the firm enters a new market, builds a new plant, launches a new product line, or creates a new distribution channel. Most tactical plans include actions that fall into all three categories. Management will be required to make choices and trade-offs among categories and to assess the overall risk/return profile to ensure that it is acceptable while offering a reasonable probability of meeting the targets.

Set Clear Targets and Objectives

Chapter 5 discussed the target-setting process, which is the primary mechanism for linking strategic planning with tactical and financial planning. Target setting occurs during the strategic planning process and requires management to do two things:

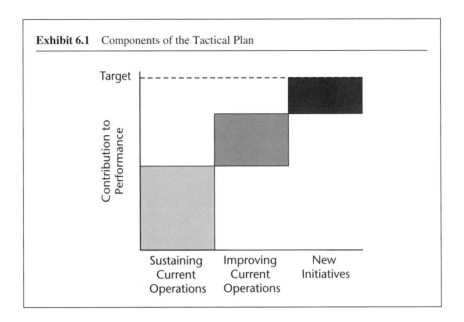

Exhibit 6.1   Components of the Tactical Plan

1. Define the key measures of strategic success.
2. Set targets for each measure to guide tactical and financial planning.

All planning must be focused on a goal or target. The tactical planning process starts with the issuance of targets that the plan needs to meet. These targets are set around the key performance measures that the organization has established during the strategic planning process and should be agreed on before detailed planning begins.

The changing of targets is one of the major causes of rework in the planning process. Changes in targets usually occur for one of two reasons.

1. The initial iteration of the budget or financial plan fails to deliver the results expected because one or more units cannot meet the targets. Typically this results in the shortfall being redistributed to the other units, often in an arbitrary manner at the very end of the budget cycle.
2. Due to the extended cycle time for developing tactical plans and budgets, a lot of new information emerges that causes management to rethink the original target.

Planning to an ever-changing target is a waste of time. The successive plan iterations increase frustration, reduce plan quality, and diminish ownership and commitment. By shortening the overall elapsed time for tactical and financial planning to 60 days or less, organizations reduce the risk that events will make targets obsolete before the plan is completed. The net result is a more robust plan.

Of course, at times events overtake a target, and it becomes clear that the original target no longer makes any sense. If this occurs, best practice organizations still have a distinct advantage. They can update their plans to reflect a more reasonable target much more easily since they do not have to rework nearly as much detail as the average company. They also can choose to use the rolling forecast process to reflect changes in the original targets and simply reflect a variance between the forecast and the original plan. Either way, they minimize the amount of rework required.

Integration Is Key

Strategy drives tactics and tactics drive results. Tactics are the means by which strategy gets implemented and form the bridge between strategic planning and tactical execution. Tactical plans should focus on the same goals, critical success factors, and drivers identified during the strategic planning process. What this means is that the tactics and initiatives defined in the tactical plan should directly link to aspects of the overall strategic plan and also to a specific measure of business performance. For example, a project to implement a new customer relationship management (CRM) system may be linked directly to a strategy of customer focus and service as well as to a measure of customer retention. Ensuring that tactics in the operating plan link both to strategic objectives and to tactical results gives management increased confidence that actions are aligned with objectives. Many organizations fail to carry the measures defined in the strategic plan through the operating plan and into the management reporting process, which makes tracking progress in any meaningful way almost impossible.

The financial plan translates the tactical plan into a set of financial statements that define the allocation of resources against specific tasks and projects and estimates the results that are expected to accrue from implementing the tactical plan. These results should be expressed in the same terms as the targets. The tactical and financial plans clearly state where the organization expects to be relative to its overall strategy at the end of the plan period. Collectively the strategic plan, the tactical plan, and the financial plan define the key management reporting requirements. They also define the set of measures that should be built into the forecast process.

Establish Clear Accountability

Tactical and financial plans must clearly identify responsibility and accountability; without doing so, the risks of failure are significantly increased. There needs to be a clear separation between the discussion and evaluation of longer-term scenarios and the explicit definition of goals and +plans that will be used to assess performance and hold people accountable. As Sun Microsystems cofounder and former CEO Scott McNealy likes to say, you need "a throat to choke."[2]

A tactic without an owner is unlikely to deliver the results expected. Blurred accountabilities lead to confusion and missed expectations. A best practice planning process clearly defines those elements of the plan that are longer-range planning assumptions and those that form part of a commitment by management to achieve certain results. Accountability is more than just identifying someone to be responsible (see Exhibit 6.2).

Exhibit 6.2   What Accountability Really Means

Capability	The individual has the skills, experience, maturity, and credibility to perform the role and accept the responsibility.
Resources	Reasonable resources are made available in the form of time, money, people, information, and management support.
Authority	Senior management delegates the appropriate organizational authority to execute. This can be in the form of the appropriate title, reporting line, approval limit, and communication.
Performance measures	Appropriate measures of performance, milestones, and overall targets are defined, agreed on, and communicated.
Incentives and consequences	The rewards for success and the consequences of failure are defined, communicated, and understood.

Define the Right Time Horizon

Defining the right time horizon for an tactical plan is not as easy as it may at first appear. Most companies develop annual plans; however, doing so is driven more by the needs of the financial community than by any operating imperative within an organization. Limiting tactical planning to the financial calendar is somewhat arbitrary and rarely reflects the appropriate time horizon to guide execution.

Many organizations adopt a variety of planning horizons based on their business needs. High-throughput or volatile businesses, such as consumer products, high technology, or retailing, find that developing a detailed operating plan for a full year is impossible. If product life cycles are short, as in many high-technology segments, or if selling cycles are highly seasonal, it makes little sense to look more than one or two cycles into the future. Such organizations can meet the annual planning requirements by developing only the minimum information needed. They then develop detailed plans for the time periods that make most sense.

Best practice companies consider three variables in determining the optimal time horizon for tactical planning:

1. *The normal cycle of product development and selling within the industry.* For example, automotive companies typically plan anywhere from two to four model years into the future, reflecting the elapsed time from conception to market for a new product. Pharmaceutical companies adopt an even longer time horizon driven by the time frame for the development and approval of new drugs. A fashion retailer may look out only two fashion seasons when develop-

ing detailed tactical plans. Toy manufacturer Mattel focuses its detailed plans on the next two toy selling seasons.

2. *The lead time required for making major resource allocation decisions.* Decisions that require significant capital investment in new plant or facilities or those that have a long cycle time before a return is realized, such as oil exploration, will have a longer time frame than tactics that can be implemented quickly.

3. *The time period that provides senior management, board members, and other stakeholders with enough information to approve plans and expenditures.* Robert Goizueta, the successful CEO of Coca-Cola who managed a rise in the company's value from $4 billion to $145 billion, was adamant in his views on the role and time horizon for tactical planning. David Greising described Goizueta's philosophy in this way: "Five year plans, he felt, were a waste of time. No one could predict with any accuracy what the world would look like in five years. He wanted three-year plans, and he told the executives that he would hold them accountable for meeting their three-year targets."[3]

Balancing the needs of the business with the organization's predictive capability defines the most practical time horizon.

Use a Common Language

Planning is as much about communication as it is about developing precise estimates of expected future performance. Well-developed plans serve as unifying forces in aligning all the priorities that need to come together to make a plan work. Effective planning demands a common language. Definitions, formats, and processes need to be defined consistently across an organization if the different elements of the plan are to be integrated successfully. Years of poorly integrated acquisitions, decentralized management models, and redundant computer systems have left most organizations with a number of different planning processes. This fact makes the consolidation, prioritization, and rationalization of resources across the different organizations extremely difficult. Senior management has to wrestle with inconsistent plans and business case justifications for projects.

Best practice organizations develop common definitions, processes, formats, and timelines for their planning processes. Business cases are created using well-established criteria that link to the overall goals of the business. The use of a common language facilitates more effective communication during the planning process and greater understanding of the plan during execution. Superior execution is based on a shared understanding of the objectives and the tactics in much the same way as all players on a football team must be clear as to exactly which play is being run for it to have a chance of success. The definition of standards does not need to limit flexibility. Within a common framework, specific issues that are unique to a particular entity can be addressed as needed.

The existence of the framework actually makes it easier to identify and manage exceptions to the rule.

Tactics Drive Budgets

One of the most common flaws in the tactical planning process is a failure to define tactics adequately. All too often, the communication of a target triggers an immediate leap to develop a financial plan or budget. By allowing the tactical planning process to default to a primarily financial exercise, a key step is missing. The importance of devoting adequate time to developing the operating plan was described by Larry Bossidy:

> An operating plan is not about green eye-shades putting numbers together . . . . It ties a thread through people, strategy and operations, and it translates into assigning goals and objectives for the next year.[4]

Defaulting to a budget at the expense of developing a sound tactical plan can be even more damaging when the process is seen as being controlled or owned by the finance organization. In this case, the plan that emerges is finance's plan rather than the business's plan. This is very dangerous since the level of ownership and hence accountability by operating management will be limited at best.

Tactical planning generally comes in two forms: tactic-centric and budget-centric. Tactic-centric planning focuses on defining tactics to meet the targets generated during the strategic planning process. Budget-centric planning has a bias toward developing a detailed financial plan that sums up to the targets. Exhibit 6.3 illustrates the line of questioning typical under each approach.

Best practice organizations start by defining the alternative actions available to them for meeting a particular target. For example, if the target calls for a 20 percent increase in sales, the discussion will start by evaluating the pros and cons of the dif-

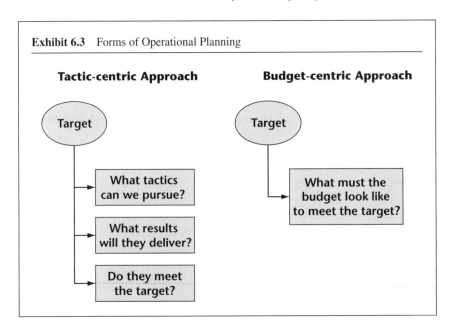

Exhibit 6.3   Forms of Operational Planning

Tactic-centric Approach

Target

What tactics can we pursue?

What results will they deliver?

Do they meet the target?

Budget-centric Approach

Target

What must the budget look like to meet the target?

ferent options for increasing sales, such as entering new markets, launching new products, or increasing sales to existing customers. The process becomes an iterative one with each possible tactic being evaluated for its ability to deliver the required level of tactical and financial performance. The result is a series of tactics that collectively can deliver the targeted level of performance.

Although best practice companies emphasize the importance of taking a tactic-centric rather than a budget-centric approach to tactical planning, that does not mean they do not address the financial implications of the operating plan. The tactical planning process and the financial planning process are inextricably linked.

Ensuring the appropriate balance and sequencing between tactical planning and financial planning not only results in a better plan but also increases the level of ownership and accountability among operating management.

Risk Weighted

One of the most tangible ways in which best practice organizations differentiate themselves is in the explicit recognition of risk throughout the planning and management reporting processes. Referring to the components of the plan, activities that simply sustain existing operations are less risky than those that target completely new activities. The dilemma many organizations face is that there is a mismatch among the risk profiles of the activities in the operating plan, the availability of good information, and management's level of comfort and experience. As Exhibit 6.4 shows, the area where data are most scarce is that which carries the highest risk.

Not surprisingly, the amount and the quality of information will decline progressively as activities farther from the current business are considered. Conversely, the risk profile of each element is the exact opposite of management's comfort level and the availability of information.

There is a real danger that plans will be most rigorous about the things that have the least risk and the least rigorous about the major, high-risk initiatives on which much of the strategic success of the organization depends. Best practice organizations recognize this dilemma and ensure that the allocation of management time and effort is driven by the risk profile of the tactics being considered, not by the level of management comfort or the availability of information.

Exhibit 6.4 Highest Risk Is Where Data Are Scarce

	Availability of Information	Management Confidence	Risk
Sustaining current operations	High	High	Low
Improving new operations	Moderate	Moderate	Moderate
New initiatives	Low	Low	High

The allocation of management time should be driven by the relative risk profile of the different activities to be planned. This means that projects and initiatives should consume the majority of managers' attention during the planning process.

Integrate Projects and Initiatives

Projects are the basic mechanism for effecting change in business. All strategic and operating plans rely on the successful execution of a wide range of projects and initiatives to meet their objectives. Project work consumes an increasing proportion of staff time in all enterprises and can account for as much as 80 percent of managerial and professional staff time. As routine operations become increasingly automated, the number of jobs that consist simply of completing repetitive tasks throughout the workday is shrinking. Tom Peters observed that the work life of many people today is defined by the projects in which they participate; he went so far as to define the equation "I = My Projects."[5] The crucial importance of projects in meeting objectives is worthy of more detailed consideration since it is an area of chronic weakness in many companies.

Meeting strategic objectives and meeting tactical plan targets are largely functions of successful execution across a range of projects. Delays in bringing a new product to market or bringing a new plant online can materially disrupt financial performance; however, project planning is rarely integrated into the overall planning process. Projects are referred to in strategic and tactical plans, but these plans provide little insight as to the objectives, expected results, or risk factors. Project reporting is rudimentary, often limited to measuring progress relative to time and budget and providing estimates to complete. Little systematic assessment of risks or measurement of value is attempted.

Successful execution requires excellence in project planning and management. To develop a comprehensive management and measurement process, each step in the project process needs to be considered. Numerous methodologies describe the life cycle of a project. Most take a procedural view of the activities and tasks that need to be completed at each stage; few address the need to link projects to business objectives and plans throughout the process. Best practices for project planning can be organized into six steps (see Exhibit 6.5).

Conception   The first step in the project process is the generation of ideas. These ideas usually surface during the strategic or tactical planning processes or are generated in response to events arising during the normal course of business. Best practice companies have a consistent, well-defined process for capturing and defining project concepts. This process includes identifying the key business measures that the proposed project will impact, linking the project directly to the business strategy, and defining the overall business case using a consistent set of assumptions and formats so that the expected return on investment is clearly defined. Projects are defined and evaluated using a published set of criteria, and those that meet the required standards are put forward for consideration during the planning process.

Exhibit 6.5 Project Life Cycle

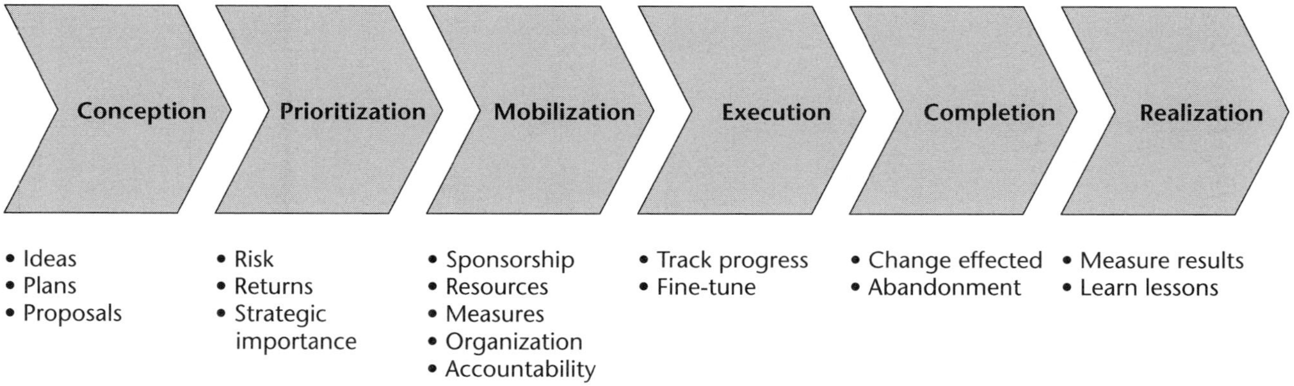

Conception
- Ideas
- Plans
- Proposals

Prioritization
- Risk
- Returns
- Strategic importance

Mobilization
- Sponsorship
- Resources
- Measures
- Organization
- Accountability

Execution
- Track progress
- Fine-tune

Completion
- Change effected
- Abandonment

Realization
- Measure results
- Learn lessons

Prioritization   All businesses have more good ideas than they can possibly act on. Effective prioritization to ensure that the most strategically important and economically attractive projects are commissioned is essential. As the planning process unfolds, significant effort is devoted toward developing detailed justifications for every initiative. In many companies, the atmosphere becomes very competitive as project owners battle for sponsorship and resources. Projects are compared using different criteria, such as ROI, strategic fit, and risk. A manageable list is agreed on and the plans get approved. Common problems include:

- Bias in the prioritization process that rewards projects that have the strongest sponsorship rather than those that deliver the most value.
- Using different assumptions in calculating project returns.
- Addressing an excess of demands over available resources by giving every project only a portion of the resources needed, thereby putting all projects at risk.
- Approving information technology (IT) projects even though no clear ROI can be demonstrated. The rationale is usually that it is a "strategic" investment, which is code for "We do not know how to quantify the benefits but the technology is awfully sexy."

Best practice organizations use an objective and systematic process that recognizes the need for a balanced and rational process for allocating scarce resources to projects. Adopting a very simple approach whereby projects are prioritized against two major criteria, the risk/return of the project and the contribution or alignment of the project with the organization's strategy, can eliminate many of the problems just described.

A common mistake that best practice organizations guard against is to assess a project's risk and return in isolation from other projects and from the business itself. Three questions can address this issue:

1. *What is the opportunity cost associated with the project?* By investing time and effort in a project, the organization is making a conscious decision not to allocate the resources to another project.
2. *What is the impact of the project on other projects or on the existing business?* For example, implementing a new set of financial systems is clearly going to have an impact on productivity and service levels within the finance department.
3. *Does the organization have the management capacity and capability to manage effectively the portfolio of projects that are commissioned?* Many organizations are responding to this question by establishing a formal project or program management office (PMO; a full-time organization staffed by professional project managers whose task is to coordinate the management of the complete portfolio of projects).

Strategic alignment assesses the relative importance of a project in enabling an organization to meet its strategic objectives or conversely in understanding the negative impact of not pursuing a particular project or initiative. Evaluating strategic alignment is important for two reasons:

1. It helps ensure that management maintains focus on the overall strategic objectives of the organization. It is easy to become enamored with a new project that promises spectacular returns but has absolutely nothing to do with an organization's strategy or its capabilities.
2. Assessing strategic importance or alignment can help management decide between projects that have similar risk and return profiles. Projects can be mapped based on their risk/return profile and strategic importance using a matrix like the one shown in Exhibit 6.6.

Clearly, projects that are both strategically important and deliver a high return at reasonable risk are the most attractive and should receive priority for funding. The hardest challenge is for management to decide between potentially high-return projects that have little strategic importance and lower-return projects that are more consistent with the strategy. Before making a choice, it is essential that the risk profiles of the high-return projects be thoroughly validated. Of course, if all the high-return projects have little alignment to the strategy, it may be time to revisit the strategy. Funding high-return projects that have little strategic value can be very tempting; best practice organizations continuously guard against the potential loss of focus such projects can cause.

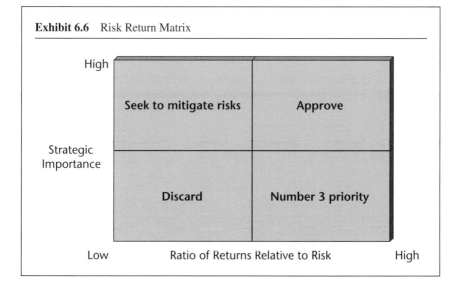

Exhibit 6.6 Risk Return Matrix

If the number of attractive projects exceeds the resources available, management has three options:

1. Reprioritize projects and eliminate a sufficient number to match the resources available.
2. Optimize the resources required for each project by looking at alternatives, such as phasing the implementation. Although doing this extends the overall implementation cycle, it can reduce the average resource load.
3. Seek alternative sourcing options if the constraint is labor, not funding. Many companies are tapping third-party resources for projects or even outsourcing entire projects.

One of the principal benefits of outsourcing is to free up internal resources to focus on those activities and projects that contribute the most to strategic success.

Mobilization   Once a project makes the cut and is approved, the next step is to develop the detailed project plan and secure the required resources. The most frequent mistake made during the mobilization phase is to restrict effort to simply assembling the project team. Mobilization is much more than assigning people to the project team; it is a disciplined process that paves the way for execution and should include:

- Solidifying sponsorship and commitment from all stakeholders
- Agreeing on appropriate project metrics and assigning clear ownership and accountability
- Developing the detailed implementation plan including key milestones, critical path, contingencies, roles, and responsibilities
- Securing commitment from all third parties contributing to the project and ensuring all appropriate contractual items have been addressed
- Agreeing and communicating the incentive plan for project team members
- Ensuring that the staffing process addresses not just the number of resources required but also the skills, experience, and motivation of the project team members

Execution   Execution is where change happens and value is created. Projects do not operate in a vacuum, so effective execution requires constant vigilance and measurement. Measures need to track not just the inputs of time, money, and resources but also the changes that are occurring during implementation and the outputs that are being delivered. Of course, in some situations a project does not work out as planned. These cases test the quality of the planning process and the resolve of senior management. Were the circumstances and criteria for abandoning a project clearly defined at the outset? Does management have the courage to abandon a project, or is it tempted to throw additional resources at the project in the hope that things may turn around?

The most important section in any project proposal is one that is most often missing—a description of the conditions under which a project should be abandoned. Clearly defining exit criteria minimizes the risk that resources will be wasted on an initiative that has little chance of success. Resources can then be reallocated to other initiatives

Establishing "exit" criteria for a project involves three steps:

1. Identifying the risk factors associated with the project
2. Setting the bounds of acceptable performance
3. Building measurement into the overall management process

Both pharmaceutical and consumer products companies make effective use of clearly defined exit criteria. Pharmaceutical companies have well-defined processes for tracking the progress of new drugs through every stage of development. At each stage, the probability of the drug being brought to market successfully is evaluated. If a drug under development falls below an acceptable threshold, development will be stopped and the resources redirected toward other projects with a higher probability of success. Likewise in the consumer products industry: The use of focus groups, pilot markets, and test rollouts are all designed to assess the likelihood of a product being successful.

Best practice companies apply similar techniques to all projects to ensure the most effective utilization of resources and that good money is not thrown after bad in a futile attempt to rescue a failing initiative.

Completion Projects by definition have a beginning and an end, or at least they are supposed to. Unfortunately, as one frustrated executive once told me, "Our projects just go on and on; in fact, in many cases they are no longer projects—they have become careers." Projects need to have a defined end point that should trigger a number of important events including:

- Redeployment of the resources assigned to the project
- Celebration and communication of successful project completion
- Tracking realization of the planned benefits
- Scheduling of the postcompletion project review to capture lessons learned

Realization Fewer than one in five projects is ever subjected to a rigorous postimplementation review to assess whether the benefits projected in the original business case have been realized. Failure to implement a review is incomprehensible, given the importance of projects in realizing any business objective and the amount of resources that organizations dedicate to projects. Measuring the results of a project postimplementation is critical. Not only does it quantify the ROI, it provides a powerful feedback process to the organization regarding what works and what does not work that can be used to enhance future project performance.

Managing Information Technology Investments at Cisco Systems

Like many companies, Cisco wrestled with the problem of how to determine the level of investment to be made in IT. Broad guidelines were established for the level of IT investment that were tied directly to the rate of revenue growth. The target for IT investment was expressed as a percentage of revenue, thereby limiting the rate of IT investment growth to that of the business. This model worked reasonably well when IT was largely focused on supporting back-office processes, such as general ledger, payroll, and accounts receivable; however, as IT moved from the back office to the front office and on into the supply chain and the customer organizations, the traditional approach was not sustainable.

Information technology had moved from being a pure expense to becoming a driver of future revenue growth. By constraining IT investment so that it lagged growth in the business, there was a risk that key customer-facing investments would not be made at the right time. In the book *Net Ready: Strategies for Success in the E-conomy*, Cisco's chief information officer, Peter Solvik, described how Cisco first recognized the risk and then moved to change the model.[6] The key elements were:

- Changing the reporting line for IT from the CFO to the CEO, thereby recognizing the strategic importance of IT and providing a balance between strategic value and cost management.
- Separating the costs of IT infrastructure from those designed to drive business growth and treating them as a general and administrative expense. This removed the need to burden every customer-facing IT project with its share of infrastructure costs. Infrastructure investments were viewed as additions to a set of shared resources that can be used by many business units.
- Funding for IT projects became the responsibility of the business unit making the request. The IT function's budget was simply to cover the cost of infrastructure.
- Clear policies were defined and implemented to manage the risk and secure the return from IT investments. These policies included:

  - Projects must show a return on investment in six to nine months.
  - Projects can last no longer than one year.
  - IT personnel assigned to a project report to both the requesting business unit and the IT organization.

Cisco realized a number of benefits from adopting this approach. First and foremost, funding responsibility was aligned with the organization best placed to manage the investment. IT infrastructure investments are managed by IT for the benefit of their customer base. The business units own the responsibility for funding initiatives that are designed to contribute directly to meeting their targets. The focus on rapid ROI and projects of manageable length ensures that projects are not overly complex or risk losing momentum as they drag on for years.

FINANCIAL PLANNING BEST PRACTICES

A well-developed tactical plan makes the financial plan or budget relatively easy to complete. Think about that statement for a moment. How many organizations do you know where that is true?

Getting the balance of effort right is essential; best practice companies devote two to three times more effort to developing the tactical plan than they devote to the financial plan.

Budgets Are a Financial Representation of Tactics

The basic purpose of a budget is to describe in financial terms the planned future performance of the organization. There are two parts to the budget: the operating budget and the capital budget. The operating budget describes the projected revenue to be earned from the organization's activities and the expenses that will be incurred. The capital budget describes the investments that will be made to sustain the current business and support future growth. Taken together, the operating budget and the capital budget provide a financial representation of how an organization will allocate resources and describe the expected returns that will be earned. Unfortunately, many organizations have budgets that bear little or no relation to the tactics that will be employed in meeting the agreed-on objectives. The budget may state exactly how much the organization will spend on office space but provide little to no insight as to how much will be spent on the acquisition of new customers. If users cannot discern the major tactics or initiatives an organization is going to pursue by reviewing the financial plan, monitoring future progress becomes very difficult.

Organizing both the financial plan and the operating plan in the same way makes measurement and management much easier (see Exhibit 6.7). For financial accounting purposes, it may be necessary to reorganize the plan around the profit and cost centers that comprise the organization, but that should not be an impediment to representing the plan in the form that is most relevant for managing execution.

Start with Business Drivers Volume drives all business activity, from the number of customers served, to the number of products offered, the number of people

Exhibit 6.7 Plan the Way the Business Is Managed

	Q1	Q2	Q3	Q4	Total
Baseline Sales	221	226	242	217	906
New Product 1	+8	+14	+19	+19	+60
New Product 2				+5	+5
Marketing Campaign 1		+3	+4		+7
Marketing Campaign 2			+3	+3	+6
Loyalty Program		+2	+2	+2	+6
Plant Shutdown	−5	−10	−9	−9	−33
Reduction in Product Lines			−7	−9	−16
Revised Baseline	*+3*	*+9*	*+12*	*+11*	*+35*
Total	224	235	254	228	941

(Rows "New Product 1" through "Reduction in Product Lines" are bracketed as Primary Tactics*.)*

employed, the number of orders received, and the number of sales calls made. Estimating volumes for key business activities is an effective predictor of many other business variables. For example, estimating the number of orders that will be generated allows an organization to develop further estimates of the number of order processing staff that will be needed, the number of invoices that will need to be generated, and the number of shipments that will be made. From each of these estimates, further projections can be made that provide a comprehensive view of the level of activity the business will need to support.

Developing a sound understanding of the relationship between different drivers is a good starting point for simplifying a complex, detailed process. In the automotive industry, volume planning has been at the heart of the planning process for over half a century. Estimating total volume, breaking it down into the likely mix of models, and then identifying the different option packages is at the heart of the planning process. When the initial volume plan has been completed, it can be matched up with the available engineering capacity to design new models and the manufacturing capacity by model. Solving the equation of balancing market demand with capacity is the key to profitability. The importance of this process was seen in the mid-1980s, when General Motors was slower than its competitors to anticipate the increase in demand for sport utility vehicles and minivans. The U.S. market changed to a point where more than half of all sales were of trucks and minivans while GM was stuck with more capacity to produce cars than trucks. Both Chrysler and Ford moved more quickly and were able to capture both market share and profits at GM's expense.

Decimate Detail   Many organizations have an insatiable desire for detail. No matter what the situation, the immediate response of many managers is to ask for more detail prior to making a decision. Unfortunately, in many situations, having more detailed information simply makes decision making harder. Managers have to digest much more data, which takes more time and does not necessarily increase their confidence.

Developing very detailed budgets is time consuming, expensive, and rarely results in a more accurate plan. Quite the contrary. The more line items that are budgeted, the less time there will be to develop a good estimate for each. It also stands to reason that the more items in the budget, the more variances that will be created as actual results are tracked against each line item. Each variance will require analysis and explanation. Again, the more variances there are, the less time an analyst will have to look at each one and the less useful the resulting analysis.

> If someone says to you, "That's a very detailed budget," is it a compliment or a criticism?

One of the primary reasons that budgets become so detailed is that many people find comfort in a financial plan that defines every conceivable line item. People mistakenly believe that more detail translates into more accuracy. The comment

"That's a very detailed plan" is almost always seen as a compliment. In reality, the more detailed the plan, the more wrong it is likely to be.

Conversely, best practice organizations match their desire for detail with their predictive capability (see Exhibit 6.8). Although the natural inclination is to make the budget as detailed and precise as possible, if there is no sensible method for developing an accurate estimate, why bother? In some cases, trying to develop a budget number with no reasonable basis for estimation can do far more damage than simply wasting time and effort.

At a large brewing company, the budgeting process started in June for the following calendar year. The process was so detailed that managers were asked not just to estimate sales by beer type but also to estimate the packaging configurations. Managers had to estimate, for each beer type, the mix between cans and bottles, the sizes of each—12 ounce or 16 ounce—and the package size—6-pack, 12-pack, or case. In total, they had to create 144 separate volume estimates. Needless to say, most of the estimates were worthless because managers had no rational basis on which to develop them. The inefficiencies were not restricted to wasted time. One purchasing manager thought he saw an opportunity to save the company money. He noticed that the consolidated budgets projected the exact volumes of each packaging type that would be needed for the following year. Using these estimates, he was able to negotiate purchase contracts with the company's packaging suppliers. By placing a bulk order in advance, he realized a significant reduction in the total cost. The discount added fractions of a penny to the margin on all products, producing a reasonable improvement in overall profits. On the surface, this looked to be a valuable benefit for the company.

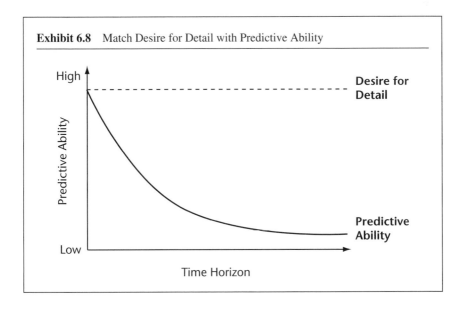

Exhibit 6.8 Match Desire for Detail with Predictive Ability

Unfortunately, as the year unfolded, it became clear that although the estimates of overall volumes by beer type were reasonably accurate, the more detailed packaging estimates were way off the mark. The company faced significant shortages of some package types while possessing excess inventory of others. Management was forced to stockpile unwanted cans and rush-order much-needed bottles at significant unplanned cost. The root cause of the problem was not an error by the purchasing manager. The issue was the requirement that detailed budgets be developed for all plan periods regardless of whether the organization had the capability to estimate the numbers effectively.

The fix was simple. The packaging detail was taken out of the budget and integrated into the six-week rolling production planning process. Doing this allowed for much more accurate estimates that were based on current information. Not only was packaging inventory managed more effectively, freeing up cash, but two weeks were taken out of the budget cycle by eliminating the need to develop the package-level detail for a full 12-month period.

Too much detail limits flexibility. An unintended side effect of driving plans and budgets to a very detailed level is limiting the speed of decision making. Instead of managers making immediate resource reallocation decisions in light of actual events, they tend to be constrained by the budget. Reducing the level of detail allows managers much greater flexibility to adapt to changing circumstances within the broad parameters of the agreed-on plan.

Do You Want Fries with That?

The absurdity of demanding large amounts of detail in a budget or financial plan is obvious when you apply the same logic to your own budget. Some budgets are as simple as a rough estimate based on income and expenses carried around in one's head. Some people simply use their credit card limit as the control process—the philosophy being that while under the limit, spend; when over the limit, stop spending. Others develop more detailed budgets using Quicken or Microsoft Money. I fall into the latter category. When developing my family budget, I start with the biggest items, such as salary, mortgage, property taxes, car payments, and so on through about 15 expense categories. After completing this process, I allocate funds to a single group called "having fun." I use this fund for dining out, going to the movies, and the like. My budget works well. There are occasional variances as payment amounts change, but generally it gives me a high degree of comfort in my spending plans.

If I were to apply the same logic used by the average organization to my own budget, the results would be absurd. Imagine the scene: I am sitting at my computer in the middle of August trying to develop next year's family budget. I have completed all the major predictable items and am now down to a single line item labeled "eating out." It has three subaccounts: upscale restaurants, family restaurants, and fast food joints. I develop estimates of spending by category, and my worksheet begins to expand as I factor in the variables associated with the family's eating habits. I estimate the number of meals with and without wine or kids—both major cost drivers in my household. I think back over the last few months and develop some estimation factors:

- About 95 percent of meals in upscale restaurants include wine, compared with only 15 percent of those in family restaurants.
- About 20 percent of upscale meals will be with the children versus 75 percent in each of the other two categories.

After a couple of hours of analysis, I come up with a very precise estimate for each subaccount. I load the final numbers into the plan and go to bed.

It is now April of the next year and I am reviewing the first-quarter results for Axson Family Inc. The numbers make depressing reading. Out of the 75 line items in the budget, more than half have material variances to budget. I did well with the big items, but many of the smaller ones including eating out are way off. After a couple of hours of analysis, I find the problem: My fast food visits were way over plan and the average spent was consistently 15 percent higher than budgeted. After a little more analysis, I realize that I super-sized all my purchases, which blew my budget out of the water. After hours spent developing very detailed estimates, my budget is in ruins because five months earlier I failed to predict my desire for a large fries with my burger.

Automatically Generate the Baseline Most companies miss a tremendous opportunity to both shorten the time to develop financial plans and focus the planning process on those key tactics that are designed to change the level of performance fundamentally. As companies have deployed new technology to track almost every aspect of the ongoing operations of their business, they have amassed a substantial amount of information regarding sales and expense trends. Using this base of information, it is relatively easy to automatically generate a baseline financial plan for the business factoring in the expected improvements that were established during the target setting process (see Exhibit 6.9). Besides eliminating the need to manually create baseline budgets for items that will not change substantially, it allows managers to focus on the impact on the baseline financial plan of the new or changed tactics. The result is a financial plan that incorporates the underlying performance trends in the business and also fully captures the expected impact of the tactics developed during the tactical planning process.

Focus on Materiality and Volatility Besides matching the level of detail to an organization's predictive capability, many best practice companies also balance detail based on the relative materiality and volatility of the item being planned. Traditional planning processes have always recognized that big numbers are more important than smaller numbers. An investment of $10 million is more material than one of $100,000. The impact of the increased speed and complexity introduces another variable into the mix: volatility. Volatility focuses on the speed with which a particular variable can change.

The combination of volatility and materiality can be very useful for selecting those items that are most relevant for planning and management reporting.

Items that are neither material nor volatile probably merit little or no attention in the planning process. They can be managed through direct monitoring of actual spending levels. If the profile of an item in this category changes and it begins to

Exhibit 6.9 Automatically Generate the Baseline Plan

	Current Quarter Forecast					Baseline Plan			
	Q1	Q2	Q3	Q4	Productivity Factor	Q1	Q2	Q3	Q4
Sales	215	219	235	211	3%	221	226	242	217
Gross Profit	86	89	94	82	3%	89	92	97	84
Net Profit	15	16	17	14	5%	15.8	16.8	17.9	14.7
Sales per Employee	$8,600	$8,760	$9,362	$8,406	5%	$9,030	$9,198	$9,830	$8,826
Close Ratio	47%	48%	53%	42%	5%	49%	50%	56%	44%
Average Order Size	$277	$267	$257	$311	5%	$291	$280	$270	$327
Employee Turnover	7%	7%	7.1%	6.8%	0%	7%	7%	7%	7%
Customer Satisfaction	83%	81%	79%	77%	0%	77%	77%	77%	77%
New Product Sales %	31%	32%	29%	25%	0%	25%	25%	25%	25%

increase in materiality and volatility, then it will move into one of the other quadrants and be subject to an increased level of scrutiny. A good example would be the changing profile of mobile phone costs as a component of communication budgets in the last 15 years (see Exhibit 6.10). Initially spending levels were low, unit costs remained high, and adoption rates were low so there was little volatility. By the mid-1990s, however, the unit costs for both equipment and minutes of use had declined to such a point as to trigger mass adoption.

Suddenly mobile phone charges became significant expenses and started to grow rapidly. Managers of communication budgets needed to manage the expenses more effectively, as they were both material and volatile. A second change occurred following the introduction of fixed-rate plans in the late 1990s. Cell phone adoption had slowed, most people who needed one had one, and now the monthly cost was fixed. Mobile phone charges remained material but volatility declined.

Tracking the importance of different variables based on their relative materiality and volatility allows an organization to direct its planning efforts toward those items that will have the biggest impact on meeting its performance objectives. Spending more time on a few important items is a much more efficient use of scarce planning resources than spending a little time on many relatively unimportant variables.

Align Detail with Responsibility   After I speak on best practices in performance management, one of the questions I am asked most often is "How many line items should be in our budget?" Many people find it difficult to grasp how less detail can ensure that plans are actionable and that budgets provide adequate control. The key difference between best practice companies and the rest is that a best practice company focuses on developing only the budget detail that it needs at

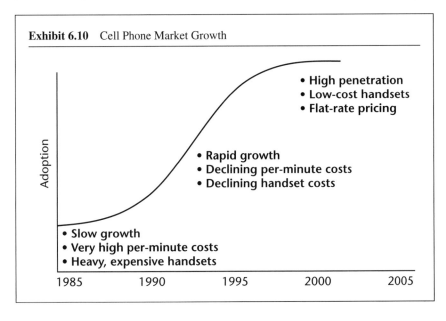

Exhibit 6.10   Cell Phone Market Growth

each level of the organization. The line items that the facilities manager needs to budget will be different from those required by a sales manager.

Budget content is driven by the role and responsibilities of the individual. Instead of a single detailed template being sent to all budget managers, the content is customized to each. Each manager completes only those budget items that are meaningful and relevant to his or her area of responsibility. Personalizing the content of the budget to the individual makes budgets more meaningful because they reflect items that the individual can control or influence and for which the person is being held responsible. This customization typically results in a more rigorous and accurate budget since each individual is being asked to budget fewer, more relevant items. Overall, the budget process can be completed in a much shorter time and its quality will be higher. Technology is a key enabler here. The budgeting system needs to support the creation of multiple different budget templates and then automatically perform the required consolidations according to agreed-on rules to ensure that the level of detail is both appropriate and manageable. As with all other aspects of planning, financial planning is a collaborative process. The ability to share budget information during the development process improves both the accuracy and ownership of the end product.

Eliminate Politics   Earlier I mentioned how best practice companies limit the criteria by which plans and initiatives are evaluated to strategic fit and economic value. Unfortunately, at many companies, a third criterion often emerges: politics. When politics enters the world of planning, decisions are not made solely on their strategic or economic merit. The process goes something like this: As budget time approaches, managers start to engage in intense lobbying to ensure that their departments or projects get preference during the planning process. Deals are brokered and alliances formed in the pursuit of patronage and sponsorship. Managers agree to support each other's initiatives or form alliances to protect cherished projects or expenditures in the hope that they will receive favorable treatment during the rationalization process that occurs toward the end of the planning cycle. The budget approval process often rewards the best politicians, not the best businesspeople. Ultimately the result simply suboptimizes overall performance as the most important criteria are subjugated.

Do not limit communication during the planning process. However, understand that effective politics in planning is about communication and education, not influence and patronage. The planning process needs to be open and candid. Making sure that good proposals are heard or that wise expenditures are approved regardless of the source of the idea is a valuable part of the overall process.

Explicitly Address Alternative Scenarios   Many executives have said that the process of planning is often more valuable than the end result. The planning process is the only time they have the luxury to ask what-if questions without directly impacting day-to-day operations. Planning focuses on asking three questions. The first two are straightforward: Where are we going? How are we going to get there? The third asks: What if things do not turn out as planned? The answers to this question provide the most value during implementation since things never turn out exactly as planned and success is a function of the speed with which variances are identified and the organization can react.

As with strategic planning (see Chapter 5), scenario planning and contingency planning are effective tools in the tactical and financial planning processes. Best practice organizations understand that it is highly unlikely that all their assumptions about the future will prove correct; in fact, they know that most of them will be wrong. Recognizing this fact allows them to make sure that the planning process allows adequate time to ask what-if questions. In many cases, a best practice organization reduces the level of detail in its plans but increases the amount of time dedicated to addressing variability in the plans. A best practice organization that is faced with the choice of detailing the expense budget to the lowest level possible or developing a series of valid scenarios and contingency plans will pick scenarios and contingencies every time. Exhibit 6.11 gives an example of the types of scenarios

Exhibit 6.11 Sample Plan Scenarios

	Plan Scenario	Upside/Strong Growth	Downside/Continued Weakness
	Moderate economic growth with sustained low inflation	Strong growth; robust economic recovery	Weak economic growth with inflation inflation trending toward zero
GDP Growth: Year 1	3.4%	4.3%	2.6%
Year 2	3.3%	4.1%	2.3%
Year 3	3.8%	4.3%	2.4%
Consumer Spending	3.0–3.5% growth due to increases in real income, tax cuts, low interest rates, low inflation.	Moderately stronger than the plan scenario	Weak and well below the historical trend
Credit Quality	Further stabilization	Significant improvement	Renewed deterioration
Unemployment	Modest employment gains; unemployment at 6.1%	5.8%	7.0%
Inflation	1.8%	3.2%	1.5%
Rate Outlook			
Fed Funds	2.0%	5.0%	0.3%
10-year Treasury	5.1%	5.8%	3.5%
DOW	10,120	12,000	8,500
S&P 500	1,088	1,220	940
Nasdaq	1,770	1,900	1,400

the planning team provided to each business at Bank of America to guide their planning process. Each organization was asked to test the sensitivity of its plan under each of the two alternative scenarios provided and to describe the changes that would be made if these scenarios played out in reality. By considering the possibility that the baseline assumptions might be wrong, which is highly likely in the volatile financial services industry, each business was able to identify the leading indicators that the plan scenario was no longer valid for its business and to develop contingency plans that could be put into action immediately, thereby optimizing performance in spite of changes to the operating environment.

Prize Flexibility   Most budgets or forecasts present a relatively static view of the world that significantly handicaps the ability to make and implement crucial resource allocation decisions in a timely manner. Best practice organizations are increasingly adopting a dynamic budgeting process that integrates the flow of actual results into the budget and forecast process, providing a continuous view of progress and alerting managers to potential problems and opportunities. For example, during the planning process, management may define a series of contingencies in the event that sales do not meet a certain level by a certain date. These contingencies could include increases in promotional spending and advertising combined with a freeze on hiring and reductions in materials purchasing. The dynamic budgeting process will identify that the threshold for triggering these actions has been reached and automatically alert managers that they need to implement the contingency plan.

The technology can go even further; instead of simply alerting management to the problem, the system can dynamically update the budgets for the affected items and send automatic alerts to managers regarding the changes in their budgets. The system also could be set up to automatically prevent new hire requests from being accepted into the human resource system and stop the generation of purchase orders for new materials. An organization without such a capability would probably not find out about the shortfall until the next month-end and will have lost valuable days in which to respond. The power of such tools is compelling. On September 12, 2001, Wal-Mart's systems alerted the business to the increased demand for U.S. flags and automatically triggered increased orders from the company's suppliers, ensuring that the retailer was able to meet demand. Many of its competitors found the supply of flags exhausted because of Wal-Mart's superior execution.

It Doesn't Have to Be Annual   The practice of annual planning has been institutionalized over many decades, largely driven by external reporting requirements. It is convenient for boards and shareholders but rarely matches the rhythm of the business. Detailed annual plans and commitments actually can be a detriment to performance as managers strive to achieve long-obsolete goals and objectives. An increasing trend among many companies seeking to develop the agility and flexibility required to compete in today's volatile markets is to dramatically limit the scale of the annual planning process to the absolute minimum necessary to meet the needs of the board of directors and external stakeholders. In its place is a quarterly or in some cases monthly dynamic planning process that updates objectives, reassigns resources, and adjusts tactics in response to the real-time performance of the business. Many leading companies, including GE, Cisco, Dell, Wal-Mart, and ExxonMobil, embrace aspects of this more continuous process.

Moving to a dynamic process that integrates real-time management reporting with the budget and forecast process can increase visibility into performance and hence shorten the time it takes an organization to respond to events.

BEST PRACTICE SUMMARY

- Targets are agreed on and committed to before the tactical and financial planning processes commence.
- Tactical planning includes the development and approval of contingency plans to meet targets under a range of future scenarios.
- Tactical plans clearly state the tasks to be completed, by whom, when, how, and with what resources.
- Tactical plans address the actions to be taken to sustain current operations, make improvements to current operations, and embark on new ventures.
- Benchmarks are utilized in setting goals to ensure that performance compares favorably with that of competitors or peers.
- Projects and initiatives are evaluated based on both strategic fit and economic value.
- Criteria for abandoning a plan or project are clearly stated and followed.
- Politics and influence are minimized throughout the process.
- Risk factors are clearly identified in all aspects of the plan.
- The trade-offs made in developing contingency plans are explicitly stated and agreed.
- Interim decision points are clearly identified together with the course of action under each likely outcome.
- The process for making decisions that impact the plan is clearly defined.
- Rewards for success and the penalties for failure are defined and communicated.
- Financial plans provide a financial representation of the operating plan.
- Agreement on the overall summary-level budget is reached prior to preparing detailed budgets.
- Baseline budgets are generated automatically based on actual trend data; managers can then focus on the "net change" that will result from new or changed tactics.
- The financial plan integrates capital budgets with operating budgets.
- The financial planning process is fully integrated with a rolling forecast process.
- The level of detail (number of line items) is greater for earlier periods and less for later periods, based on the organization's predictive ability.

- Financial plans are fully linked to strategic plans through tactical targets derived from strategic objectives.
- Current-year budgets are seeded using inputs from multiple sources (the latest forecast, variances from prior year, competitor assessments, internal/external information, etc.).
- Budget reiterations are focused on identifying actions to achieve tactical targets.
- Each level of the organization budgets a limited number of line items that are relevant to its area.
- Line-item detail is derived from the key performance drivers and is based on materiality and volatility.
- Measures defined in the tactical and financial plans directly feed into the management reporting process.
- Tactical and financial planning is a collaborative, cross-functional process.

NOTES

1. Greg Myers, Symantec Corporation Speech to the CFO Excellence in Finance Conference, Phoenix, February 2002.
2. Scott McNealy, CEO, Sun Microsystems, interview, Gartner IT Expo, Orlando, FL, October 2000.
3. David Greising, *I'd Like the World to Buy a Coke: The Life and Leadership of Roberto Goizueta* (New York: John Wiley & Sons, Inc., 1998).
4. Larry Bossidy and Ram Charan, *Execution: The Discipline of Getting Things Done* (New York: Crown Business, 2002), p. 228.
5. Tom Peters, "The Wow Project," *Fast Company* (May 24, 1999), p. 116.
6. Amir Hartman and John Sifonis, *Net Ready: Strategies for Success in the E-conomy* (New York: McGraw-Hill, 2000), pp. 245–246.

Chapter 7

Management Reporting: From Information to Insight

The worth and value of knowledge is in proportion to the worth and value of its object.

—Samuel Taylor Coleridge

In 1963 *Business Week* commented that "the great day—when all the information for solving a management problem is only a push button away—is closer than you think."[1] Well, over 40 years have passed, and we are still waiting.

Information is the lifeblood of the modern corporation. Without it, decisions cannot be made, customers cannot be served, and earnings cannot be grown. Management reporting has been the focus of billions of dollars' worth of technology investment. Management information systems, data warehouses, and data marts litter the business landscape. Yet despite these massive investments, surveys consistently show a high level of dissatisfaction. Fewer than 1 in 5 managers believe they have all the information they need to perform their jobs effectively, and fewer than 1 in 10 believes that they have realized the full return from their technology investment. In interviews with numerous executives over the years, the same phrases keep cropping up:

"I don't have the information I need to manage the business effectively."

"It takes too long for our management reports to be produced."

"Given the amount of money we spend on information technology, we seem to have a lot more T (technology) than I (information)."

The problem is not lack of data—most organizations are drowning in data, and much more are on the way. The increasing digitization of information flows within and between organizations is creating vast new reserves of data. Emerging technologies such as RFID (Radio Frequency Identification Devices) promise to create even more data for people to analyze: "Why has that can of beans moved from aisle 2 to aisle 7?"

However, such sophistication is beyond most companies, where even the most basic reporting tasks take too long. The average organization takes five working days to close its accounting books and another four days to produce the requisite management reports. For an organization that closes its books on a monthly basis, this means that accurate financial information is not available until over halfway through the next month. The advent of Sarbanes-Oxley has actually extended the closing cycle for many companies, further delaying the delivery of critical management information. Computer systems moved from batch processing to online processing during the 1980s; most management reporting did not.

Given the volatility and speed with which events occur in today's globally connected markets, management is at a significant handicap. Managers are trying to manage a real-time world with batch reports.

Without an effective reporting process management is flying blind, forced to adapt to changing business conditions with little timely or relevant information. Best practice organizations seek to match the information that is reported to the needs of the recipient at a specific time. Management reporting is a systematic process that starts with an event—all events create data. An event may be a customer walking into a store, an employee arriving at work, or a phone call to a customer service center; they all create data that may be subsequently used for management reporting. Data about the nature, timing, location, and impact of any event can be captured for subsequent use. The challenge for the management reporting process is to synthesize and structure all the data into relevant, actionable information and then deliver it to the right person at the right time.

This increasingly complex process requires the successful collation, processing, and reporting of three different types of information:

1. Measures of performance; for example, sales, profit, productivity
2. Reporting of events; for example, launch of a new product, acquisition of a new customer
3. Provision of context or analysis; for example, the negative sales variance was caused by warmer-than-expected weather in the Northeast

Most traditional management reporting systems handle only the reporting of performance measurement information. Reporting of information concerning events within the organization or the marketplace relied on informal processes, and the provision of analysis was largely ad hoc. The emergence of new technologies and tool sets in the last few years has allowed organizations to combine performance measurement information with news of relevant events and appropriate analysis into an integrated performance management system. Exhibit 7.1 shows the five major steps involved in translating data into useful management information.

The first step, data collection, assembles data from multiple internal and external sources. Data are collected from internal transaction processing systems, such as sales, order processing, inventory management, production, distribution, finance, human resources, and customer service and also from external sources, such as supplier and customer systems, marketplaces, and third-party information sources. The second step is to organize the data into logical groups (e.g., by customer, product, geography, department, or time period) and perform appropriate validation checks to ensure integrity, accuracy, and consistency. The third step, storage, ensures that the data are housed in a suitable place, such as a general ledger or data warehouse, in such a way as to facilitate easy access for multiple different reporting purposes.

Transformation converts the data into information. This step involves the sorting and selection of the appropriate data, execution of calculations or manipulations,

Exhibit 7.1 Five Major Steps Involved in Translating Data into Useful Management Information

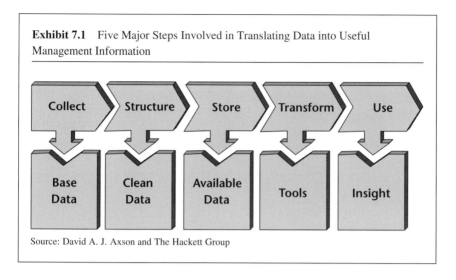

Source: David A. J. Axson and The Hackett Group

and creation of the required reports. Reports can be traditional paper-based ones or can include online access, e-mail distribution, Web-based delivery, and increasingly wireless delivery to a variety of portable devices, including cell phones and personal digital assistants (PDAs). This step also includes the provision of the appropriate tools to enable effective use of the information, including drill-down capability, spreadsheet modeling, and other analytical tools. The final step is the most important of all. Use ensures that the right distribution and access methods are in place to enable a legitimate user to access the data and also ensures that each user is equipped with the necessary tools, skills, and training to use the information effectively.

Best Practices Are Now a Necessity

The sudden collapse of a number of high-profile companies during 2001 and 2002 prompted calls for greater disclosure and improved financial reporting. The apparent fraud behind the collapses of Enron and WorldCom combined with a litany of other accounting irregularities not only rocked investor confidence but also served as a wake-up call to regulators. The likely result is that companies will have to make more and more information public, and do it faster. Xerox Corporation's 2002 annual report was 1,000 pages long; many others check in at over 500 pages. In the United States, deadlines have been shortened to 30 days instead of 45 days for submitting quarterly reports and 60 days instead of 90 days for annual reports.

Will the requirements to provide more information faster solve the problem and transform corporate reporting into a transparent lens through which all behaviors can be analyzed? Probably not. The problem is not necessarily the quantity or speed of reporting but the quality of the information. Information quality is the most important attribute of a management reporting process, whether for external or internal purposes. As regulators' demands for quantity and speed are satisfied, there are real risks that the overall quality of the information will suffer. Best practice companies understand that effective management reporting is a balance among quality, quantity, and speed.

TYPICAL PROCESS

Management reporting is time consuming and labor intensive. Reporting frequency is tied to the calendar and driven by the accounting close, irrespective of the underlying needs of the business. Very little information is available more frequently than monthly; many measures are reported on only quarterly or annually. Information is gathered from many different systems and manual sources. Information needs have evolved over time as numerous ad hoc reports have become institutionalized as part of the routine reporting process. It is very rare for any report to be canceled. This fact increases the volume of reports and creates redundancy; the same information appears in multiple reports, often in different formats. It is unclear which reports are the most important ones. The ability to relate information contained in a report back to specific elements of the strategic, operating, or financial plans is limited. Consolidation and formatting are largely manual processes. Much effort is expended in reconciling multiple inconsistent definitions for even the most basic data elements, such as customer, product, business unit, and sales, across different organizations and systems. Most management reporting is a function of the data available rather than the information that is needed.

The general ledger and related consolidation system serve as the only common source of management information. The accounting process relies on a series of manual interventions and reclassifications to ensure accuracy. Often the general ledger is used to compensate for lack of more appropriate management reporting systems. To provide more detailed management reporting, the general ledger chart of accounts may contain 5 to 10 times the number of accounts actually needed to fulfill the basic requirements to close the accounting books. This unnecessary detail extends the closing cycle and creates many more journal entries that combine to drive up costs and consume significant staff time. A series of partially built-out data warehouses may support the overall reporting process; however, because they have been developed on different technical platforms, they simply add to the overall complexity of the reporting environment. This complexity makes the rapid restatement of management reports to reflect organizational changes, acquisitions, or divestitures time consuming and largely manual. Requests for reports outside of the standard reporting calendar require significant manual effort and frequently bypass the usual systems with a consequent loss of accuracy and integrity.

Reports are paper based and contain mostly internal financial information with perhaps some internal operating statistics. Minimal external information concerning customers, competitors, and markets is provided. Information cannot be filtered or personalized based on user needs. The emphasis is on volume with multiple different users receiving the same set of standard reports. Many managers find the reports so difficult to navigate or so unreliable that either they do not use the standard reports or they get their staffs to create more usable ones. Professional staffs spend significant time rekeying system-produced reports into alternative presentation formats to make the information more usable or to satisfy managers' personal preferences.

The average management report is 30 to 40 pages long and contains 12,000 to 15,000 data points, yet managers typically use less than 5 percent of the information contained in any report. Users, unable to access data for themselves, must rely on analysts to extract information for ad hoc reporting. Little time is spent on understanding the numbers or, more important, determining the key drivers of the reported results. In global companies, the problems are even worse as each country typically maintains its own systems. Additional data are captured through numerous ad hoc methods including paper reports, fax, e-mail, and verbal inquiry.

In response to these problems, many organizations have created work-arounds, one of the most popular of which is the flash closing report. Flash reports are developed in response to an extended accounting close cycle and provide a preview or estimate of what the final numbers will look like. The reports typically are produced on the first or second workday after the accounting period ends and consist of a series of estimates of the most important accounting numbers, such as sales, margins, and profits. Often these numbers are generated outside of the main general ledger system using a series of independent spreadsheets to organize and consolidate the data.

In many organizations, management relies on flash reports to make critical decisions. The arrival of actual financial results a few days later is a minor event if the flash report was accurate. The accounting organization typically creates a rigorous reconciliation process to ensure that the final numbers tie to those in the flash report. The whole process is hugely inefficient and wasteful. If the organization fixed its accounting close process, the total effort involved in creating flash reports would be unnecessary A number of organizations have recognized this fact and have worked assiduously to fix the problem with impressive results; in Alcoa and Cisco, for example, accounting books are closed in eight hours or less and no flash reports are needed. Unfortunately, these organizations remain the exception. Most organizations persevere with a completely redundant process that consumes valuable time and resources rather than fixing the problem.

Work-arounds are not the sole preserve of the accounting department. Flash reports often are created to report sales, monitor inventory, and track outstanding receivables. Their creation consumes valuable time that could be spent elsewhere if reporting processes were attuned to the needs of the business. The inability to access basic management information easily and quickly severely handicaps an organization's decision-making ability.

MANAGEMENT REPORTING BEST PRACTICES

Effective management reporting is about delivering the right information to the right people at the right time. Best practices are built around these three basic principles of content, delivery, and people.

Decisions Drive Information Requirements

Perhaps the most important management reporting best practice is that the reporting requirements are driven by the needs of the information recipient. This may sound obvious, but all too often management reporting is driven more by the information that is available than by the information needed to make decisions. Management information needs are defined by three factors: the business, the individual's role and responsibilities, and the current situation (see Exhibit 7.2).

Different businesses need different measures. Measuring units of production is relevant for a car factory but has little relevance to a law firm. One of the distinguishing characteristics of a best practice organization is that it factors in the situational aspects of management reporting needs. For example, the information that managers need when developing an operating plan is different from what they need when reviewing customer profitability or deciding which projects to approve. The information needs of a chief executive officer (CEO) change depending on the current situation; for example, if sales are declining, greater emphasis will be placed on monitoring the sales pipeline and closely scrutinizing the impact of changes in advertising and promotional strategies. Structuring management information around events or situations enables managers to focus their decision making and make better decisions faster.

Focus on Relationships, Not Organization Structures

Most management reporting is structured to provide an organizational view of the business; information is reported for each business unit, department, or other organizational dimension. This focus seems to make sense; however, it raises three major issues that contribute to many problems organizations face with management reporting:

1. *Organization structure tends to change frequently; in many large organizations, weekly changes are not unusual.* This creates a problem in keeping the management reporting consistent with the most recent organization chart. The

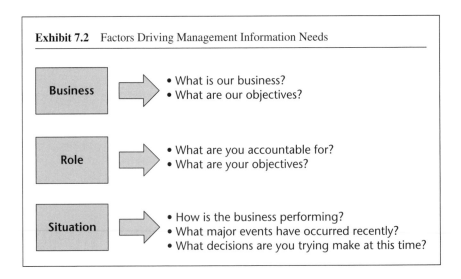

Exhibit 7.2   Factors Driving Management Information Needs

Business →
- What is our business?
- What are our objectives?

Role →
- What are you accountable for?
- What are your objectives?

Situation →
- How is the business performing?
- What major events have occurred recently?
- What decisions are you trying make at this time?

restatement of management information to reflect organizational changes consumes significant resources. In fact, it provides good job security for finance staffs, since few companies can keep up with the pace of organizational change.

2. *Structuring management information around the organization chart provides a largely internal view of the business.* Business is about selling products and services to customers. The organization of different departments and functions is simply a way to accomplish this objective. Management reporting structured solely around the organization chart can make the reporting of valuable information, such as customer and product profitability, very difficult.

3. *Organizational silos can make it very difficult to view information across other dimensions.* Many organizations find it very difficult to report information that cuts across the organization in a consistent manner. Organizational reporting tells managers everything they need to know about what happened in a particular department or business unit in a prior period but provides very little insight into the complete picture of a particular market, customer segment, or product line. Adopting a relationship or cross-functional view (see Exhibit 7.3) helps managers understand the total picture.

Besides structuring management information around a number of different dimensions, best practice organizations also understand the need for both a hierarchical and a linear view. An example of the hierarchical relationship between measures would be to take a profit and loss report and break it down into the subsidiary measures that add up to the profit. An example of a linear relationship would be the links among inquiries received, orders booked, product shipped, invoices issued, and cash received (see Exhibit 7.4).

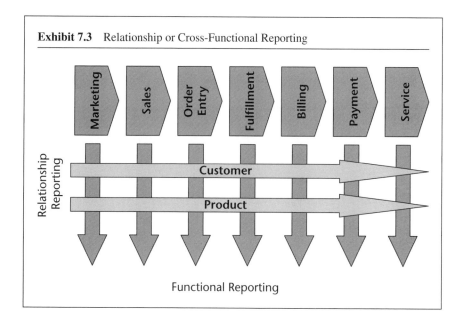

Exhibit 7.3 Relationship or Cross-Functional Reporting

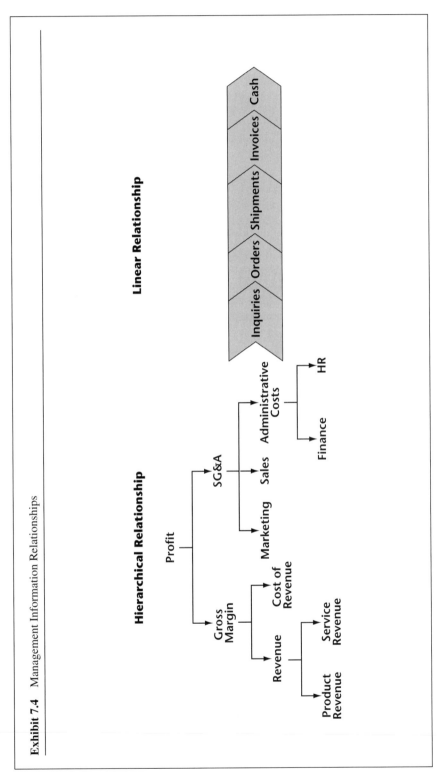

Exhibit 7.4 Management Information Relationships

Understanding these relationships is important in defining who needs what information and how that information should be organized. The hierarchical driver tree depicts the relationships among different attributes of the business and links them directly to specific business strategies or goals. This framework is used in slightly different forms by many best practice organizations to organize their overall management reporting and performance measurement processes. The linear flow is organized around a business process and shows the flow of information through the process. Linear flows provide information not just about outputs or results but also about inputs and activities. Input measures include hours worked and capital invested; process measures include cycle time and work in process; output measures track units produced, revenue earned, and customer satisfaction. Combining input, process, and output measurements offers a complete picture of the overall execution efficiency of the organization. A measurement process that provides management with an integrated linear view of the inputs, processes, and outputs of key business processes enables management to better manage the allocation of the resources to different activities.

It's All About Content

Information must be tailored to users' needs. Best practice practitioners have moved beyond a one-size-fits-all approach to the delivery of information. Personalized management reporting views are built for each individual or group of like users based on their needs and preferences. Information needs are closely matched to roles and responsibilities of the individual and are focused on the same goals, critical success factors, and drivers of the business used in the development of strategic, tactical, and financial plans.

Management reporting should provide a complete picture of key business measures across three primary dimensions:

1. Operational/financial
2. Internal/external
3. Leading/lagging

Operational information describes the level of activity occurring within an organization. It includes measures of volumes, cycle times, resource utilization, productivity, and quality. Financial information translates operational measures into financial results, such as sales, expenses, and profit. Internal information relates to all activities within an organization. External information comprises measures relating to customers, suppliers, competitors, and more macro factors, such as regulation, politics, and the economy. Leading or predictive information provides estimates or forecasts of future measurement values and can be developed for operational, financial, internal, or external measures. Lagging or historic information reports actual results for the current or a prior period.

Much of the management information available to organizations today is internal, financial, and lagging; ironically, this is the exact opposite of what most managers value.

Best practice companies understand that they need a better balance across each dimension. Operational measures are excellent leading or predictive indicators of future financial results—orders predict sales, returns predict credits, complaints predict customer satisfaction, quality is a predictor of cost of goods sold. A sound understanding of the trends in key operating measures provides managers with a powerful early warning mechanism that can buy them time. For example, if the level of calls coming into the telesales department is declining, there is a good chance that sales will decline unless there is a compensating increase in the number of calls that result in a sale. By tracking the level of telesales activity and the close ratio of calls to sales, managers will be able to react faster and take immediate corrective action. Identifying operational measures that can serve as good leading indicators is a hallmark of a best practice reporting process.

It has always been easier for an organization to accumulate internal than external information. Internal systems generate large amounts of information about internal operations. External data are another issue. Most organizations have very unstructured processes for collecting and analyzing external data. Separate reports are prepared about customer satisfaction, competitive positioning, and market evolution. A manager seeking to understand the implications of external information on internal operations often needs to manually combine external data with internal data, which takes time and slows down decision making.

The comparison of performance relative to peers has increased significantly in recent years. Many leading companies have made competitive performance measurement an ongoing part of their performance management processes. This should not be limited to comparisons within your own industry. Steve Ballmer, CEO of Microsoft, says that some of the best insights can be gleaned from other industries that share similar characteristics: "There's a lot you can learn from the automotive industry. You have to look at the people in this world who have big R&D [research and development] budgets—and that basically means pharmaceuticals, autos, chips, and network-equipment makers. At Microsoft, we're spending $4 billion a year in R&D. If you want to find people up in our range, they're basically almost all within those industries."[2]

Effective integration of external information into the management reporting process provides management with a rich source of comparative information that can help ensure that internal performance improvements keep pace with the market.

Even more valuable than external information is good predictive information. Leading indicators should be sought out aggressively and prized above all other measures. A leading indicator provides insight or early warning into a future event. The low-fuel warning light on a car's dashboard is a perfect example of a leading indicator. It comes on when the car has enough fuel to travel another 50 or 60 miles—a perfect leading indicator, since it gives the driver advance warning of a future event, in this case running out of fuel. Forewarned, the driver is able to develop a plan—here find a gas station—before any damage is done. The warning light would have significantly less value if it came on only when the fuel tank was empty. Many business measures fall into the too-late-to-do-anything-about-it category.

To complete the basic framework for best practice management reporting, measures can be reported and analyzed by each major relationship or dimension, such as line of business, customer, product, or supplier. The mapping of the relationships of measures and dimensions provides the overall inventory of management information (see Exhibit 7.5).

Define the Right Information Requirements

Defining the right information requirements is becoming more important every day. The proliferation of data is increasing exponentially the potential amount of information that could be created. Organizations need to select those measures that best track the progress or results of a particular process, activity, or project relative to their overall objectives.

For a commercial entity, the only measure that counts over the long term is earnings growth. Many failed companies were market leaders by one measure or another but were unable to translate that position into profits. Think of Polaroid, Braniff Airlines, Burroughs, and Netscape. All were leaders in their respective markets at one time by measures other than profitability, yet none was able to translate that leadership into sustained success.

Best practice organizations recognize that leadership in a single category must translate into profitable growth if their competitive position is to be sustained. The ability to identify the impact, either positive or negative, of every operational action on an organization's ability to meet its strategic and financial objectives is at the heart of a best practice management reporting process.

The three steps in defining what needs to be measured are straightforward:

1. Understand how the business creates value (i.e., makes money or adds value).
2. Understand the organizational model employed.
3. Define the appropriate measures to ensure alignment and accountability.

The starting point is the strategic plan. From the strategic plan, it should be possible to identify the major goals and objectives of the organization, the revenue

Exhibit 7.5 Mapping Relationships

| | Dimensions | | | | |
Measure	Customer	Product	Geography	Business Unit	Employee
Sales	X	X	X	X	
Profit	X	X	X	X	
Productivity			X	X	X
Sales calls	X		X	X	X
Returns		X	X	X	
Turnover			X	X	X

and profit model, and the major strategies that the organization has defined. The strategy provides the set of basic information needed to track progress. The same process can then be applied to the tactical plan and the financial plan. At each stage, three questions should be answered:

1. Which information provides the best measures of progress made and results achieved?
2. What additional information can help manage progress toward the agreed-on objectives?
3. Who needs the information?

Once this process is completed for all aspects of the strategic, tactical, and financial plans, the core set of management information requirements that need to be satisfied is evident. There are two important benefits of this approach. First, by defining the information requirements of the organization based on the plans that have been developed, there is guaranteed alignment. Second, given that plans change over time, it follows that an organization's information requirements also will change. Defining the management reporting requirements of an organization is not a one-time event. It is not unusual for 10 to 15 percent of the information needs of a business to change each year as plans, organizations, and priorities change. Best practice organizations have established an ongoing process for updating their management reporting. It involves not just adding new information as needed but also removing information that is no longer relevant—another step many organizations ignore.

Learning from the Master

Peter Drucker has defined the questions executives need to be able ask if they are to fully leverage the information potentially available. Here Drucker describes the best practice challenge:

Few executives ask:

- What information do I need to do my job?
- When do I need it?
- In what form?
- And from whom should I be getting it?

Still fewer ask:

- What new tasks can I tackle now that I get these data?
- Which old tasks should I abandon?
- Which tasks should I do differently?

Practically no one asks:

- What information do I owe? To whom? When? In what form?

An executive or an organization that can successfully answer all these questions is well positioned to achieve best practice benchmark performance in management reporting.[3]

Use Measures to Define the Criteria for Success

Understanding how an organization creates value is an essential step in defining the right measures. This task requires clear focus and a little creativity. Best practice organizations avoid relying on what exists today; they seek out measures that provide a distinct competitive advantage in better anticipating customer needs and in quickly fixing operational problems. Jim Collins, in his 2002 book, *Good to Great*, identified an organization's ability to understand and hence measure the single most significant economic denominator of its performance as one of the characteristics of companies that made the transition from being just good to being great.[4] Exhibit 7.6 shows two examples drawn from Collins's research.

Two other examples illustrate the power of redefining measures. For many years, Coca-Cola measured market penetration in much the same way as most other companies do: by measuring how many people in a particular market drank its products. However, as the company came to dominate in many of its markets, with a 50 percent share of the total carbonated beverage market, this measure ceased to have as much relevance. Coke needed a new measurement basis; it needed to increase its share of a person's total liquid intake. For example, if the average person consumes five beverages a day, Coke's aim was to increase its share of those beverages. Coke referred to this new measure as the "share of stomach." Coke was no longer satisfied with getting people to choose its product occasionally; it wanted to persuade people to make Coke their primary beverage choice. At a stroke, Coke's "share" declined dramatically to a meager 2 percent, allowing management to set new stretch performance targets.

General Electric adopted a similar approach to redefining its markets. GE had long established the maxim that it must be the number-one or the number-two player in every market in which it competed. Over time, the company realized that as its business grew more successful and management understood the need for market

---

Exhibit 7.6 Identifying the Critical Performance Measure

Company	Denominator of Economic Performance	Key Insight
Walgreens	Profit per customer visit	Shift from profit per store to profit per customer visit reflected the symbiotic relationship between convenient and expensive store sites and sustainable economics
Nucor	Profit per ton of finished steel	Shift from profit per division to profit per ton of finished steel reflected Nucor's unique blend of high productivity culture mixed with mini-mill technology, rather than just focusing on volume

Source: Jim Collins, *Good to Great* (New York: HarperCollins, 2002), pp. 106–107.

leadership, it was quite possible to define a market so narrowly that it was easy to demonstrate that GE was number one or number two. Having achieved its objective, management often moved from an aggressive growth strategy to one more focused on defending the company's position; one result was a loss of ambition. This insight led the company to redefine its markets much more broadly. GE created a whole new series of measures and stretch goals that reinvigorated the organization's competitive zeal.

Use Insightful Analysis to Compete

The best companies are now moving beyond the simple processing and reporting of business information. They are using insightful analysis of business information as a means for identifying and exploiting profitable opportunities. In this environment, companies can easily quantify the investments they make in systems, analytical tool sets, and talented analysts directly through top- and bottom-line growth.

In an article entitled "Competing on Analytics," Thomas H. Davenport, a professor at Babson College, described how many companies are seeking to use sophisticated analytics as a core basis for competing, be it Capital One in the credit card industry, Harrahs in the casino business, or Procter & Gamble in consumer products.[5] Davenport describes how "virtuosity with data is often part of the brand." For example, in the late 1990s FedEx went so far as to advertise itself through its ability to provide real-time tracking of packages at a time when many of its competitors could not match that capability. Progressive Insurance has long advertised its ability to offer a range of competing quotes for insurance; LendingTree.com and perhaps most significantly Google both use their analytical horsepower as their key competitive distinction.

Developing an ability to compete based upon insightful analysis requires that the basics of data standards, information management, and technology infrastructure are in place.

Make Reporting Relevant

Making sure that management reporting is relevant goes a long way to guaranteeing effective use of the information to improve overall performance. Burying relevant information among the irrelevant increases the risk that it will be missed. A simple test for measuring the relevance and value of reporting is to look at each report and see if it meets these seven attributes:

1. Relevance
2. Trend
3. Tolerance
4. Early alert
5. Call to action
6. Forecast
7. Context

What Constitutes a Great Management Report?

The best management reporting processes deliver precisely the right information, not too much and not too little, to maximize the probability of the intended recipient being able to make the most informed decision possible. Great management reports go far beyond simply reporting events. For a management report to fulfill its purpose, its must answer four questions:

1. What happened?
2. What was the impact?
3. Why did it happen?
4. What can we do about it?

All decision making is predicated on being able to answer these four questions.

Value Accuracy over Precision

Most people interpret accuracy as being synonymous with precision. For example, a number extended to two decimal places is somehow more accurate than a number extended to only one decimal place; however, this is true only if the measuring equipment is capable of two-decimal-point precision. By definition, plans are forward looking and hence uncertain; therefore, trying to predict with more precision or detail rarely translates into more accuracy.

Information for decision making, as opposed to information for accounting and compliance, does not always need to be 100 percent accurate. Ask a CEO which he or she would prefer, to wait six days and get an absolutely precise number for today's sales or get a good estimate in 20 minutes, and the answer can be predicted. In a perfect world, such a choice would not be necessary since precisely accurate data would be available instantaneously. Balancing the trade-off between precision and accuracy requires that an organization understand its measurement capability. If precise and accurate information is readily available, all the organization must do is determine whether the information is useful to anyone. If such information is not readily available, the organization should acknowledge the fact and provide the most relevant detail it can and not seek to deliver information whose accuracy cannot be assured.

People have a natural tendency to believe that the more detail they have, the more accurate and relevant a picture of events they have. In many cases, however, exactly the reverse is true.

Not Actionable = Not Useful

The metrics explosion of the last few years has not always delivered information that is actionable. The term "management information systems" should be banished and replaced with the term "management decision-making systems." There is no reason to deliver information without understanding what to do with it.

Management reporting has two purposes: Either it confirms to management that everything is on track and that no action is needed, or it points out the need for a potential change in plan to capture a new opportunity or correct a problem. Information that does not contribute to management's ability to do one of these two things is superfluous. The acid test of any piece of management information is to ask "So what? Who cares?" "So what?" tests the information for relevance to the organization. "Who cares?" identifies the people who can benefit from the information. If a piece of information does not pass both parts of the test, it is irrelevant.

Manage Data as an Asset

Much has been written about viewing data as an asset. What does this mean? An asset is defined as something that has value. However, assets in and of themselves are not of much use; the opportunities that ownership of the asset creates are the source of its value. Owning a factory does not have much inherent value unless the factory is used to produce something that can be sold or if the factory itself can be sold. Similarly, having a few million dollars in the bank is by itself not much use unless it is invested, spent, or borrowed against. The same is true with respect to data. It is an asset only if it used correctly.

Understanding how data deliver value and hence are assets is a critical element in the process of deploying best practices. Data deliver value through their effective transformation into an action or decision that results in a positive change in performance. For this reason, the subtitle of this book is *From Data to Decisions*. For data to translate into decisions, they must pass through a number of stages (see Exhibit 7.7).

An example will illustrate how this process works. Start with a data set that includes all orders by placed by all customers for all products over the last month. The data comprise thousands of individual transactions. Scrutinizing each individual transaction does not provide management with any real information; however, aggregating the transactions in different ways provides information regarding total sales for each product and total sales to each customer. Such information provides more value to management, which can discern which products are selling the most and which customers are buying the most. Yet this still does not tap into the real value of the data.

The next step is to combine this set of information with information concerning sales by product and by customer for the previous year and then rank the products and customers with the greatest increase or decrease in sales over that time. Management now has some knowledge about the trend in orders over time; again, this is interesting but not really actionable. Management will seek to understand why certain products or customers account for more or less sales over time. Adding an analysis of why the demand for certain products or from certain customers has changed equips management with insights into why performance has changed. This knowledge allows management to make decisions that will influence the drivers of the change and improve future performance. The results of making and im-

Exhibit 7.7   Translating Data into Decisions

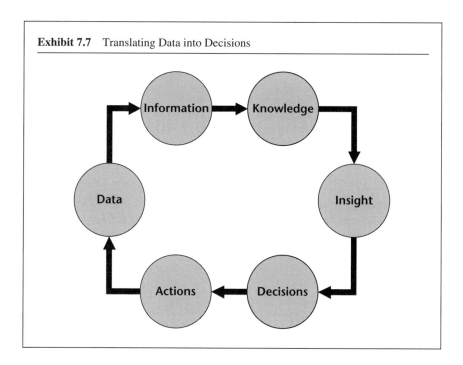

plementing these decisions will be reflected in data reported in the future, and so the cycle starts again.

Best practice companies focus on the delivery of insight, not information. For this to happen, the processes and systems that generate data and produce information and knowledge must be synchronized with the processes and people who derive insight, make decisions, and put them into action. Although this sounds obvious, the disconnect between the mechanistic and the humanistic part of the cycle is the most common cause of poor decision making. More simply, it becomes very difficult to improve decision making if:

- Management reporting is incomplete or contains incorrect information.
- The right people get the right information at wrong time.
- The right information is in the hands of the wrong people.
- The right information is provided at the right time to the right people, but they do not know how to use it effectively.

Managing data as an asset means understanding how the use of data generates value. Stockpiling data in a data warehouse is about as much use as storing computers in a closet. The potential for performance exists but is not being exploited.

Leverage the Balanced Scorecard

Tom Peters, in his 1987 book, *Thriving on Chaos*, considered the sins of traditional accounting to be so significant that he underlined this passage for emphasis:

> Our fixation with financial measures leads us to downplay or ignore less tangible nonfinancial measures, such as product quality, customer satisfaction, order lead time, factory flexibility, the time it takes to launch a new product, and the accumulation of skills by labor over time. Yet these are increasingly the real drivers of corporate success over the middle to long term.[6]

Abraham Briloff, professor emeritus of accounting at New York University, described the problem thus: "Corporate financial statements are like bikinis . . . what they show is interesting; but what they hide is vital."[7]

The balanced scorecard was a response to these concerns. Robert Kaplan and David Norton introduced the concept in the *Harvard Business Review* in 1992.[8] They developed it as a way to help translate an organization's vision and strategy into a coherent set of performance measures. The concept involves using a balanced set of performance measures across four dimensions to describe and track the key elements of strategy. The four dimensions are:

1. Financial
2. Customer
3. Internal process
4. Learning and growth

The financial perspective incorporates the traditional measures of growth and profitability. The customer dimension focuses on measures such as acquisition of new customers, satisfaction, retention, and growth that lead to the desired financial results. The internal process perspective combines measures of both operational processes that produce and deliver existing products and services and innovation processes, such as product development that create new products and services. The learning and growth dimension focuses on those activities that support long-term growth, such as the development and retention of talented people, the organization's ability to leverage technology successfully, and its ability to adapt to new competitive threats.

Kaplan and Norton's timing was impeccable. The concept of the balanced scorecard played perfectly into the increasing awareness that planning and management reporting was about more than manipulating spreadsheets. Recognition of the critical importance of the customer and the emergence of new tools and technologies, such as the Internet, knowledge management systems, reengineering, and data warehouses, provided a foundation on which to build a new measurement model.

Integrating the balanced scorecard into the overall management reporting process can provide management with a valuable tool for tracking the key performance measures for the organization across a range of different dimensions.

Using Metrics to Translate Strategy into Action

Since the emergence of the balanced scorecard in the early 1990s, many companies have adopted the framework in an attempt to develop a more comprehensive view of business performance and ensure greater alignment between strategic intent and operational action. For some the path has been rocky, with multiple scorecards competing for attention creating confusion instead of clarity. For those companies that maintained focus, the benefits can be attractive, as the experience of Cognos, a leading provider of the very software that supports performance management, demonstrates.

The company's challenge was a good one—explosive growth. Revenues grew from $491 million in 2002 to $877 million in fiscal year 2006; earnings increased more than six times from $20 million to $125 million over the same period. Managing rapid growth while also operating in the ever-changing technology market posed significant challenges for management. They needed confidence that the company's evolving strategy was consistently executed. CEO Rob Ashe and CFO Tom Manley led a major effort beginning to 2003 to develop a corporate strategy map that expressed the company's objectives in terms of 13 goals, such as "Build great products" and "Drive customer value at every step." Having synthesized the strategy down to a manageable 13 objectives, the team then set about defining meaningful measures for each objective. As the work progressed, it became clear that there were significant gaps between the information being used in different parts of the business. The company was able to use the analysis of these gaps to create a common information set that could support the four-quarter rolling plan process across different business functions, such as sales, marketing, product management, finance, and information technology (IT). By 2006 the company found that its scorecard-based measurement process combined with the rolling four-quarter plan served as an effective management process for translating strategic intent into consistent operational execution while also serving as a great communication vehicle to the board, managers, employees, and other associates. Manley and Ashe use Cognos' own software daily to track significant performance indicators such as sales pipeline.

"Our new executive portal is the ideal one-stop information hub for real-time insights into performance activity," said Manly. "Combined with our initiatives scorecard, this innovative portal helps us continually extend our view from pure financial metrics to operational, market, customer and employee business drivers and indicators."

A side benefit has been that the company has been able to use its own products to support the whole process—a great advertisement!

Guard Against Measuring the Wrong Things

It is as important to understand the possible negative impact of measuring the wrong things or measuring the right things at the wrong time as it is to identify what should be measured. Xerox spent millions of dollars on customer surveys under the assumption that there was a strong link between the level of customer satisfaction and overall financial performance. Subsequent analysis found no such linkage. Customer loyalty was found to be a far better predictor of financial performance. Loyalty went beyond merely satisfying the customer to assessing the likelihood of a customer either continuing to do business with the company or increasing its level of business. This subtle but crucial insight had profound implications for Xerox's business as its came under assault from new entrants into its core market.

Measuring the right things at the wrong time can be equally as damaging. Measuring customer satisfaction after the customer has defected to a competitor is akin to shutting the stable door after the horse has bolted. Timing is everything.

More Than Just Numbers

Earlier I defined the three types of information contained in management reports: performance measurements, reporting of events, and contextual information. Unfortunately, almost all traditional management reporting consists of quantitative information. Numbers drive everything. They can be added up, compared to each other, graphed, tabulated, and subjected to multiple manipulations. There is a certain elegance to a report that contains neat rows and columns of perfectly formatted information. The abstract is somehow made less abstract. However, many of the most important insights cannot be reduced to numbers. The act of quantifying everything can mask the truth.

As the saying goes, "There are lies, damn lies, and statistics." Numbers are very good at telling you what happened, but they rarely tell you *why* it happened. Numbers will tell you that sales were down, expenses were up, and hence profits were down; it is much harder for numbers to tell you why sales were down. Was it a pricing problem, the loss of a key customer or salesperson, or product obsolescence? Although numbers may help you identify these reasons over time, they are unlikely to jump out at you.

Many organizations address this problem by annotating management reports to explain the contextual reasons why the numbers look the way they do. Analysts conduct detailed investigations of the reasons behind particular variances—almost all of it after the event. Best practice organizations take a much broader view of information. Instead of just focusing on what numbers to report to which people, they look beyond simple quantitative data to other types of information that help provide context and insight. Sources of such data can include news media, analyst opinion, research bodies, academia, government, customers, suppliers, and employees. An organization may combine customer sales information with news relating to the customer's business in order to understand better future opportunities with that customer.

Start with Users, Not Data

Too many designers of management reporting systems make the mistake of starting with the data. What are they? Where are they? How should data be defined? These are important questions, but the two most crucial questions are: Who needs the data? and Why? Adopting a user- or decision-centric approach rather than a data-centric approach is the hallmark of an effective management reporting process. Historically IT professionals have used the term "user" almost as an insult, saying such things as: "The users just don't get it" or "It's a user problem." In many organizations, the biggest barrier to systems development is the inability of IT staff and users to communicate effectively. Many IT professionals take pride in their ability to master the technical, acronym-laden language that dominates their world. If the humble users do not get it—well, that's their problem.

Best practice IT organizations adopt a strong customer- or user-centric approach to designing, developing, and supporting management decision-making systems. Design is a collaborative process where user or customer needs are paramount and the technology is secondary. Functional areas often define what needs to be reported in different ways. For example, a British financial institution used to produce four different product profitability reports, all of which showed different profit numbers for the same product. Some products were shown as being profitable on one report while appearing to lose money on another report.

Today, companies have a wonderful opportunity to dramatically improve both the accessibility and the integration of external information into their management reporting processes. Two major technological advances are extending an organization's ability to collect external information and integrate it into the management reporting:

1. *The deployment of new systems in supply chain management and customer relationship management allows organizations to capture data that were not historically available.* These systems extend the data collection process beyond the boundaries of the organization, providing management with access to valuable information about customer buying patterns, supplier inventory, shipments, and the like. As a general rule, the earlier in a business process that data can be captured, the more potent the information is for improving internal decision making.

2. *The emergence of the Internet as an information source combining a low-cost, ubiquitous, and easy-to-use access method has spawned an explosion of information sources.* In less than a decade the Internet has become a kind of global data warehouse. As one executive said, "It is easier for me to search for information on the Internet than it is to search for it within my own organization." Judicious use of the Internet can provide organizations with a wealth of information to support decision making. Access to data about customers, products, markets, regulations, prices, innovations, and other research can be integrated into the internal management reporting process. Best practice practitioners aggressively seek to integrate a broad cross-section of external intelligence into their management reporting processes.

Make Online Real Time a Reality, Not a Slogan

The information delivery process defines the means by which data are transformed into information and made available to end users. In addition to improved access to external information, the advent of true online, real-time transaction processing is driving the availability of much richer information about current and past performance. The ability of organizations such as Wal-Mart and Dell to track the flow of transactions through their business in real time allows them to spot trends much more quickly than an organization that reports such information on only a monthly or quarterly basis. Many best practice organizations use the phrase "managing from the actuals" to explain how the continuous flow of real-time information allows them to fine-tune their business constantly.

The real-time flow of information through an organization allows for much more sophisticated modeling and forecast development to provide management with a complete view of past, current, and likely future performance. One of the earliest examples of an industry leveraging the availability of such information was the airline industry's development of sophisticated yield management models to optimize the revenue from each seat on an airplane. By tracking the sales of tickets continuously, airlines can dynamically adjust the pricing of each seat to maximize the total revenue earned from each flight. As Continental Airlines CEO and former chief financial officer Lawrence Kellner explained in a May 2000 interview: "It used to take us weeks to find out if a particular flight was profitable, now we have a pretty good idea of how profitable each flight will be before it takes off and accurate results the next day."[9] The availability of such information gives management much greater flexibility in decision making. The correlation between companies that have invested in world-class management information systems and those that dominate their markets is increasingly strong. GE, Wal-Mart, Federal Express, Dell, Schwab, and Amazon.com not only dominate their respective markets but also are recognized as some of the most information-savvy companies around; this is not a coincidence.

Information Delivery Best Practices

Collection
- Capture data once, right at the source.
- Enforce standard definitions across all systems and processes.
- Minimize the manual collection of data.
- Identify the most credible source where multiple potential sources exist.
- Seek to capture all required attributes of a transaction at the same time.

Structuring
- Perform all validation and reasonableness checks at the point of data capture.
- Aggregate like data into logical groupings; for example, group all sales transactions together.

Storage
- Ensure adequate replication and redundancy for security purposes.
- Seek to optimize storage based on frequency and nature of likely usage.

Transformation

- Execute all commonly required manipulations, calculations, and other transformations according to a predefined schedule, and store the results for subsequent access and use.

- Apply all required tolerance and exception checks and trigger appropriate alert mechanisms.

Use

- Make all information available to all legitimate users as soon as possible.

- Ensure all reported information is accompanied by appropriate demographic data; for example, time period, comparison basis (actual, budget, forecast, etc.), or unit of value.

Invest in Education

As Peter Drucker succinctly described:

> [Executives] know how to get data. But most still have to learn how to use data.[10]

Much of the potential of new management reporting processes and systems is lost not because of any technical failure but because inadequate investment is made in educating intended users on how to make effective use of the insights now at their fingertips. Over the last few years, I have conducted an informal survey of all the people who have attended my speeches—over 5,000 people. I ask them: "How many of you use a spreadsheet application as a tool for performing analysis of major business decisions?" Over 90 percent of those surveyed answered yes.

Then I ask: "How many of you have had more than one day's formal training in using the spreadsheet application?" Less than one-third answer yes to this question. Although they lack the rigor of a formal survey, the results clearly demonstrate how little most organizations invest in training people how to use the tools and systems at their disposal. Even if adequate training is provided in using the new systems, most organizations fail to provide much guidance on how to make best use of the new information. The availability of rich new information sources can fundamentally change the way an organization makes decisions. In the traditional model, problems usually are not identified until it is too late. Providing managers with access to richer leading or predictive information presents an opportunity to prevent a problem from escalating; however, managers must have the confidence and knowledge to act on the information in a timely fashion. Best practice organizations invest in educating their people on the tools and the technologies that deliver management information and on how to use the information most effectively.

Dialogue, Debate and Discovery

One of the biggest negatives associated with the deployment of computer technology through business has been the isolation of analysts and managers and the stifling of group communication. Analysts have become slaves to their spreadsheets who rarely emerge from their cubicles to engage in dialogue with their peers. Communications are limited to e-mail and instant messaging. In many organizations, there are almost no corridor discussions about the impact of an event. Organizations are losing one of the most effective tools they have for developing insightful analysis: dialogue and debate. Best practice organizations strive to ensure that technology does not isolate managers and analysts. New tools and systems should free up time for discussion and debate. The most insightful analytics rarely spring from solitary staring at columns and rows of numbers in a spreadsheet. Take your analyst team into a conference room, shut off all phones and PDAs, and spend an hour discussing the most significant performance variance; the quality of the insights that emerge from smart people engaging in constructive debate will always surpass those realized alone.

When Alcoa built its new headquarters building in Pittsburgh, which opened in 1998, then chairman and CEO Paul O'Neill demanded that the design facilitate impromptu dialogues between employees. The result is a bright, airy, and totally open plan facility—no corner offices—that embodies a number of design principles that force collaboration and cooperation:

- Nonhierarchical: "mobility rather than status"
- Large open floors: "productivity rather than privacy"
- Ubiquitous access for all to all at all times: "bring down the walls"
- Flexibility, adaptability: "the only constant is change"

O'Neill believed that the fully open office plan would encourage all employees to collaborate more completely and productively. Organizations that effectively integrate best practice tools and technology for management reporting with people refocus the role of their analysts. The priority is not on crunching numbers but on delivering high-quality insights to support decision making, educating end users on how to make best use of the available information, and providing insightful analysis of material business events.

Separate the Frequency of Measurement from the Frequency of Reporting

Recognizing that simply because something has been measured does not mean that is has to be reported is a big step toward managing the growth in the amount of information available in most organizations. All too often, reports are generated every time a new measurement is captured. If sales are measured hourly, a sales report probably is generated hourly and sent to a group of people regardless of whether hourly sales information is relevant to them. The advent of real-time systems provides the opportunity to report much more information much more often. The result can be a severe case of information overload, which at best slows down decision making and at worst can paralyze an organization.

Best practices focus on matching the frequency with which information is reported to the specific needs of each user. Although a specific measure may be updated continuously, few users will need such constant updates. Take share prices as an example. Most share prices are updated in real time; however, only a few professional traders need to track their continuous movement and then only in a few select stocks. Despite the advent of Web-based tickers, most investors need no more than daily or weekly updates to manage their portfolios. For long-term investors, a single annual review may be adequate. Those who own a particular stock through a mutual fund require no updates on individual stock prices. This single measure—a stock price—is updated in real time, but the frequency with which it needs to be reported varies greatly. The same logic applies to a best practice reporting process. Many more things will be measured much more often than any single user needs or can accommodate. The key is to match the right information to the right user and deliver it at precisely the right moment to maximize the chance of making a good, timely decision.

Flexible Delivery

In the early days of business computing, there was only one medium for information delivery. Whole forests were sacrificed to make green-and-white lined computer paper that was fed in never-ending streams through industrial-strength printers. Sophisticated printing, bursting (tearing the reports along the perforations), and collating operations hummed away in every large company. Trolleys were wheeled around office buildings groaning under the collective weight of the reports.

Myth of the Paperless Office

The concept of the paperless office became a powerful marketing theme for most computer companies. In 1970 futurist Alvin Toffler wrote, "Making paper copies of anything is a primitive use of machines and violates their very spirit."[11] The gap between the promise of the paperless office and the reality was humorously demonstrated in 1979, when a consulting firm in Washington, D.C., opened a prototype of a paperless office. During the initial demonstration, things did not proceed exactly as planned. The telephone started ringing and would not stop; eventually the exasperated tour leader answered it and rather sheepishly asked if he could borrow a piece of paper from someone in the group to take a message! Few people talk about the paperless office anymore. Paper remains a useful medium for management reporting.

The demise of the traditional mainframe computer and the rise of the graphical user interface and laser printer marked the end of the green-and-white paper report for all but a few users. Today technology offers a wide range of potential media for information delivery. Of course, paper remains a powerful delivery vehicle; the average office worker uses around 10,000 sheets of paper for printing and copying every year, and consumption has increased sixfold in the last 50 years. The combination of low cost, flexibility, and portability make paper an unbeatable option.

Reporting should be designed and organized around the user's work style. Today's systems are capable of supporting multiple different reporting mechanisms at the user's choice. The optimal medium can be a function of the type of information being delivered, the user's preference, and the user's current situation. For example, the same information may be delivered to the same people by e-mail if they are in their office or by voice mail or text message if they are traveling.

Design Matters

One of the most neglected areas in the development of most management information systems is the design of how information is presented to the user or customer. All too often design is left to the systems developer. The process is limited to a few brief discussions of alternative formats based on the standard templates that come with the software package or tool set being used. At its worst, poor design can result in critical business information being ignored by decision makers. At the very least, poor design inhibits understanding, increases the risk of misinterpretation, and slows down decision making.

The challenge facing designers of management reports is to effectively balance content with format. Many of the most valuable management reports in a company can be almost unreadable, consisting of page after page of narrowly spaced numbers. Conversely, well-designed reports may contain data of questionable value or accuracy. Good design takes complex information and makes it easy to understand and use. Used correctly, design can improve decision making significantly by drawing the user's attention to the important information, presenting it in a way that is easy to understand, and thereby shortening the cycle time to make a decision.

Technology is increasingly capable of supporting design that makes information easier to interpret and act on. Design is becoming more widely recognized and can contribute significantly to productivity. Edward Tufte, in the epilogue to his excellent book *The Visual Display of Quantitative Information*, sets out the purpose of good design: "What is sought in designs is the clear portrayal of complexity. Not the complication of the simple; rather the task of the designer is to give visual access to the subtle and the difficult—that is, the revelation of the complex."[12]

The use of graphical representations to portray key business information is increasing, yet care is necessary. The use of inappropriate graphical representations can be more damaging than burying key business data in the depths of spreadsheet hell. Great design should be a requirement of all efforts to improve management reporting. The translation of complex information into easy-to-understand representations is the final step in translating data into actionable information.

Tufte defines excellence in the design of statistical ideas as consisting of "complex ideas communicated with clarity, precision and efficiency"—a fitting test for all management reporting.[13]

BEST PRACTICE SUMMARY

- Management information requirements are driven by the needs of the user, not the data that are available.

- Equal focus is given to defining the right information, identifying the appropriate users or customers, and ensuring that the information is available when needed: right content, right people, right time.

- User needs address the overall business environment, the individual's role and responsibilities, and the user's current situation.

- Management reporting balances three key types of information:
  - Operational and financial
  - Leading and lagging
  - Internal and external

- Management reporting balances performance measurement, the reporting of events, and the provision of contextual information relevant to decision making.

- Leading indicators are aggressively sought out, but the organization understands the inherent uncertainty in any predictive information.

- Reporting is not tied solely to an organizational view of the business.

- Reporting can be readily provided around multiple dimensions or relationships, including customers, suppliers, products, geographies, organizational units, and business processes.

- Appropriate external benchmarks are used to monitor internal performance relative to peers, competitors, and other standards of performance.

- All performance measures can be linked to strategies, tactics, or financial objectives.

- Performance measures track inputs, processing, and results.

- A process is in place to review the continued usefulness of all reports and performance measures over time.

- The "So what? Who cares?" test is rigorously applied to ensure information is relevant and actionable.

- Management reporting focuses on delivering insight that accelerates and improves the quality of decision making.

- Balanced scorecards are integrated into the management process of the organization and are not simply other management reports.

- Reporting is tailored or personalized to the individual recipient.

- Self-service reporting tools allow the customer or user to access information directly when and how desired.

- The information technology organization works in partnership with the rest of the organization sharing a common, easily understood language to ensure that management information systems support the organization's overall needs. The approach is customer-centric, not data- or technology-centric.

- Full leverage is made of new systems and data sources to feed the management reporting process.

- The frequency of measurement differs from the frequency of reporting—online real time is a reality but is combined with selective rather than broadcast reporting.

- Reporting is triggered by the needs of the user or decision maker, not the calendar or the systems processing cycle.

- The difference between accuracy and precision is well understood and factored into defining the level of detail that is reported.

- Delivery mechanisms and formats leverage best practice design principles to enhance readability and use of the information.

- A comprehensive education program is in place to ensure productive use of systems, interpretation of management information, and selection and use of analytical tools.

- Care is taken not to isolate managers and analysts. Debate, dialogue, and collaboration are actively encouraged.

NOTES

1. *Business Week.*
2. George Anders, "Steve Ballmer's Big Moves," *Fast Company* (March 2001): p. 142.
3. Peter F. Drucker, *Managing in a Time of Great Change* (New York: Penguin Books, 1995), p. 109.
4. Jim Collins, *Good to Great.*
5. Thomas H. Davenport, "Competing on Analytics," *Harvard Business Review* (January 2006): 99–107
6. Tom Peters, *Thriving on Chaos* (New York: Harper & Row, 1987), p. 589.
7. Quoted in Jeffrey Bronchick, "We Need Better Stock Analysis Not More Info," *Wall Street Journal*, August 6, 2002.
8. Robert S. Kaplan and David P. Norton, "The Balanced Scorecard—Measures that Drive Performance," *Harvard Business Review* (January–February 1992).
9. Interview with Lawrence Kellner by the author, May 2000.
10. Drucker, *Managing in a Time of Great Change* (New York: Bantam Books, 1984), p. 109.
11. Alvin Toffler, *The Third Wave* (New York: Bantam Books, 1984).
12. Edward R. Tufte, *The Visual Display of Quantitative Information* (Cheshire, CT: Graphics Press, 1983), p. 191.
13. Ibid., p. 13.

Chapter 8

Forecasting: Pass the Crystal Ball

He who can see three days ahead will be rich for three thousand years.

—Japanese proverb

The *Oxford English Dictionary* defines a "forecast" as a "conjectural estimate of something future." "Conjecture" is defined as the "formation of opinion on incomplete grounds; guessing." So forecasts are just guesses about the future.

In 1922 Thomas Edison predicted that "the radio craze . . . will die out in time." Of course he was wrong; most forecasts are. When asked to construct a forecast, the fact that most are wrong is perhaps the hardest concept for most people to come to terms with. Everything we have been taught conditions us to believe that right answers are good and wrong answers are bad, yet when faced with developing a forecast, the odds are stacked against us. Getting over the fear of being wrong is the first step toward developing a best practice forecasting process.

Why do organizations spend so much time and money trying to predict the future? First and foremost, the process of forecasting can be an invaluable aid to making decisions. As Peter Schwartz comments in his discussion of scenario planning, *The Art of the Long View*, "The end result . . . is not an accurate picture of tomorrow, but better decisions about the future."[1] Many companies fail to understand this crucial insight. The real value of a forecast is not the accuracy of the answer but the insights into how current decisions and future events interact to shape performance. The forecasting process serves as a vehicle to increase management's confidence in the decisions it makes by taking a rational view of the most likely future outcomes based on currently available information. Forecasting is not a single, discrete process. Forecasts are being developed constantly in every area of business. Salespeople are assessing the likelihood of certain deals closing in the near future; factory personnel are forecasting the need for more materials to maintain production; and the corporate treasurer is forecasting cash flows to ensure that the business has adequate money on hand.

The differences between planning and forecasting are subtle and can be confusing. J. Scott Armstrong, professor at The Wharton School, University of Pennsylvania, and Fred Collopy, of the Weatherhead School of Management, Case Western Reserve University in Cleveland, offer a practical definition of the difference: Forecasting is concerned with what the future will look like, while planning is concerned with what it should look like.[2]

This definition acknowledges the different principles on which plans and forecasts are based. Plans are designed primarily to meet some predefined and agreed-on objective, whereas a forecast seeks to understand the impact of events on the likelihood of achieving the objective.

Forecasting includes the activities related to assessing the financial and operating impact of current tactics and events on future results.

TYPICAL PROCESS

Most organizations develop multiple forecasts. Marketing, sales, operations, and finance develop independent forecasts, each of which uses different assumptions and is developed using different tools, information, and time horizons. Significant time is spent reconciling the different forecasts; however, reconciliation usually occurs too late to impact decision making. The financial forecast is prepared on a monthly or quarterly basis and looks out no farther than the end of the current fiscal year. In exceptional circumstances, an organization may develop a revised forecast in response to a major event that fundamentally alters the assumptions on which current tactics and resource allocations were made. For public companies, the forecast cycle usually is timed to provide input for the quarterly reporting process and conference calls with investment analysts.

Forecasting cycle times vary widely; however, it not unusual for a complete companywide forecast to take more than two weeks to develop. This length of time is unacceptably long for a critical aid to dynamic management decision making.

Cycle times are extended for three reasons:

1. It is difficult to get timely information, particularly if the organization has a long accounting close process.
2. The level of detail required in the forecast is so great that managers require significant time to develop estimates for each line item.
3. The tools available to support forecast development are limited to a series of disconnected spreadsheet models.

Since the enactment of Sarbanes-Oxley in the United States and similar legislation in other countries, forecasting cycle times have generally become even longer as companies spend more time ensuring the integrity of the actual results on which their forecasts are based.

Developing the forecast is a purely financial process with little or no reference to the underlying tactics that generate business results. Given the lack of rigor, most forecasting processes are subject to manipulation and game playing, which obscures their potential value. In part due to the effort required to develop a forecast, few organizations include corrective action plans to guide management decision making. Financial forecasts are completed at the same level of detail as the financial plan or budget, regardless of an organization's predictive capability. Few organizations monitor the accuracy of their forecasts on a systematic basis, and forecast accuracy is rarely built into the overall performance measurement system. There is little integration among forecasting, reporting, and financial planning. Notwithstanding the challenges that organizations face in developing a credible forecast, there is significant internal demand for more accurate and timely forecasts.

FORECASTING BEST PRACTICES

Forecasts seek to estimate the results of a given strategy or set of tactics based on two major inputs:

1. Data concerning external events and trends combined with internal performance detail
2. Updates to a set of assumptions about the future environment.

Best practices organizations take a very pragmatic view of what it is realistic to expect from a forecast. Forecasting is not a precise exercise with predictable outcomes; rather, forecasts seek to offer some insight into likely future performance, typically under a range of different assumptions. The objective is to equip managers with information that enables them to make timely tactical decisions that can mitigate risks and leverage opportunities. The first step it to make forecasts relevant.

Make Forecasts Relevant

In much the same way as management reports need to be relevant (see Chapter 7), forecasts must contribute to an organization's ability to develop plans, allocate resources, or execute more effectively. For a forecast to be relevant, four elements need to be defined:

1. Purpose
2. Subject
3. Time horizon
4. Scenario

The *purpose* defines the reason for developing the forecast in the first place. Forecasting without focus is a waste of time, yet many organizations religiously forecast the same items regardless of whether they are still relevant. The purpose should describe the business decisions or plans that the forecast is designed to support. For example, a forecast of new product sales can be used to adjust advertising and promotional support, ensure adequate capacity is available to meet expected demand, or identify new products that are failing. The *subject* of the forecast defines the variables that are to be forecast; in the example, it is new product sales. Clearly defining the subject helps define the drivers and information requirements that can best support the development of the forecast. The *time horizon* defines the period for the forecast, which can vary from a few minutes to many years. The *scenario* describes the assumptions under which the forecast is being developed. The most basic scenario is to attempt to forecast the most likely future outcome based on the information currently available. Best practice organizations also use forecasts to evaluate alternative scenarios based on different sets of assumptions, such as forecasts that address the best-case or worst-case outcomes or that model specific events, such as the merger of two competitors, a new technological innovation, or a change in regulation. Best practice organizations develop multiple forecasts for a single subject area under a number of different scenarios as part of their overall management process. Clearly defining the purpose, subject, time horizon, and scenario sets the stage for making further choices in designing the forecast process.

Start with the Right Information

It is difficult to forecast the weather by studying the thermostat in your house. The thermostat does measure temperature, which is a variable in developing a weather forecast, but it does not provide the right temperature information. Sound absurd? It is no more absurd than trying to forecast employee turnover by asking employees if they plan to quit, as one company did. Or forecasting traffic use of London's orbital motorway, the M25, simply by estimating the number of current trips that would use the new motorway without factoring in new trips that construction of the motorway made possible. Developing an effective forecast is as much about assembling the right information as it is about developing an accurate estimate of the future. The company in the first case was shocked to find that its employees lied when asked if they were going to quit, while the M25 acquired the moniker "the biggest car park in western Europe" soon after it opened, as usage rapidly exceeded all forecasts. Within two years of opening, the first construction project to add more lanes began.

Basing forecasts on the best available information underpins a best practice process. Typically three types of information combine to frame a forecast:

1. The original plan or previous forecast that sets out the organization's strategies and tactics, the allocation of resources, and the expected results under a given set of assumptions
2. Details about the current situation in the form of actual results, events in the marketplace, and forecasts from other sources
3. A series of assumptions about the future, which can include estimates of factors such as inflation, market growth, or interest rates as well as definitions of different scenarios that will be evaluated

Forecasting is about identifying possible relationships between different variables. The key is that the relationship needs to be more than coincidental; there must be some causal relationship that can be inferred. For example, around the time of the Super Bowl, someone always brings up the fact that there has been a striking correlation between the rise and fall of the stock market in any given year and the conference affiliation of the Super Bowl champions. To all but the wildest speculator, there is no possible causal relationship between the two events. Conversely, the battery maker Duracell, part of Procter and Gamble, has been able to consistently develop forecasts of battery demand using the relative growth in gross domestic product (GDP) as a leading indicator. As a country's GDP grows, the population's desire and ability to purchase portable electronic devices increases and hence so does battery consumption. Ensuring that the relationships between different pieces of information implied during a forecast process are valid is an important test of forecast effectiveness.

Southwest Airlines: Developing Credible Forecasts in a Turbulent Industry

In an industry where many major players (Northwest, USAirways, United, and Delta) have filed for bankruptcy protection since 2001, Southwest Airlines has consistently delivered industry-leading performance. Part of Southwest's success can be attributed to a series of performance management practices that are tuned to the volatile business environment in which the company operates.

The airline industry is subject to significant variability in both revenues and costs; these trends have been magnified in recent years as the cumulative effects of 9/11, Hurricanes Katrina and Rita, and $70-per-barrel oil make the continuous understanding of current and likely future trends essential. Southwest has not abandoned the annual budget, which serves as a basis for estimating the resources required to deliver income and cost estimates within manageable ranges; however, these budgets are updated every quarter for the quarter ahead to reflect the best currently available information. The quarterly budgets are then further supported by 12-month rolling forecasts. These forecasts have no bearing on incentive compensation so the risk of sandbagging is minimized and accuracy is consistently good.

Southwest also recognizes that its ability to develop accurate long-range forecasts is limited so it matches its desire for detail with its predictive capability—a notable best practice. The combination of the annual budget with quarterly revisions and rolling forecasts allows Southwest to adapt its resource allocations to volatility in the market. Key attributes of the Southwest process include:

- Setting a realistic planning horizon—quarterly budget updates are for the next quarter only
- Matching the level of detail to its predictive ability—for example, revenues are updated daily and the forecast horizon is monthly; maintenance is updated semimonthly and the forecast horizon is six months
- Integrating the budget, quarterly updates, and forecasts but with a clear purpose for each
- Using the annual budget as a resource allocation process, not a negotiated target-setting process

For over 30 years Southwest has been able to deliver consistent results in the face of numerous competitive and economic challenges. The adoption and adaptation of best practices allows Southwest to understand and adapt to volatility without losing sight on its number one focus—the customer.

Sources: The Beyond Budgeting Round Table and Southwest Airlines

Forecasting Is a Decision Support Process

Forecasting is a mechanism for refining an organization's thinking, plans, and re- source allocation to adjust to changing events. Some organizations have allowed the forecasting process to become so entwined with the financial planning process that the two are indistinguishable. The forecast simply updates the original budget and becomes an exercise in further validating the inaccuracy of the original as- sumptions. To be a powerful management tool, forecasting must be positioned as a positive, forward-looking exercise rather than a mechanism for apportioning blame for inaccuracy in the original planning and budgeting process. Management sets the tone; this can be as simple as altering the way questions are phrased. Instead of reacting to a forecast variance by asking "Why didn't we anticipate that in the budget? Who screwed up?" a more positive tone can be established by saying "Okay, clearly things have changed. What are the major drivers of the change? What are the implications for our business going forward? And what actions should we be taking as a result?"

Forecasts are based on the extrapolation of the expected results of an organi- zation's tactics subject to the impact of any material changes in the operating en- vironment. The primary purpose of the forecast is to uncover potential future variations in performance against plan based on current tactics. When a material variance is identified, it will trigger an assessment of the impact on the organiza- tion's ability to meet its objectives and direct management to evaluate possible changes in tactics to minimize the negative impact or take advantage of the opportunity.

Positioning the forecast process as a decision support tool that seeks to provide insight into future opportunities and threats reduces the pressure to develop ab- solutely precise estimates. The uncertainty inherent in any future projection should guide the organization to develop as much flexibility as possible in the forecast.

It Starts with Sales

The most basic component of a forecast is sales. As Jack Stack comments in his 1992 book, *The Great Game of Business*, "There's a reason the sales line is at the top of the income statement."[3] Without sales, all other elements of a financial plan or forecast become irrelevant. The sales forecast drives decisions across the whole organization, from the number of people that need to be hired to the funds available to invest in new product development. Given the pivotal role of sales in all aspects of decision making, it is amazing how many organizations pay little or no attention to the process by which the sales forecast is created. Typically the sales forecast is extracted under duress from the sales organization. This forecast is then second- guessed by marketing, production, and finance with the result that eventually sales throws up its hands in frustration and simply says, "Just tell me the number you want." At that point, all hope of commitment to deliver on the forecast by the or- ganization most responsible for sales is lost. This is a very unsatisfactory way to de- velop the single most important element of any forecast. Make no mistake: Sales forecasting is hard. Any activity that seeks to predict future human behavior is fraught with uncertainty; however, it behooves all executives to pay special attention to the sales forecast process. While there is no guarantee of success, there are some clear best practice rules that can improve the quality and ownership of the forecast.

Best Practices Guidelines for Sales Forecasting

- The sales forecast must be owned by sales. It must become the sales department's commitment to deliver.

- Developing the forecast should be a collaborative process with open discussion of assumptions and tactics.

- Balance sales potential with delivery potential. Sales translate to revenue only if the product or service can be delivered and the customer pays the bill.

- Leverage all available information. A good sales forecast requires an understanding of many things, including marketing and promotional plans, product launch plans, inventory, market share, competitive position, production capacity, material supply, and outside influences on customer buying decisions.

- Set near-term milestones. Ensure that any sales forecast establishes intermediate targets that can provide an early warning of over- or underperformance. The earlier these are identified, the more time an organization has to adjust its plans.

- Ensure incentives are tied to results. As the sales forecast is so crucial to making many decisions, the sales organization must feel the pain of failure and share the rewards of success.

- Recognize that overachievement can be as big a problem as underachievement. Many organizations suffer from endemic "sandbagging" in their forecast processes. People purposely underestimate what can be achieved so that they look good when they blow away their target.

Use a Rolling 90-Day Forecast

Most forecasts follow the fiscal calendar. For example, if an organization operates on a calendar-year basis, each forecast prepared during the year will extend through December 31 of that year. Over the last few years, an increasing number of organizations have modified this approach and implemented a rolling forecast process that extends the forecast over a consistent time horizon, typically four to eight quarters out, depending on the nature and cycle of the business; however, the results have not been what were expected (see box).

Since the first edition of this book, the rolling forecast has come to be seen as an almost universal best practice truth. I was part of the chorus. I was wrong. Four, six, or eight rolling forecasts are not a silver bullet. What has caused this revisionist thinking? Two things: practical experience and common sense.

Best Practice Health Warning: Rolling Forecasts Can Seriously Damage Your Performance Management Process—Use with Care

---

In many situations a rolling forecast is neither desirable nor practical. This was brought home to me during my time as head of corporate planning at Bank of America. The bank had discussed moving to a rolling forecast for some time but had made little progress. Upon taking up my position at the bank, this seemed like a simple step to take. I explained all the perceived benefits and met little initial resistance. My finance colleagues counseled me to test the idea with the business before going further—very sound advice. I started my discussions with the retail banking, credit card, and mortgage businesses. Although there was some debate over the details, no major roadblocks were raised. Next I ventured up to New York from the bank's Charlotte headquarters to meet with the asset management and investment banking groups. The asset management executives were a little less sure of the benefits; they said that the key measure in their business, "assets under management." was very closely related to two metrics that were very difficult to predict with any degree of certainty: overall investment returns in different categories (e.g., equities, bonds, real estate, and commodities) and the returns delivered by the bank to its customers.

While they did not completely reject the concept, their enthusiasm was lukewarm at best. My next stop was the investment bankers. Our first conversation went something like this:

Axson: "We are thinking of moving to a rolling four- or five-quarter forecast for the bank in order to provide better visibility and a more consistent forecast window to support decision making. How applicable would that be in your business?"

Investment Banker/Master of the Universe: "Look, I can barely forecast what might happen tomorrow. So you can ask me for whatever you want but what you will get back will be less than useful. [The executive actually used slightly stronger language.] If I could predict where the markets will be four or five quarters out, I would not be sitting here talking to you. I would be on a very big yacht somewhere very warm."

I got the point.

As companies grew increasingly frustrated with the value of rolling forecasts with long time horizons they began to take a closer look at the relationship between increasing volatility and the role of the forecast. As we discussed in Chapter 1, volatility and uncertainty are two of the reasons why managers have become frustrated with the annual budgeting process, which produces plans that almost immediately become obsolete. Many organizations have now moved to a different type of rolling forecast—one that looks out only for the next 90 days. A 90-day rolling forecast works like this: For the first quarter of the year, the plan serves as the performance commitment for the organization; after two months of actual results have been recorded, the organization develops an updated forecast for the second quarter and evaluates whether the end-of-year projection contained in the plan remains valid or needs to be changed. The detailed forecast for the second quarter serves as an updated performance commitment by management and records the impact of changes in tactics in response to events occurring in the first quarter. This process then repeats itself each quarter. In effect, the organization is moving to a rolling quarterly plan process where commitments are updated in response to the real-time performance of the business rather than tracking performance against an already obsolete plan. Exhibit 8.1 illustrates a typical rolling 90-day plan/forecast process.

In designing a rolling forecast, it is critical to select the time horizon that is most appropriate for the business. This horizon typically is determined by the lead time for making key decisions. For example, consider a retailer, where sales are subject to significant seasonal patterns and supply chain responsiveness is key to profitability. Here a rolling forecast should seek to look out no more than one or two selling seasons, typically no more than six to nine months for most forecast items. A six- or eight-quarter rolling forecast is unlikely to be of much value for most items with the possible exception of capital planning regarding store development and refurbishment.

Potential pitfalls of a longer-term rolling forecast:

- *Failure to match the desire for detail with predictive capability.* Most companies have an almost insatiable desire for detail, which pervades reporting, budgeting, and forecasting. However, for both budgeting and forecasting, more detail does not equate to greater accuracy since you are trying to predict the future. Many organizations fail to leverage a rolling forecast because they insist on forecasting all subsequent periods in the same level of detail. Not only is this a waste of time, but it also increases the risk that decisions will be made based on detailed future forecasts that have no sound basis and are simply extrapolations of current performance or worse simply guesswork. As a general rule, the level of detail in a forecast should decrease the farther out you look.

- *Focusing exclusively on financials.* Rolling forecasts offer the greatest value when they link key operational drivers of the business to expected future financial results. If the rolling forecast is created simply project the financial results

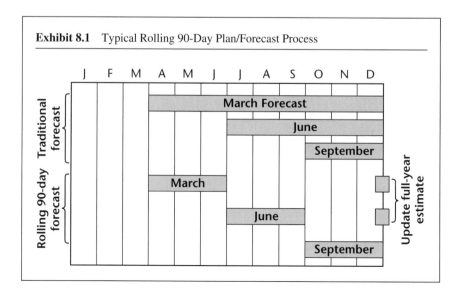

Exhibit 8.1   Typical Rolling 90-Day Plan/Forecast Process

of the business into future periods, it ceases to offer any real value to business management as a decision-making aid. The objective should be to develop a driver-based rolling forecast that projects both the key operational variables of the business and the resulting financial results. For example, an effective rolling forecast should include projections for items such as inventory turns, customer conversion, promotion response rates as well as sales, gross margin, and operating expenses.

Is a Rolling Forecast Right for You?

A rolling forecast can be most valuable when four conditions are met:

1. Material decisions will be significantly enhanced by the move to a rolling forecast.
2. Reasonable projections of future performance over the rolling forecast time horizon can be made based on information available at the time of forecast creation.
3. There is a good understanding of the relationships between key business drivers and financial results.
4. If the proposed time horizon of the forecast is four quarters or more, current fiscal year– or calendar-based forecasts should be accurate to an average level of +/– 2 percent over a five-year time period.

Implemented in the right environment, a rolling forecast can be a powerful tool to increase the visibility into the drivers of future business performance. Rolling forecasts can also dramatically reduce the pain associated with traditional budgeting processes. However, they are not a silver bullet. The design and implementation of an effective rolling forecast process requires careful thought and preparation.

Driver-Based Rolling Forecasts

One distinguishing feature of a best practice forecast process is that the financial forecast is not based solely on the analysis of financial measures. The forecast is constructed by estimating changes in the key drivers of the business. The quality of a financial forecast improves dramatically if the projected change in financial results is based on a rigorous understanding of the likely changes in the key drivers of each financial measure. For example, developing a meaningful sales forecast requires the consideration of a broad range of drivers, including the number of salespeople, the productivity of each one, the schedule of planned new product introductions, product pricing relative to competitors, and future advertising and promotion. All these factors can influence the number of new customers the company expects to acquire, the level of sales to existing customers, and any change in the customer attrition rate. The deeper the understanding of the relative impact of each driver and of the interaction between the different drivers, the more accurate the forecast.

Another advantage of using a driver-based approach is that it facilitates more collaboration. By translating a financial measure into its component drivers, it is possible to engage different functions and organizations in the development of the forecast. Doing this increases the rigor of the forecast process and also the ownership of the result. Instead of the forecast being a creation of the finance department alone, it becomes a shared result of all contributors. Frequent measurement of the key drivers of an organization's business provides a sound base of information for constructing a forecast.

Deploying an Adaptive Forecasting Process at American Express

The volatile economic environment that followed the terrorist attacks on September 11, 2001, has triggered major performance management process changes at many companies. For American Express, it served to highlight the limitations of the company's traditional, relatively static planning process and the lack of consistency in forecasting approaches and systems across its three businesses. The $29 billion company with 76,000 employees operating in 26 countries needed a more flexible, integrated, and responsive process to deal with the uncertain and volatile economic environment. Building on the principles set out in Hope and Fraser's *Beyond Budgeting*, American Express has implemented a progressive new rolling forecast process.[4] The key elements in the transformation have been to:

- Base business forecasts on key drivers of activity, such as the number of American Express cards in use and the average spending per card.
- Set credible top-down targets for each business unit.
- Move to a rolling five-quarter forecast.
- Introduce scenario planning beginning in 2002 to evaluate the potential impact of a range of uncontrollable events and create a management playbook to mitigate the risks and take advantage of the opportunities.
- Standardize tools and methods while still allowing for local customization for unique business conditions and drivers.
- Eliminate the traditional annual budget in 2005.

From the initial introduction of the new process in 2002, the company has rolled the process out across 26 countries and further refined it, adding new features such as an investment optimization framework that allows managers to make investment trade-off decisions as part of the overall portfolio evaluation process. The new process allows the company to reassess its investment priorities on a more frequent basis. Jaime Croake, American Express's vice president of planning transformation, commented, "Where we used to do quarterly reviews, and we'd have three opportunities during the year to release investments, now we've got 12." Thus, when the company identifies an opportunity and has funding, it can quickly act. In 2003, this flexibility allowed the company to increase funding over the base plan, which contributed to an 8 percent rise in new cards. Anand Sanwal, Vice President of Investment Optimization adds, "Beyond making us a more flexible organization, investment optimization has driven changes in organizational behavior. Decision-makers better understand that investment decisions cannot be made in a vacuum within a business segment but across the enterprise in order for us to best achieve our company-wide financial and strategic objectives."

The combination of a driver- and risk-based process demonstrates how leading companies are deploying new performance management techniques to sustain growth in an increasingly volatile and uncertain world.

Sources: The Beyond Budgeting Round Table and American Express

Forecast Fewer Things More Often

The dominance of detailed centralized planning processes tended to drive a commensurate level of detail into the forecast. Rarely was the result more accurate forecasts; however, cycle times lengthened as organizations struggled to construct all the required detail. Some organizations compensated by reducing the frequency with which forecasts were developed, often moving from a monthly to a quarterly forecast.

In the last few years, best practice organizations have moved in the opposite direction. Instead of reducing forecast frequency and increasing detail, they are forecasting more frequently and reducing the amount of detail in each forecast. These organizations understand that not only does more detail not equate with more accuracy, but also that excessive detail limits the rigor that can be put into each element. By forecasting fewer items more often, these organizations are able to develop more experience and knowledge that can only enhance the quality of the forecast. Organizations that rely on real-time information as a source of their competitive advantage have made forecasting of the most volatile or fast-moving elements of their business a near-continuous activity. The emergence of tools and technologies that support rapid forecasting offers organizations much more choice in the frequency, level of detail, and scope of their forecasting activities.

Events, Not Calendars

The calendar has always been the governing factor in triggering all aspects of planning and management reporting. Today, however, an increasing number of organizations are moving to event-driven forecasting. This means that forecasts are triggered by external events that may impact the business, such as competitor action or regulatory change; or by internal events, such as the start of the strategic planning process or a delay in the launch of a new product.

Event-driven forecasting is very compatible with forecasting less detail more frequently. For example, an event that may be material to one business unit may not be material to the organization as a whole, so it makes sense to develop a forecast for the affected unit but not for the whole organization.

Define the Appropriate Time Horizon

Forecasts can address different time horizons. Long-term forecasting, or scenario planning, typically looks more than three years out and is used to guide more speculative investments in research and development or long-term capital planning. Medium-term forecasts typically are used to develop performance targets, prioritize capital investment decisions, and crystallize market and product strategies. Short-term or real-time forecasting is used to set pricing, predict near-term demand, translate demand into requirements for the supply chain, and set specific marketing and promotional spending plans. Forecasts that address the same time period and scenario should use the same set of assumptions. Forecast recipients must understand exactly which assumptions were used in its development.

The time horizon also influences the level of detail in the forecast. Long-range forecasts should be developed around a few, typically less than 10, macrovariables. Medium-term forecasts usually address the next four to eight quarters and are based around the same key drivers that are addressed in the operational plan. These forecasts typically are done at least quarterly but can be executed more often, depending on the specific needs of the organization. Short-term forecasting focuses on the current business cycle and is designed to support day-to-day decision making. Such forecasts focus on one or two key business drivers and are designed to optimize short-term performance.

Forecasting at Google

Eric Schmidt, chief executive of Google, explained why Google does not provide earnings guidance in a January 2006 interview; "There is a cost to not providing guidance and I understand that. The reason that we don't is our business is so dynamic we'd have to give very broad ranges and I don't think that would be constructive."[5]

Use Forecasting as a Risk Management Tool

All businesses have to deal with uncertainty. The forecast process is the perfect time to address uncertainty explicitly. A forecast that relies only on what is known and certain offers little value to management in making decisions. All too often forecasts appear to reduce uncertainty by translating a whole series of imprecise assumptions into a precise estimate of future results. This is the exact reverse of what is required. Dealing with uncertainty is one of the hallmarks of a best practice forecast process. Forecasting business drivers that are both highly volatile and material requires a different approach. Generally best practice companies use two methods to handle such items:

1. Develop a series of forecasts based on a reasonable range of values for each key driver rather than rely on a single-point estimate.
2. Decompose the driver into a series of more predictable elements that can be forecast with some confidence, and use the results to gain insight into the likely behavior of the unpredictable variable.

The oil industry offers a rich case study as to how to deal with a key variable that is both material and volatile. Oil companies have become very adept at developing operating plans and forecasts under different oil price assumptions. They have well-thought-out forecasts that assume various price points for a barrel of oil. Each forecast sets out the strategic and tactical changes that the company will employ under each scenario. Companies closely monitor a whole series of drivers that can influence the price of oil, including the size of known reserves, the political stability in key oil-producing nations, the aggressiveness of environmental legislation in major oil-consuming countries, and other variables that can provide insight into likely oil price movements.

In the movie business, companies have become much more creative at managing risk. The response to the 1-hit/100-miss cycle has been to diversify. Film producers attempt to spread the risk through both complex funding and distribution deals that limit the risk of one disaster sinking a whole studio. The industry has become much more savvy at understanding the overall economic drivers of the business. Instead of relying solely on movie studio funding to pay for the production and marketing and box office receipts for revenue, producers now have a myriad of options, all of which can help reduce risk. In addition to box office receipts, revenue can be derived from promotional tie-ins with fast food chains or beverage companies, licensing of merchandise, video and DVD rights, and computer games, to name a few. Funding typically is shared by a number of partners in exchange for a share of the profits and acceptance of some risk. Even directors and film stars are getting in on the act. James Cameron, the director of *Titanic*, sacrificed his up-front fee for a share of the profits as the movie's costs spiraled out of control and predictions of huge losses mounted. His gamble paid off handsomely; the film became the highest-grossing film of all time. The less successful *Pearl Harbor* still paid off big for director Michael Bay and lead actor Ben Affleck, both of whom opted for a profit share instead of most of their fees. In both cases the major players were willing to accept more risk in return for a potentially greater return. The studios and producers were happy to sacrifice possible profits for lower risk. Both times the directors and actors won big time.

In each situation, forecasting played a crucial role in making decisions. Participants have to balance their confidence in the forecast with their personal risk profile and make a judgment as to the right decision. Cameron, Bay, and Affleck all had supreme confidence in their product and were willing to take on additional risk in exchange for higher returns.

Play the What-If Game

Beyond addressing the trade-off of risks and returns, forecasting is the perfect forum for testing alternative views of the future. Two components need to be addressed when evaluating different scenarios: the probability that the particular scenario will play out and the impact the scenario will have on the business. It makes sense to address a few high-impact scenarios that can fundamentally restructure a particular economy, market, or business as part of the longer-term forecast process completed in support of strategic planning. Examples of such scenarios could include increasing commercial development in China, the potential offered by the decoding of the human genome on healthcare, and the availability of universal broadband connections in the home. Exhibit 8.2 illustrates a few scenarios that at one time would have been thought to be highly improbable.

As part of the forecast process, best practice companies define the measures that help predict whether a particular scenario is likely to happen. For example, consider a scenario that assumes that fixed-line telephone service will be replaced,

Exhibit 8.2	Improbable Scenarios
Date	Scenario
1960	• Foreign automakers will own more than half the U.S. market. • A person will land on the moon.
1980	• Germany will be unified in less than 10 years. • The LP record will disappear.
2000	• Enron and WorldCom will both collapse. • The Nasdaq will close below 1,300.

not just supplemented, by wireless service. Leading indicators that may precede the unfolding of this scenario could include a decline in the number of fixed telephone circuits being used and a decline in the number of calls made over fixed lines matched by a corresponding increase in the traffic over wireless circuits. Building these leading indicators into the management reporting process enables management to monitor the emergence of a new scenario.

Developing and testing different scenarios allows management to model the likely impact on current decision making and future results. In effect, management is creating a series of contingency plans that define how it will respond should one of the scenarios become reality. The impact on overall results can be significant. The ability to spot major trends or shifts rapidly and act on them is a key driver of competitive success. In cellular phones, Nokia's rise and Motorola's relative decline can be attributed largely to Nokia more accurately forecasting the speed with which the mobile phone market would switch from analog to digital service.

The Process Is as Important as the Result

The process of developing a best practice–based forecast can be just as important as the end result. Executed correctly, the forecast process will gather input from many different internal and external sources, test the likelihood of different scenarios, and allow the organization to test its thinking about different courses of action. The most valuable outcome may not be the quantitative results of the forecast but management's increased confidence in the chosen course of action and in the organization's ability to respond quickly and positively to changing events.

Providing time for management to plan how it will react under different sets of circumstances is one of the biggest benefits of the whole forecast process. As the famous South African golfer Gary Player once commented, "The more I practice the luckier I get." His point was that the more he practiced bunker shots, for example, the more likely he was to be lucky and have one of them go in. In business, there is tremendous value to having confidence based on prior consideration, experience, or anticipation of a particular situation. Best practice companies use the forecast process for testing their thinking about the future and gaining a better understanding of how their actions will change under different scenarios. Forecasts should focus on identifying the need for changes in tactics to meet established targets or exploit emerging opportunities. Forecasting requires that a series of detailed inputs are translated into clear, actionable information that enables adjustments to be made to plans and tactics.

Penalties of Success

Beating a forecast sounds like good news, but it can have dire and expensive consequences. In the early 1990s, Hoover UK, a division of Maytag, ran a promotion that offered free airline tickets with the purchase of a vacuum cleaner. Not an unusual idea; such promotions appear all the time. However, the crucial difference here was that the price of the airline ticket exceeded the price of a vacuum.

For a $100 purchase a customer could get a $500 plane ticket to the United States—an attractive proposition. Hoover executives assumed many buyers would not claim the free flights because of the onerous restrictions placed on travel. They were wrong. Over 200,000 people bought inexpensive appliances and demanded their tickets. Hoover tried to extricate itself from a dangerous situation by offering vouchers or refunds, but consumers and, more important, England's notorious tabloid press were having none of it. Hoover became front-page news, and the company was facing a pubic relations disaster that could have destroyed its reputation in the United Kingdom. Eventually the company was forced to honor all the tickets at a cost of more than $70 million, which proves that beating a forecast is not necessarily a good thing.

Ensure Consistency

One of the more valuable uses of forecasting is to monitor the changes that occur over time. This is possible only if there is a high degree of consistency in the assumptions used in the forecasting process. Best practice companies ensure that a common set of assumptions is used for all forecasts to increase comparability over time. Recently many organizations have begun to reduce the importance placed on the quarterly financial forecast as a tool to manage external expectations. Both Gillette and Coca-Cola went so far as to stop providing such guidance. Taking the lead from the regular sales forecasting process that has existed within sales teams for years, organizations are developing more comprehensive short-term forecasts aimed at fine-tuning operations. Two factors, one external and one internal, are driving the change. Externally increased volatility and speed across all aspects of business have made annual, quarterly, and even monthly business reviews obsolete as a means of managing performance. Organizations must respond in days, hours, or minutes if they are to take advantage of short windows of opportunity or avoid taking a major hit. In most markets, the luxury of reviewing past performance, conducting broad analysis of options, and making decisions has been eliminated. For example, in late 2001, General Motors announced a radical new zero-percent financing program across its whole product line to try to sustain demand following the events of September 11, 2001. GM's major competitors, Ford and Chrysler, did not have the luxury of time to contemplate how to respond. The decision to match GM's offer was instant despite the high cost. Internally, companies are seeking to realize the potential offered by many of the new technologies that provide access to valuable data not readily available in the past. The capturing of sales data through sales force automation systems, the integration of the total customer view through customer relationship management systems, and the aggregation of supply chain data from newly deployed supply chain systems provide a vast new source of real time data. The collection of this vast stream of real-time transactions provides companies with a continuous view of how their business is operating, in stark contrast to the staccato monthly reports of old. Taking the flow of data and rapidly synthesizing it enables companies to discern trends much more rapidly than in a batch-processing world. A softening in the sales pipeline, an impending shortage in the supply chain, or a potential expense overrun can be detected as it happens. The knowledge gained by comparing forecasts can be built into future forecasting efforts and improve both the consistency and the accuracy of the forecast process. These learnings can help eliminate the traditional hockey stick effect that many organizations see in their forecasts (see Exhibit 8.3). All too often, the forecast process merely pushes sales and earnings that were originally expected in the current period into later periods while keeping the year-end target the same. The manifestation of such a pattern is a pretty good indicator that the forecast process is broken. Developing a consistent basis for developing forecasts and monitoring the trend over time allows an organization to identify the hockey stick effect much more quickly.

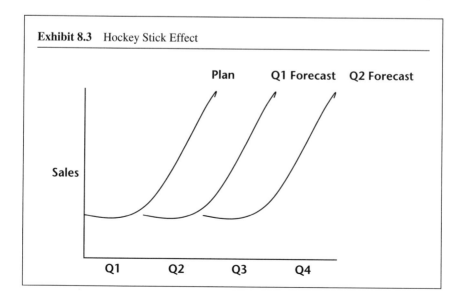

Exhibit 8.3 Hockey Stick Effect

Balance Statistical Analysis with Gut Feel

There are a number of schools of thought about the most effective approach to forecasting, ranging from highly complex statistical models to subjective management opinion based on limited analysis. During the 30 years after World War II during which large-scale formal planning was dominant, there was a trend toward developing highly scientific, statistical models that attempted to forecast the future. The last 20 years have seen a move away from such a programmatic view of the future. In 1992 Peter Drucker went so far as to declare: "Uncertainty—in the economy, society, politics—has become so great as to render futile, if not counterproductive, the kind of planning most companies still practice: forecasting based on probabilities."[6]

Drucker advocated that the primary question asked during the forecast process should change from "What is most likely to happen?" to "What has already happened that will create the future?" By focusing on already observed trends, organizations can begin to develop a series of forecast scenarios. These scenarios then can be matched to an organization's capabilities to identify potential opportunities and threats. Today a number of academics and business leaders subscribe to a view of forecasting that is much more active. Instead of simply projecting the future impact of current events or trends, they advocate moving from speculating on what might happen to imagining what you can actually make happen. Gary Hamel, in his 2000 book, *Leading the Revolution*, comments: "Companies fail to create the future not because they fail to predict it but because they fail to imagine it."[7]

The practical application of these different approaches is a function of an organization's ability to construct meaningful estimates (see Exhibit 8.4). Generally speaking, forecasts focused on more predictable variables over short time horizons lend themselves to a more statistically rigorous approach. The more unpredictable the outcome and the longer the time horizon, the greater the value of forecasting approaches that explicitly address uncertainty.

BEST PRACTICE SUMMARY

- Forecasts are based on an assessment of the same goals, critical success factors, and key drivers of the business that are used in strategic, operational, and financial planning process.
- The forecast is not simply an extrapolation of the financial plan. The financial forecast is derived directly from the forecast of key business drivers.
- The start point for forecasting is a robust, systematic sales forecast that defines the organization's future revenue expectations.
- Longer time horizon rolling forecasts (typically four, six, or eight quarters) are used only when an organization's decision-making ability and predictive capability support their development.
- Forecast detail is less in later time periods, reflecting reduced predictive capability.

Exhibit 8.4 Selecting a Forecasting Approach

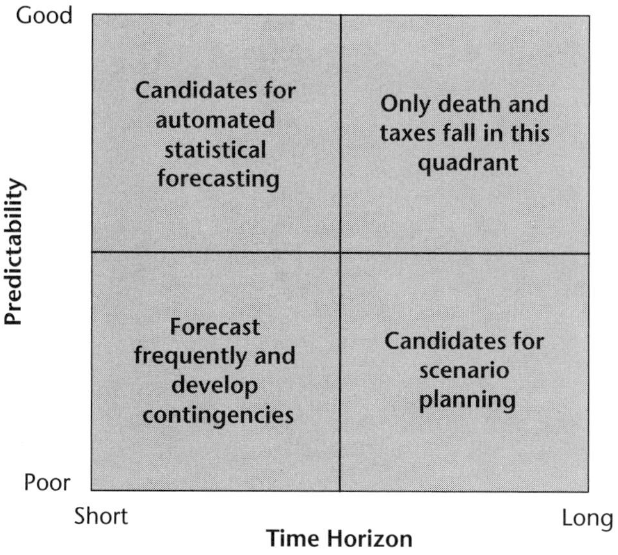
Good
Candidates for automated statistical forecasting
Only death and taxes fall in this quadrant
Predictability
Forecast frequently and develop contingencies
Candidates for scenario planning
Poor
Short
Long
Time Horizon

- Marketing, sales, production, and financial forecasts are developed using the same assumptions.
- Forecast trends over time are analyzed, and the knowledge gained is fed back into the overall process.
- Forecasts contain an explanation of material variances in performance, an explanation of the drivers or causes of the variance, an assessment of the materiality of the variance, and guidance as to the likely actions available to management.
- Forecasting is a collaborative process that seeks to gather the richest possible insight into future performance regardless of the source.
- Forecasts are revised only on an exception basis and only when projected results differ from plan by a predetermined range.
- Forecasts are actionable—they do not just identify problems but explain why the problems exist and explore the options for fixing them.
- Forecast consolidations are executed automatically through a single common tool. Consistency and simplicity are the hallmarks of a good forecasting process.
- Forecasts should use modeling tools with multiple what-if scenarios, and sensitivity analyses should be developed.

NOTES

1. Peter Schwartz, *The Art of the Long View* (New York: Doubleday, 1991), p. 9.
2. J. Scott Armstrong, "Forecasting Principles at Wharton," copyright 1997–2002.
3. Jack Stack and Bo Burlingham, *The Great Game of Business* (New York: Currency Doubleday, 1994), p. 154.
4. Jeremy Hope and Robin Fraser, *Beyond Budgeting* (Boston, Harvard Business School Press, 2003).
5. Kevin J. Delaney, "Seeking Guidance from Google," *Wall Street Journal*, February 25, 2006.
6. Peter F. Drucker, *Managing in a Time of Great Change* (New York: E.P. Dutton/ Truman Talley Books, 1995), p. 39.
7. Gary Hamel, *Leading the Revolution* (Boston: Harvard Business School Press, 2000), p. 120.

Chapter 9

Risk Management: Place Your Bets

The past seldom obliges by revealing to us when wildness will break out in the future.

—Peter L. Bernstein

Uncertainty, volatility, and unpredictability have come to characterize the environment in which most organizations now operate. Although the luxury of detailed long-term plans predicated on a stable view of the future has long gone, as we have seen, such practices remain at the heart of most performance management processes. Many managers are beginning to understand the futility of trying to plan out future performance precisely; hence the emergence of risk-based planning techniques over the last few years as managers seek to adapt to ever more volatile and uncertain markets. Even a cursory review of recent events is enough to illustrate the need for more dynamic, responsive performance management processes (see Exhibit 9.1). Changes occur with such frequency and velocity that static annual plans simply cannot hope to plot a course that remains valid for more than a few weeks.

The first step on the road to developing a set of risk-aware management practices is to recognize that simply ignoring risk does not make it go away. In fact, the elimination of risk is not the objective. As Peter Bernstein succinctly described: "The capacity to manage risk, and with it the appetite to take risk and make forward-looking choices, are key elements of the energy that drives the economic system forward."[1] Risk-taking is fundamental to a company's ability to create value. The primary objective of the commercial enterprise is to generate returns that more than compensate investors for the risks they assume. Investment in new products, research into new technologies, and even the redesign of core business processes all incur risk; those organizations that can manage these risks effectively while also executing successfully emerge as leaders.

The volatility and uncertainty of the last few years are driving investors, regulators, and managers to seek greater insight into both the positive and the negative impact of risk on future performance. While most companies have made good progress in improving the quality and availability of financial information (with the occasional prod from regulators), leading companies are simultaneously upgrading the processes, measures, and tools they use to manage business risk. Risk identification, monitoring, and management are now integral parts of any effective performance management process. Increasingly, success is being defined by those organizations

Exhibit 9.1 An Increasingly Volatile World

Unpredictable One-Time Events	Rapidly Emerging Trends
◆ 9/11	◆ Offshoring
◆ Asian tsunami	◆ Broadband
◆ Hurricane Katrina	◆ Sustained high commodity prices
◆ Long-Term Capital Management	◆ Economic rise of China and India
◆ Enron, Worldcom, Qwest	◆ Aging population

Source: Sonax Group, Performance Management Research Program

that can anticipate and react best to changes in the marketplace. These changes are being fueled by two forces:

1. Unpredictable one-time events that have rapid and broad global impact
2. Acceleration in the pace at which external and internal trends become material

NO EXCUSES

Managers have historically used the negative impact of one-time events that are outside of their control as excuses for shortfalls in performance, and that trend continues to this day. Numerous companies cited the impact of 9/11, Hurricane Katrina, or the Asian tsunami as explanations of poor results; however, we are seeing a significant change in how these excuses are being viewed by investors and other stakeholders. Instead of giving management teams a free pass for the impact of such events, many observers are looking at how an organization responds to such challenges. Those that handle adversity the best can command a premium relative to their excuse-giving peers. An excellent example of this was the stellar performance of Southwest Airlines in the months after 9/11, in stark contrast to peers such as United, US Airways, Northwest, and Delta, which all filed for Chapter 11 bankruptcy protection. The impact of 9/11 and Southwest's ability to withstand the enormous challenges it posed to the airline industry served to highlight the company's significant advantages over its competitors.

The reality is that events that once had relatively limited local impact now ripple rapidly across the globe. The global economy is no longer comprised of a number of largely isolated national economies and industries where the impact of events in far-flung corners of the world is minimal. Global markets and integrated supply chains accelerate the effect of unpredictable events on companies and markets around the world. An organization's management processes must adapt to this changed reality.

GLOBAL INTERDEPENDENCE

The degree of interdependence among companies, markets, and economies, combined with the increasing speed of communications, is accelerating the pace at which trends move from emerging and interesting to established and dominant. It took decades for consumer ownership of cars, telephones, and televisions to reach critical mass; contrast that with the adoption rates of personal computers, cell phones, and MP3 players, which went from cool new technologies to mass market staples in 10 years or less. For managers trying to preserve leadership positions in fast-changing markets or establish leadership positions in new markets, the need for adaptability, speed, and not a little luck is clear. The last few decades offer numerous examples of the speed with which once-dominant companies can find their market leadership positions rapidly undermined by aggressive new competitors offering innovations in product or service or simply executing far more efficiently (see Exhibit 9.2). Of the over 7,400 companies that have gone public since 1980, 25 percent have gone out of business—and no, they were not all dot-coms.

For many, the terminal effects of these changes did not show up in the company's financial statements immediately; however, the signs were there for all to see if only they had been recognized. In his 1995 book *Managing in a Time of Great Change*, Peter Drucker isolated the problem of relying solely on a financial view of an organization's health:

> Financial accounting, balance sheets, P&L, cost allocations, etc. are an X-ray of the enterprise's skeleton. But just as [many of] the diseases we commonly die from—heart disease, Parkinson's, AIDS—do not show up on an X-ray, so too a loss of market standing or a failure to innovate do not register in the accountant's figures until the damage is done.[2]

Recent events make the truth of Drucker's statement more apparent than ever before. The speed with which many major companies met their demise rocked the confidence of investors, put board members squarely in the spotlight, and placed chief executive officers and chief financial officers on the firing line. The public had little warning that the collapse of these companies was imminent. Only when the financial impact of management mistakes had crystallized on the balance sheet or profit-and-loss account—in other words, when it was too late to do anything—did the full magnitude of the problems become clear. No more compelling argument for integrating a sound risk management capability into an organization's performance management processes should be needed.

Exhibit 9.2   Changing Market Leadership

Product or Industry	Established Players	New Entrants/Innovators
Airlines	PanAm, TWA, American	Southwest, JetBlue
General merchandisers	Sears, J.C.Penney	Wal-Mart, Target, Kohls
Portable music players	Sony	Apple
Automotive	GM, Ford, Chrysler	Toyota, Honda, Subaru
Film rental	Blockbuster	Netflix
Reference source	Libraries, Encyclopedia Britannica	Google

Regulatory Pressure

Legislators and regulators have moved quickly, passing new rules requiring greater disclosure of financial information in an attempt to improve transparency. The demands for more accurate and timely distribution of financial information are appropriate; however, the message behind Drucker's comments has gotten lost in the governance rhetoric. Few voices calling for improved corporate reporting acknowledge that the financial results of any business event are the last step in the process. To improve the management of overall business risk and performance, companies need better insight into the operational drivers of future results.

The need to develop a broad, systematic, and rigorous approach to risk management is perhaps most widely understood in the financial services industry. One of the major elements in the Bank of International Settlements (BIS) Basel Capital Accord, published in January 2001, is the definition of operational risk. The accord defines "operational risk" as "the risk of direct or indirect loss resulting from inadequate or failed internal control processes, people, and systems or from external events." Andrew Crockett, general manager of the BIS commented: "We need to find ways for firms to provide a richer set of information about risk than is normally included in accounting standards."[3] In other words, financial information is not enough to gauge a company's overall business risk.

In April 2006 Timothy Geithner, president of the New York Federal Reserve Bank, noted that the measurement and modeling of risks is not enough:

> Stress testing and scenario analysis is an important part of the process of calibrating this relationship between risk and capital and margin. The test of a sufficiently strong process is not simply the realism of the process used to measure potential losses, but the impact that it has on the decisions made.[4]

This captures the essence of an effective business risk management process: It is not just about the process of measurement; the decisions that managers make are what will determine the success or failure of an organization's risk management process.

Threat of Irrelevance

Perhaps the biggest risk organizations face, and also one of the least understood, is the threat of becoming irrelevant to one's customers. From the days of the oft-cited buggy whip manufacturers whose whole business became irrelevant upon the introduction of the automobile, companies have been exposed to the risk that customers simply no longer want, need, or value their goods and services. The economic landscape is littered with the relics of once-mighty companies that lost a vital connection with their customers. Building intelligence into an organization's performance management processes to assess the continued relevance of products and services is crucial if an organization is to identify and respond to the threat adequately. While this sounds like an obvious point, few organizations seriously consider the possibility that their business may become irrelevant until it is too late. As

Exhibit 9.3 Drivers of Change

Factor	Examples
Consumer taste	Atkins Diet
Technology innovation	Video to DVD, CD to MP3
Regulation	IRAs, Health Savings Accounts
Competitive model	Wal-Mart, Dell, Southwest
New product innovation	iPod
Execution failure	Kmart
Foreign action	Concorde
Current events	9/11—Homeland Security
Collusion	Archer Daniel Midland, Sothebys
Ethical failure	Tobacco companies
Technology/process failure	Northeast U.S. blackout in 2004
Leadership	Sunbeam, Enron, Worldcom
Values	Mothers Against Drunk Driving
Environment	Toyota Prius, aerosol cans

Source: Sonax Group, Performance Management Research Program

discussed in Chapter 6, few managers are willing to contemplate failure—yet it is essential if the right decisions are to be made and the organization is to survive, never mind prosper. Measuring the risk of irrelevance first demands that an organization understand its attraction to customers. As the examples in Exhibit 9.3 illustrate, many factors increase the risk of irrelevance.

How relevant would H & R Block be if the United States introduced a flat tax with no deductions, Exxon Mobil if non–oil-powered vehicles and sources of electricity predominate, Starbucks if caffeine were found to cancerous, or Blockbuster if broadband video on demand becomes ubiquitous? After all, it is not that long ago that Wang, Woolworth, AT&T (the old one, not the reincarnation), Pan Am, the American textile industry, the British mining industry, and network television dominated their respective markets.

Developing an Effective Business Risk Management Capability

Historically risk has been defined narrowly as the measurement and management of financial risk. Market price, interest rate, credit, and exchange rate risks have dominated management's attention and are well understood, if not always managed effectively. However, such a narrow view is no longer sufficient. The impact of specific risk factors, from the stability of global supply chains to the threat of attack from special interest groups, represents just some of the increasing portfolio of potential risks that can impact performance. As Exhibit 9.4 illustrates, no company is immune.

Exhibit 9.4   Expanding Portfolio of Risks

Company	Risk Type	Examples
Microsoft	Regulatory	• Settlement costs of $700 million in the second quarter of 2005 alone
Wal-Mart	Numerous	• Use of illegal alien workers to clean stores • Wage discrimination lawsuits by female workers • Rezoning of land to prevent store expansion • Union organization efforts
Google	Governmental	• Voluntarily agrees to censor service in China
eBay	Special interest	• Concerns over privacy of personal data
Nike	Special interest	• Use of child labor
Levi Strauss	Demographics	• Aging of customer base
	Competitor action	• Changing tastes and brand preferences
Kodak	Technological	• Move to digital photography

Personal Experience at Bank of America

The impact of various categories of risk was brought home in a powerful way to me during my time as head of corporate planning at Bank of America. In a single 12-month period, the bank was exposed to numerous unforeseen events from investigations by New York State Attorney General Elliot Spitzer into late trading of mutual funds, to the collapse of the Italian dairy company Parmalat, and to the accidental disclosure of personal customer information by one of the bank's third-party suppliers. Each event could have materially impacted performance and required that the bank's risk management team rapidly assess the likely impact and recommend appropriate action. The bank's systematic approach to evaluating risk and developing appropriate mitigation strategies helped minimize the impact of such events. By taking rapid, decisive action, Bank of America was able to maintain customer and investor confidence; deliver a record year of profits; complete the acquisition of FleetBoston for $47 billion; and still demonstrate adherence to its tagline, "Higher Standards."

Integrating an effective risk management capability into the performance management process requires that an organization is able to:

• Identify the risks to which the organization is exposed
• Quantify the materiality and probability of occurrence
• Determine the need for mitigating strategies to be developed
• Develop appropriate mitigation plans
• Drive timely decision making
• Monitor execution and results

A systematic approach starts with the routine review of many factors that are not typically addressed by traditional planning, budgeting, and reporting processes, such as: the quality of the corporate governance, employee management, and customer management processes; the company's use of technology and its business interruption plans; the deployment of best practices; the sensitivity of the company's products to technological obsolescence; the adequacy of contingency plans against possible pandemics (e.g. SARS, avian flu); and the degree to which the company is subject to attack from special interest groups.

Numerous tools are already available—including the balanced scorecard, activity-based costing, driver-based forecasting, real options, Monte Carlo simulations, stress testing, and scenario planning—that are designed to provide insights beyond pure financial results. They all can add value if used appropriately; however, many techniques for measuring risk are ad hoc; few organizations have universally agreed-on processes. Best practice organizations have established a process for translating the information generated by these tools into an understanding of risk that then leads to better decision making. A systematic, objective, and comprehensive framework that assesses all of the nonfinancial variables contributing to an organization's risk profile provides the foundation for understanding risk and then managing risk.

Integrated Framework for Enterprise Risk Management

In late 2004 the Committee of Sponsoring Organizations of the Treadway Commission (COSO), a voluntary private sector organization focused on improving the quality of financial reporting, published its thinking on enterprise risk management. Following the passage of Sarbanes-Oxley, the resulting practices have become an integral part of many organizations' adoption of enterprise risk management (ERM). The so-called COSO framework sets out six objectives for effective ERM:

1. *Aligning risk appetite and strategy.* Management considers the entity's risk appetite in evaluating strategic alternatives, setting related objectives, and developing mechanisms to manage related risks.
2. *Enhancing risk response decisions.* Enterprise risk management provides the rigor to identify and select among alternative risk responses—risk avoidance, reduction, sharing, and acceptance.
3. *Reducing operational surprises and losses.* Entities gain enhanced capability to identify potential events and establish responses, reducing surprises and associated costs or losses.
4. *Identifying and managing multiple and cross-enterprise risks.* Every enterprise faces a myriad of risks affecting different parts of the organization, and enterprise risk management facilitates effective response to the interrelated impacts, and integrated responses to multiple risks.
5. *Seizing opportunities.* By considering a full range of potential events, management is positioned to identify and proactively realize opportunities.
6. *Improving deployment of capital.* Obtaining robust risk information allows management to effectively assess overall capital needs and enhance capital allocation.

Source: Committee of Sponsoring Organizations of the Treadway Commission

Framework for Measurement and Management

It is no coincidence that many of the companies that have established leadership positions in their markets are also those that have most effectively harnessed the power of technology to turn operational information into insight. Wal-Mart tracks the flow of products through its stores to ensure that shelves are never empty; Toyota dynamically adjusts its production schedule based on the flow of orders for different vehicles.

In the future, perhaps we will have a standard measure of business risk not unlike a Moody's or Standard & Poor's rating that provides all interested parties with an objective and credible assessment tool. Such a system might offer business managers both an aggregate corporate score and a series of more specific predictive measures, which together could form a comprehensive early-warning mechanism for trends in different risk factors. To be effective, the framework would need several key attributes: The measurement basis would have to be objective, fact-based, and consistent to ensure comparability and credibility. The model would have to acknowledge the unique characteristics of every organization and be able to adapt to changing situations. And, above all, it would need to deliver insights that are easy to understand and actionable.

The result of such a rating system would be that business managers would make better decisions because they would understand the implications of different operational risk factors on future performance. An impossible goal? Challenging, but not impossible. The magnitude of the challenge should indicate the potential value of the journey.

In the absence of such a universal measurement framework, many companies are establishing a risk-based early-warning system as part of their overall ERM process. The objective is to identify and quantify major trends and assess the degree of exposure. These insights are typically assembled by planning, finance, or, if the company has established one, the risk management team. In many companies the emerging role of chief risk officer (CRO) is charged with developing a comprehensive understanding of the overall risk profile. The CRO serves as the eyes of the corporation, externally as well as internally, scanning the outside world and the organization for threats and opportunities.

A starting point for developing an effective risk management framework is to understand the level of business risk—and hence future financial risk—to which an organization is exposed. An organization must fully leverage many of the tools it has become accustomed to using in recent years, such as contingency planning, market and competitive intelligence, scenario planning and data mining—but with a new focus and discipline. Many components of this approach exist today. The challenge is that much of the information is assembled in an ad hoc manner, and there is no unifying process to provide a complete organizational risk profile. Moving from an ad hoc and largely subjective process to a systematic, fact-based measurement system is the objective. Business issues and opportunities can emerge over many years. Rarely do they occur overnight. The emergence of Japanese automotive manufacturers as a potent competitor in the United States, the Internet, outsourcing, biotechnology, budget deficits, even the collapse of the Soviet Union all were years in the making.

To prepare for and respond to such threats, organizations need to be able to identify trends and to determine materiality and probability; the combination of these two factors sets the parameters for the type of risk mitigation strategies that need to be employed (see Exhibit 9.5). A starting point is to analyze drivers of external change and determine how they will affect the organization by assessing what the company already knows. In most organizations vital risk management information is buried in silos with two damaging consequences:

1. The aggregate impact of different risks is missed until it is too late.
2. Data gathered in one part of the business that could prove invaluable to another are never identified or communicated.

All available intelligence must be collated and synthesized; new technologies that enable the aggregation and organization of data from multiple sources can speed this process greatly. Establishing a risk-based early-warning system demands that companies look beyond the data in their enterprise resource planning (ERP) or general ledger systems. In parallel with collating the internal data on opportunities and threats, organizations must look outside, seeking those trends or events that

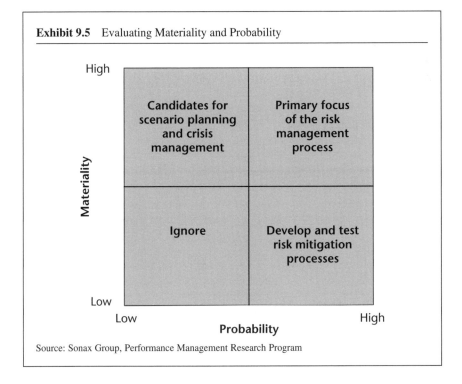

Exhibit 9.5 Evaluating Materiality and Probability

High	Candidates for scenario planning and crisis management	Primary focus of the risk management process
	Ignore	Develop and test risk mitigation processes
Low		

Materiality (vertical axis)

Probability — Low ... High (horizontal axis)

Source: Sonax Group, Performance Management Research Program

signal opportunity or threat. Quantitative data are important, but companies must look to obtain and synthesize qualitative data.

After completing the initial intelligence gathering, an organization can begin to identify gaps in its intelligence and proceed to fill them. What emerges is an organizational risk profile of the corporation that can serve as the trigger for thinking about how to respond and embed the appropriate actions in strategic and operating plans. A company's organizational risk profile is made up of three elements (see Exhibit 9.6). The first three steps are to:

1. Establish the external risk profile of the organization by assessing overall market complexity and volatility.
2. Determine the organization's internal risk profile based on its chosen business model and structure.
3. Evaluate the execution efficiency of the organization in each core business process and in aggregate.

An organization's risk profile is a function of the environment and market in which it operates, the choices it makes about how to organize and serve that market, and its ability to execute. Over the last 20 years, tremendous focus has been given to the third factor through the use of tools such as total quality management, Six Sigma, reengineering, and the like. From a risk management standpoint, these practices have reduced the risk that a company becomes irrelevant simply because it products and services are of poor quality. Levi Strauss did not lose market share because the rivets started to fall out of its jeans; Xerox did not make copiers that failed to copy; Kodak did not lose market position because its film was defective; Sun Microsystems did not go from sales of almost $16 billion in 2000 to barely $11 billion in 2005 because its computers failed to work. However, the intense

Exhibit 9.6 Components of an Organization's Risk Profile

Source: Sonax Group, Performance Management Research Program

focus on operational excellence has distracted many organizations from the risks posed by market and structural issues that can be far more damaging. Consider the performance challenges in recent years of Texas Instruments, Motorola, Dana Corporation, Boeing, AT&T, Cadillac, and Westinghouse, all companies that are former winners of the Baldrige Award for Quality. Great quality is no defense to irrelevance. Performance management processes need to adequately address risk factors in all three categories (see Exhibit 9.7) and not become so overly focused on one that the organization is blindsided by risks in the other areas.

External Risk Profile

An organization's external risk profile is a function of the strategic choices a company makes regarding the business it is in, the markets it which it will participate, and its positioning in those markets. An organization incurs certain risks simply through the choice of the markets in which it will participate. Business complexity and revenue volatility are directly impacted by the structure of the market. Changes in market structure are driven by several factors, including technology, the regulatory environment, local customs, and consumer behaviors. Technology is altering fundamental, long-established characteristics in many industries. The ubiquity and low cost of Internet-based services have demolished barriers to entry in many markets, including auctions, book selling, and banking.

Both the telecommunications and utility industries offer graphic examples of how a company's risks can increase exponentially in a very short period of time as a result of regulatory change. In a period of less than 10 years, telecom companies and utilities were transformed from staid and predictable organizations into volatile, high-risk businesses; in 1984, Enron was still a sleepy manager of gas pipelines, AT&T and British Telecom operated monopolies in their respective markets, the PC was in its infancy, and Starbucks had not yet opened its first coffee bar. Similar

---

Exhibit 9.7   Potential Risk Factors

External	Model and Structure	Execution
• Industry risk profile	• Governance	• Growth rate
• Channel complexity	• Process complexity	• Market position
• Rate of change	• Technical complexity	• Earnings quality
• Product churn	• Staff quality	• Productivity
• Customer loyalty	• Organization structure	• Cycle time
• Regulation	• Management practices	• Service levels
• Globalization	• Process discipline	• Process costs
• Barriers to entry	• Best practice utilization	• Process quality
• Special interest	• Information architecture	• Staffing levels
	• Systems architecture	• Staff leverage

Source: Sonax Group, Performance Management Research Program

shifts took place in the brokerage and airline industries during the 1970s and 1980s. The transformation was devastating for some established players (e.g., Eastern and Pan Am).

Local customs can impact risk as a company seeks to enter new markets. After a number of missteps, Wal-Mart has learned that simply exporting its successful U.S. model is no guarantee of success in markets such as Mexico and Germany resulting in its 2006 withdrawal from the latter market; even McDonald's adapts its menu to local tastes: a Samurai Pork Burger in Thailand, curry in India, and spicy fries in Hong Kong.

Missing a Trend Can Be Painful, Even Deadly

In the autumn of 2004, Lee Scott the CEO of Wal-Mart, admitted that his company had been somewhat blindsided by some external events that were threatening the company. From investigations into the use of illegal aliens by contractors hired to the clean their stores, through discrimination lawsuits filed by female workers, to local communities changing their planning regulations to prevent Wal-Mart building new stores, the company had come under attack on many different fronts—none of which has been led by competitors. A few months later a full-page advertisement in the *New York Times* was headlined "How Much Does Wal-Mart Cost American Taxpayers Every Year?"[5] This was followed by the call: "It's time to Rollback Wal-Mart." The irony that a company noted for its command of information could be blindsided by such attacks was not lost on many. These trends did not emerge overnight; in fact many had been a decade in the making. Wal-Mart was surely aware of the threat but failed to recognize its impact. The company has since embarked on an aggressive campaign to explain its value both to the community and the economy, but it has been a rearguard action—the damage to the company's reputation has been done. Failing to identify the impact accurately and then act on an identified trend can be damaging. For the British in 1944 it was deadly. British intelligence learned of Germany's program to build unmanned rockets as early as 1940, but it was not until V-2 bombs rained down on London in 1944 that they took the threat seriously. Prime Minister Winston Churchill was prompted to exclaim that "We've been caught napping."

Changes in consumer behavior can be more subtle to detect but no less significant in their impact. The ready acceptance of self-service at gas stations and supermarkets, social attitudes toward smoking, the rise of wine drinking relative to beer consumption, increased environmental awareness, and the change in family structures and work habits all serve to increase uncertainty and volatility. Assessing the impact of changing market dynamics must be a key element of any effective performance and risk management process. Exhibit 9.8 gives an example of the evaluation results for one of my clients, a large, global pharmaceutical company.

Business Model and Structure

A company's operating model comprises its organizational structure and processes, and its choices in these areas can have a major effect on its operational risk. For

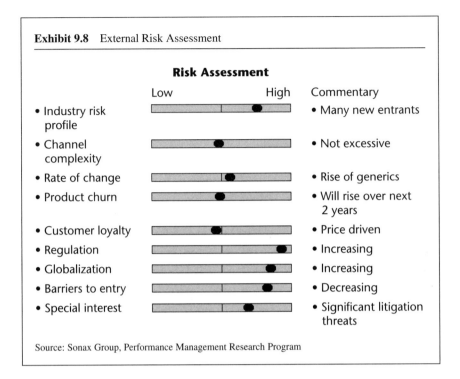

Exhibit 9.8 External Risk Assessment

Risk Assessment

	Low — High	Commentary
• Industry risk profile		• Many new entrants
• Channel complexity		• Not excessive
• Rate of change		• Rise of generics
• Product churn		• Will rise over next 2 years
• Customer loyalty		• Price driven
• Regulation		• Increasing
• Globalization		• Increasing
• Barriers to entry		• Decreasing
• Special interest		• Significant litigation threats

Source: Sonax Group, Performance Management Research Program

example, both State Farm and Progressive Insurance are major players in the U.S. auto insurance market, yet they have adopted very different business models. State Farm sells through 16,000 agents across the United States, while Progressive has chosen a direct sales model.

Choices that organizations make about their business model and structure are frequently the biggest determinant of overall risk. In addition to the choice of sales model, choice includes the degree to which a company standardizes policies; leverages technology; recruits, trains, and retains its staff; deploys best practices; manages suppliers; and structures compensation (see Exhibit 9.9). It also includes the quality of the overall performance management process—companies that wrestle with detailed, sandbagged budgets that are merely negotiated performance targets incur significantly higher risks of poor performance than those organizations where plans define an optimal level of performance and also embrace contingencies to accommodate the inevitable variability that will occur.

Execution Capability

The third component assesses the risks associated with an organization's execution capability. Execution is perhaps the area that is best served by today's business performance management systems. Measures of execution risk include most output- or results-based metrics; for example, revenue, earnings, cycle time, service levels, and productivity all measure an organization's execution efficiency. To measure

Exhibit 9.9   Structural Risk Assessment

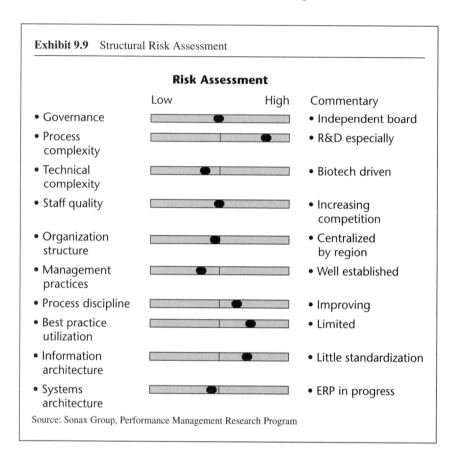

Risk Assessment

	Low	High	Commentary
• Governance			• Independent board
• Process complexity			• R&D especially
• Technical complexity			• Biotech driven
• Staff quality			• Increasing competition
• Organization structure			• Centralized by region
• Management practices			• Well established
• Process discipline			• Improving
• Best practice utilization			• Limited
• Information architecture			• Little standardization
• Systems architecture			• ERP in progress

Source: Sonax Group, Performance Management Research Program

execution risk, a company focuses on the results it realizes given the nature of the markets in which it participates and the business model and structure it has chosen to adopt. Exhibit 9.10 illustrates some of the typical variables that make up execution risk.

Our research at the Sonax Group has looked at the organizational risk profiles of over 50 companies. One of our major findings is that the first two variables—the company's external risk profile and its business model and structure—are major drivers of its execution efficiency. For example, a company that operates in a fast-moving, highly volatile market and chooses a decentralized organizational model with few standardized processes incurs higher risks than a company that competes in a more mature market and operates within a more centralized, uniform business model. The first company has not necessarily made mistakes; it simply operates in a different environment and adheres to a different strategy. For both companies, the important thing to understand is the implications their level of organizational risk should have for management decisions.

Even within an industry, two organizations can have very different risk profiles, based on their choice of business model and their ability to execute. The relative

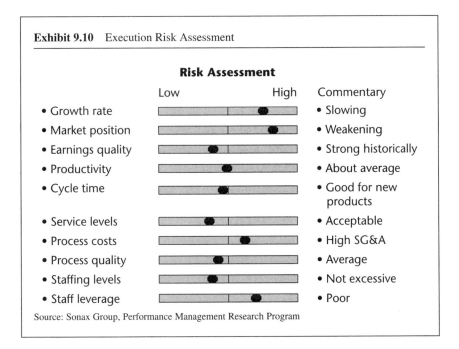

Exhibit 9.10 Execution Risk Assessment

Risk Assessment

	Low	High	Commentary
• Growth rate			• Slowing
• Market position			• Weakening
• Earnings quality			• Strong historically
• Productivity			• About average
• Cycle time			• Good for new products
• Service levels			• Acceptable
• Process costs			• High SG&A
• Process quality			• Average
• Staffing levels			• Not excessive
• Staff leverage			• Poor

Source: Sonax Group, Performance Management Research Program

dominance that market leaders such as Wal-Mart, Southwest Airlines, and Dell Computer have achieved illustrates the importance of making the correct business model choices, then executing well. Each of these leaders started with the same opportunities as companies that ended up struggling, acquired, or bankrupt. Their business model choices and method of execution are the elements that separated Wal-Mart from Kmart and Sears, Southwest from United Air Lines, and Dell from Compaq and Gateway.

The implication of these conclusions is that there is relatively little an organization can do to mitigate organizational risk by solely focusing on its execution capability. This fact may partially explain why high quality and low cost provide little immunity from the threats associated with changes in markets, customer preferences, or many of the other risk factors discussed earlier.

Many components of this approach are in use today. The challenge is that much of the information is assembled in an ad hoc manner, and there is no unifying process to provide a complete operational risk picture. For example, assessments of market structure lie at the heart of companies' analysis of possible entry into a new market or determination of the right investment allocation in a particular sector as part of the portfolio management process. However, the tools and methods for these assessments vary widely, and many of the conclusions drawn are subjective. Organizations need to move to a series of systematic, fact-based metrics. They must start by ensuring that they are collecting the right data. Doing this requires developing a complete and balanced picture of key business measures across the three dimensions discussed in Chapter 7: operational versus financial, internal versus external, and leading versus lagging.

By tracking operational indicators, organizations can identify opportunities and threats before they affect financial performance. For example, if a company sees that the proportion of candidates accepting its job offers is falling, it can surmise that it is becoming a less attractive employer. The underlying reason could be that the company's reputation is deteriorating or that its competitors are offering better compensation packages. Early identification of this type of trend gives management time to react before the problem manifests itself in a labor shortage, decline in productivity, or increase in labor costs.

External information includes measures relating to customers; suppliers; competitors; and more macrofactors, such as regulation, politics, and the economy. Leading, or predictive, information estimates future measurement values and can be developed for operational or financial, internal or external measures. Lagging, or historical, information reports actual results for a current or previous period. The fact that most information available today is internal, financial, and lagging is the main impediment to effective risk management. Instead of just-in-time warnings of risks or opportunities, organizations get information just too late to do anything about it.

External information gathering is episodic and fragmented, with the data buried in silos and not shared. Individual issues are monitored in different parts of the company—marketing conducts its own research on customer preferences and competitive trends; sales talks to customers; finance analyzes credit risk—but no one is observing external and internal risk factors holistically to assess their implications on the health of the company. Companies miss the danger signs for a number of reasons. For one, the challenge of running day-to-day operations is so great that little time is left to look outside. In addition, management and stakeholders have a short-term focus. Typically no one has had responsibility for understanding the external and internal environment—hence the emergence in recent years of more and more chief risk officers. No early-warning mechanisms existed. Plans provided great detail on what an organization was going to do and the results it expected, but little consideration was given to uncertainties in the outside world and how they could impact these carefully crafted strategies and plans.

To overcome this information deficit, companies are combining operational and financial information to form a more complete and timely picture of their risk profile than historical financial reports can provide. Operational measures are excellent leading indicators of future financial results: A material change in a key operational measure not only foreshadows a change in financial performance but can also indicate a change in the organization's risk profile. For example, an increase in quality problems with shipments from a key supplier could easily indicate that the supplier is experiencing significant operational problems that may lead to its inability to ensure future shipments. This should trigger an investigation of the underlying issues and the discussion of the need to reduce dependence upon that particular supplier. Building a mechanism that not only reports trends in key operating measures but alerts managers to potential future risks sits at the heart of an effective risk management process.

Companies must seek out leading indicators aggressively and prize them above all other measures. An organization should assemble a list of possible predictive measures for its business and then subject those options to statistical testing to determine the strength of the correlation and the time lag between changes in the indicator and the financial result. Pinpointing which indicators offer the most relevant information for decision making might take one or two iterations. It is difficult to assess a metric's value until managers make real decisions based on real information, so after determining which measures are predictive, decision makers should develop a series of alternative reports using candidate metrics and test them with different audiences to isolate those that are most valuable. Then they can develop the appropriate reporting, modeling, planning, and decision-making processes.

Ultimately, business risk measures can be built into the target-setting process that guides planning; however, companies should continuously evaluate the relevance of each measure over time, as the indicators themselves are subject to the same forces that increase or diminish the importance of the factors they measure. Not that long ago, phone companies touted the quality and availability of their dial tone as a competitive feature; banks, their ATM network coverage; and car makers offered antilock brakes and side airbags as options. Now all are competitive necessities and have little value as measures of differentiated service.

The value of building a systematic data collection and analysis framework for monitoring organizational risk goes beyond the one time assessment of risk. Over time a set of risk factors will emerge that requires ongoing monitoring. These leading indicators can be programmed into the organization's performance management system to provide early warning as a prompt for management action.

Measurement Demands Action

Unfortunately, some organizations do a good job of assessing their overall risk profile but fail to educate managers on the emerging threats, the likely consequences, and, more important, the action that needs to be taken. The challenge is not just to scan the horizon, but to transmit the information across the company and to drive through to planning, action, and realignment of the culture. To ensure full leverage of data regarding risk—and to eliminate the silos of external intelligence—companies are establishing ERM teams led by a CRO. Emerging first in the financial services industry, ERM teams are now well established in many companies including Sprint, BP, Chevron-Texaco, IBM, and Cisco. These teams are not staffed by accountants; many companies employ futurists, economists, sociologists, anthropologists, and the like, with the requisite skill sets and expertise predicated on the factors that present either opportunities or threat to a company. As these insights emerge, business plans can be adjusted to explicitly address organizational risk, which enables managers to be much better equipped to react and respond.

Providing new information that anticipates future opportunities and threats will be vital to corporate survival, permitting companies either to stay in the business and get ready for future trends, or to prepare to exit a business at the most attractive moment. A risk-based early-warning system buys time to change direction.

Adding a systematic assessment of organizational risk benefits many different constituencies. First of all, investors, lenders, and regulators can better understand the drivers of overall financial performance and derive insight into potential risks or opportunities that may lie ahead. For example, if an organization is about to embark on a major acquisition, the knowledge that the acquiring company does not have a stable, scalable, and standardized computer systems environment should alert investors that there is a significant risk of integration problems if the deal is consummated. Understanding an organization's risk profile allows stakeholders to better answer key questions such as:

- Does the company's chosen business model and execution capability support the financial results and targets?
- How well positioned is the company to respond to emerging trends—both opportunities and threats?
- Does an organization's strategy effectively recognize the varying types of risk it will encounter, and is management taking adequate steps to ensure that the appropriate skills are available?
- Does management make effective and timely decisions based on the insights gleaned from its risk management processes?

Board members also benefit from an increased understanding of an organization's risk profile. In addition to exercising fiscal stewardship over the companies on whose boards they serve, directors must also seek assurance that the organizations' management processes are effective in capitalizing on new opportunities, while assuring an acceptable level of risk and control.

RISK MITIGATION TECHNIQUES

Effective identification and measurement of risk only goes so far. The two crucial management decisions are:

1. Is the risk significant enough to require mitigating action?
2. What is the most appropriate mitigation strategy?

Determining whether a risk requires mitigation requires that managers not only understand the likely probability and impact of the risk but also the risk appetite of the organization and its owners. The same risk can be viewed differently by two different groups, which can impact the choice and appetite for different mitigation strategies. For example, many companies choose to self-insure themselves against worker compensation claims; others buy insurance.

For risks that an organization chooses to mitigate, management's default action is to accept the risk to avoid spending more on managing the risks than the potential harm. However, if managers decide that a risk requires mitigation, the next decision is to agree on an appropriate approach. Generally speaking, there are five different types of approach:

1. *Avoid.* Redesign the process or eliminate certain activities to avoid particular risks with the aim of reducing overall risk. Many of the innovations in supply chain management over the last two decades have sought to reduce the risks of tying up too much capital in inventory and ensuring that risks of stock-outs or surpluses are avoided.
2. *Diversify.* Spread the risk among numerous assets or processes to reduce the overall risk of loss or impairment. Examples include building redundancy into communication networks and control systems, or backing up business critical data.
3. *Control.* Design activities to prevent, detect, or contain adverse events or to promote positive outcomes. An example would be to demand positive verification that a person's bank account has adequate funds in it before processing a payment as opposed to performing this check after the payment has been cashed.
4. *Share.* Distribute a portion of the risk through a contract with another party, such as insurance. Numerous examples of this approach can be found; however, the recent trend of investor groups combining their resources to make acquisitions is a good example.
5. *Transfer.* Distribute all of the risk through a contract with another party, such as outsourcing or factoring.

Deciding on and implementing a risk mitigation strategy is not the end of the process. The effectiveness of the chosen strategy needs to be measured and, if necessary, the strategy must be modified. Also, risks do not remain static; for this reason, risk management processes must adapt constantly to the changing risk profile of the organization as well as to changes in the organization's risk appetite.

Effective risk management is no longer optional; it must be an integral part of any performance management process. All improvements in the ability to predict future performance—either positive or negative—offer managers the most valuable commodity of all: time to think and act.

NOTES

1. Peter L. Bernstein, *Against the Gods: The Remarkable Story of Risk* (New York: John Wiley & Sons, 1996), p. 3.
2. Peter F. Drucker, *Managing in a Time of Great Change* (New York: E.P. Dutton/Truman Talley Books, 1995).
3. Speech given at the 36th SEACEN Governors' Conference held in Singapore, 1 June 2001.
4. Timothy F. Geithner, Remarks at the New York Bankers Association Financial Services Forum Chairman's Reception, New York City, April 6, 2006.
5. "How Much Does Wal-Mart Cost American Taxpayers Every Year?" *New York Times*, April 20, 2005. Ad sponsored by WalMartWatch.com

Chapter 10

Technology:
Panacea or Pain?

Alas, technology has not allowed us to see into the future any more clearly than we could previously.

—Alan Greenspan

Picture the scene—the chief executive officer (CEO) paces a conference room, brandishing a thick report. He gazes impatiently at his senior managers. "You've all read this," he says. "Top-shelf consultants. Two million bucks. Pure strategic thinking. This could put us years ahead. The board is psyched. I'm psyched. It's a brilliant plan. One question: Given our current technology, is this implementable?" The response, from five different chairs in the room: "No." The CEO looks frustrated but not surprised.

Strategy being constrained by technology is not an uncommon occurrence. Ironically, the scene just described is not drawn from an executive suite but from a television advertisement for IBM that ran in early 2002. It accurately captures much of the frustration managers feel about the gap that exists between the promise of technology and the reality.

Holy Grail, silver bullet, or sinkhole? Technology has been seen as both the engine and the enemy of effective planning and management reporting. After all, automating inefficiency just gives you bad data faster. Billions of dollars have been spent on technology, and Alan Greenspan's statement remains as true today as it was then, yet the appetite for new technology continues largely unabated. Notwithstanding the economic slowdown that started in 2000, Gartner Group estimated that global information technology (IT) spending totaled $2.1 trillion in 2005 and IDC predicts annual growth rates of 6 percent a year through 2009.[1]

Technology has been the primary driver of productivity improvement over the last 20 years. The journey has just been more painful and less potent than many expected. Despite the variable track record, the potential is clear. As the Economic Report of the President of United States in 2001 said:

> The spread of information technology throughout the economy has been a major factor in the acceleration of productivity through capital deepening.

Increasingly, companies have been eager and able to buy powerful computers at relatively low prices. The rapid advances in computer technology, together with favorable economic conditions, have fueled a computer and software investment boom. Outside the IT sector, organizational innovations and better ways of applying information technology are boosting the productivity of skilled workers.

The productivity benefits mentioned in the report have been focused in three areas: automation of manual tasks, improved access to information, and improved communications. These changes have allowed managerial and professional staff to reduce the amount of time they spend on routine administrative or transactional activities. Unfortunately, much of the time that was freed up was consumed quickly in managing the exponential growth in the amount of information now available.

FOURTH TIME LUCKY?

We are embarking on a new age in the use of technology in business. By my reckoning, this will be the fourth age of business computing (see Exhibit 10.1).

The first age was focused principally on data processing. Computer departments were called EDP (electronic data processing) departments. Computer technology was used primarily to process transactions. The data processing age lasted for almost 30 years, from the late 1950s until the mid-1980s.

The second age was the information age. The EDP departments were renamed information systems (IS) or information technology (IT) departments as information replaced data as the primary output of business computing. Starting in the mid-1980s and still going strong today, this wave was fueled by three primary technologies:

1. The personal computer (PC)
2. The spreadsheet
3. The database

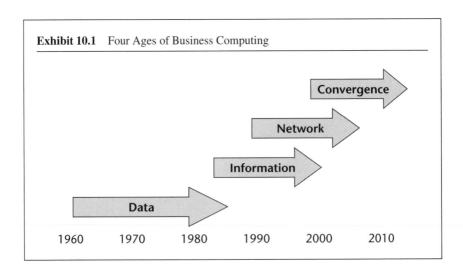

Exhibit 10.1   Four Ages of Business Computing

The PC moved computing from the data center to the desktop and into the hands of nontechnical users. The spreadsheet provided users with tools to analyze and manipulate data at their desks, and the database allowed data to be stored and organized in a way that supported multidimensional management reporting.

The third age, the network age, built bridges between multiple islands of automation that existed both within and between organizations. Physical limitations on the movement of data and information were broken down.

The cumulative effect of the first three ages of business computing was profound but has not yet delivered the ubiquitous, low-cost, seamless, and dependable environment that has been promised since the earliest days of computing. Organizations are wrestling with a patchwork quilt of partially implemented, poorly integrated, and expensive systems that, despite all their shortcomings, have woven themselves into the fabric of business to such a degree that most organizations are totally dependent on them to function.

Despite all the challenges that remain, there are some glimmers of light. We are embarking on a fourth age of business technology, which I call the age of convergence or, more practically, the payoff. Convergence in this context means the integration of four elements: computer technology, communications, information, and people (see Exhibit 10.2).

To date, the impact of computer and communications technology has been focused on the automation of existing tasks or the leverage of existing information through enhanced access, analysis, and communication. Relatively little in the way

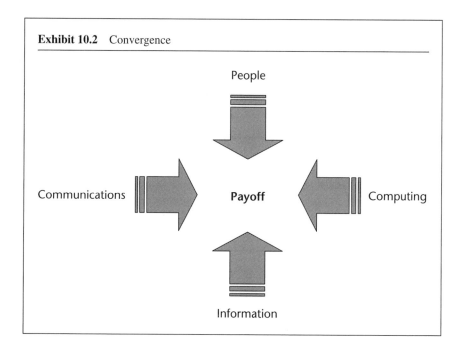

Exhibit 10.2   Convergence

People

Communications → Payoff ← Computing

Information

of new capabilities or insights has been delivered. Convergence centers on the people who use technology. The payoff is not simply a return on investment but real value in terms of tangibly improving quality of life. In business terms, this means new and better products and services at no incremental or even at lower cost. The first three ages of technology demanded too much from people. People were tied to their desks to access information or use the network; people became slaves to technology. Convergence promises to make technology work for people, not the other way around. The early signs already exist. The advances in nanotechnology and biotechnology promise to make real improvements in the quality of life. Digital technology is transforming communications and entertainment, and Internet commerce is a reality, offering choice and convenience to many. This is technology working for the benefit of people.

WHY THE TIME FOR CONVERGENCE IS RIGHT

A number of forces are powering the convergence of computer technology, communications, information, and people:

- Software support for best practices is rapidly increasing. Software vendors are finally beginning to understand that best practice compliance is a necessity. Business application providers can now support more than 90 percent of the commonly accepted best practice standards, compared with only 40 to 50 percent in the mid-1990s.

- Plunging computer and communications costs, the ongoing effect of Moore's Law, have placed highly advanced technology within reach for all organizations. No longer do users have to be a multibillion-dollar company to take advantage of the latest best practice–enabling technologies.

- The digitization of information flows between individuals and organizations is growing at a rapid rate, increasing the pool of available data that can be turned into useful information and insight.

- Tools to support integration and communication between disparate systems and technology platforms have, and will, continue to improve dramatically.

- Executive tolerance for expensive, late, and disappointing technology projects has worn thin. Organizations are adopting a much more systematic and disciplined approach to evaluating the return on their technology investments. Instead of technologies searching for applications, the start point will be customers or users: What do they need and how can technology help?

Personalizing content, combining performance measurement and contextual information, event-triggered reporting, and collaborative planning applications all seek to leverage technology. In the last few years a new class of software focusing on performance management has emerged that seeks to combine and integrate support for planning, forecasting and reporting.

APPLYING TECHNOLOGY TO PERFORMANCE MANAGEMENT— DAWN OF THE DIGITAL MANAGER

The last few years have seen an explosion in the introduction of new tools and systems designed to support an organization's performance management processes. Old terms such as "data warehouse," "decision support system," and "executive information system" have been replaced by terms such as "CPM" (corporate performance management) and "BPM" (business performance management) which generally refer to broad enterprise-level systems together with more niche-oriented applications supporting portals, dashboards, and scorecards. Regardless of the terms used, these systems are designed to support one of more of these processes:

- Performance reporting—either financial, nonfinancial, or both
- Budgeting and forecasting
- Business analysis

Beyond the Hype

No self-respecting software vendor would ever launch a product in the marketplace that could not be described as integrated, flexible, dynamic, secure, or best practice compliant; so how do you separate the hype from the reality when looking to identify the right tools for your organization?

Over the years I have reviewed numerous requirements documents developed by organizations seeking to select new systems to support their performance management processes. Guess what? They all look the same! This is both good and bad. The high degree of uniformity makes it very easy to develop a requirements document, or even purchase a ready-made one from one of the number of vendors that offer such things. It also makes it easy for the potential vendors to develop rapid responses to your requirements. Unfortunately, this has two big drawbacks:

1. It is almost impossible to tell most of the vendor offerings apart.
2. The requirements documented over the years have not been updated to reflect what is (a) desirable and (b) possible. Most organizations are still selecting systems using requirements that are derived from the very management processes they are trying to change.

Advances in technology—hardware, software, and communications—open up new avenues that can be realistically exploited by any organization seeking to upgrade its management processes.

These advances make the requirements development process a little harder but well worthwhile since you will find it much easier to discern the real differences between different vendor offerings and also determine those systems that can support where you want to go, not just where you are today. To make the process easier I have divided the requirements into two categories: the basics (or boilerplate) and the value-adding. The first category closely aligns with those requirements you typically find in requirements documents and that make the selection process so hard since nearly all vendors can handle these. The second category illustrates those requirements that separate a basic solution from one that can support your organization as its moves toward its best practice goal. The lists are not complete or exhaustive but should serve to illustrate the value of taking a more disciplined approach to identifying those truly value-adding requirements.

Examples of "the Basics"

- Ability to consolidate multiple organizational units
- Automatic restatement in response to changes in the organizational hierarchy
- Maintenance of a "single version of truth" that ensures the application of common definitions and rules
- Ability to automatically disseminate outputs to all legitimate rulers
- Ability to support multiple reporting formats (hard copy, graphical, tabular, web, wireless-PDA, etc.)
- Ability to drill down to lower levels of detail
- Enforcement of data standards and calculation rules

Examples of "Value-Adding" Performance Management System Capabilities

- *Exception based reporting.* The system has the ability to automatically identify trends and exceptions in key business measures and alert the appropriate individuals based on predefined rules.
- *Risk-based early warnings.* Can the solution automatically deliver early alerts of potential opportunities or threats based on monitoring of leading indicators?
- *Context-based filtering.* The system has the ability to organize and deliver information based on a user's role, situation, and current task. For example, a manager's information needs will be different when reviewing sales performance as compared to conducting performance reviews for staff. Is the system capable of supporting this "decision"-oriented approach, or is information locked into predefined "reports"?
- *External data integration.* Does the solution support the capture and integration of external data into the performance reporting process? Are powerful search tools provided that allow for the aggregation of all internal and external data about a specific customer, product, or market?
- *Scenario and sensitivity testing.* Are tools available to dynamically test different scenarios based on trends in the underlying drivers of the business, or does this require creation of offline spreadsheet models?
- *Dynamic reforecasting.* Can users initiate a reforecast of one or more elements of the business on demand, or are they constrained to a predefined forecast cycle?
- *Personalization.* Can content be personalized to the needs and preferences of the end user without necessitating manual manipulation and configuration?

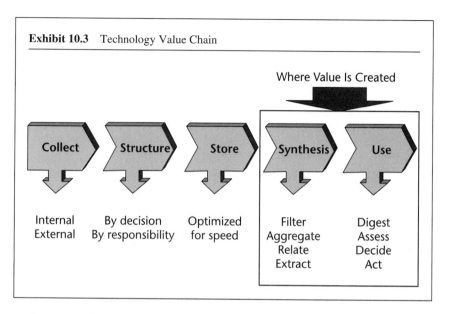

Exhibit 10.3 Technology Value Chain

Where Value Is Created

Collect	Structure	Store	Synthesis	Use
Internal	By decision	Optimized	Filter	Digest
External	By responsibility	for speed	Aggregate	Assess
			Relate	Decide
			Extract	Act

For technology to really pay off in the performance management process, it needs to focus on the filtering and selection of meaningful data. Typically systems developers have focused on the first three steps in the information value chain (see Exhibit 10.3): collect, structure, and store. Make no mistake: These three steps are critical. However, the real payoff comes from enabling steps 4 and 5: synthesis and use.

The Real Value of Technology at Princess Cruise Lines

One of the biggest challenges organizations face is developing a sound financial justification for investing in systems to support performance management. After all, how do you value a better business decision? Traditional cost benefit analysis has a place but is not the sole criterion on which investment decisions should be made. The experience of Princess Cruises, a unit of Carnival Cruise Lines, illustrates that the value of fully leveraged technology is not solely cost reduction.

Princess Cruises operates 15 cruise ships and serves over 1.2 million customers a year. The cruise line business is complex, combining all aspects of a full-service hotel, including spas, bars, retail stores, and casinos, with a shipping business operating on a global basis. In late 2001 Princess, like the rest of industry, was struggling to adapt to a world changed by 9/11, which made all previous plans, forecasts, and budgets obsolete. The finance team spent many hundreds of hours reworking numerous spreadsheets as the company sought to establish a new baseline from which to manage. The job got done but all agreed that it was painful and lacked the necessary value-added insights. In 2002 the company embarked on an ambitious program to completely reinvent its planning, budgeting, forecasting, and analytical processes and take advantage of the new planning and performance management tools that were increasingly available. As Greg Bozigian, director of financial planning at Princess, commented, "We needed to be able to rapidly adapt our plans and forecasts to changes in our markets or operating model and spreadsheets simply could not cope."

Princess selected software from Cognos, a leading player in the fast-growing market for performance management applications, and targeted the development of the plan for fiscal 2004 developed in second half of 2003, as the dawn of a new era for the company's planning processes. Looking back on the decision, Bozigian has no regrets: "The benefits have exceeded our expectations; not only can we support a bigger business with no increase in staffing but we have transformed the role of the finance team—we are able to consistently deliver high value analysis in very short cycle times, allowing our operators to make much better decisions, much faster." Princess's experience demonstrates that the value of effective technology leverage can be felt in many ways:

- *Speed.* Budgets, forecasts and plans can be developed and consolidated across the company in minutes where it formally took days; management requests for focused analysis can be answered in hours. For example, a manager in the retail division can see the projected revenue and cost of sales for every voyage by every ship based upon the forecast of passenger numbers; previously such information would have required days of data collection and consolidation.
- *Accountability.* Perhaps the greatest benefit Princess has gained is the increased level of accountability that enhanced visibility provides. Business managers can see daily analyses of performance, flowing into monthly forecasts and annual plans. Princess has gone so far as to project the Cognos plans on a screen during the quarterly forecast and annual budget review meetings. Managers then use the tool to dynamically make changes as a result of the decisions made. A crucial side benefit of increased visibility has been to minimize the potential for any type of sandbagging—the curse of planning in many other organizations.
- *Operational relevance.* Many companies struggle with budgets or forecasts that present an accountant's view of the business rather than one that reflects the strategy and tactics managers deploy. Princess has successfully integrated the key operational drivers of its business into the financial representation of that business. For example, the cruise line equivalent of a retailer's same-store sales metric is $ per available lower berth day ($ per ALBD). Princess is able to rapidly model changes in projected revenues and costs based on changing patterns of berth utilization and pricing, thereby allowing operational managers in all departments to better optimize their own operations.
- *Flexibility.* Right in the middle of developing the fiscal 2005 plan, administrative and operational departments of Princess Cruises took over responsibility for Cunard, the venerable British operator of the *QE 2* and the new *Queen Mary 2*. The planning team was able to seamlessly replicate their base planning model and tools to allow for a plan to be developed for Cunard without adding any additional resources.
- *Responsiveness.* A major cost driver for Princess is fuel. With the rapid increase in oil prices to over $70 a barrel in early 2006, the finance team was able to run multiple scenarios looking at the relationships between operating days of each ship, fuel consumed, and the cost per metric ton so that the company could optimize its profitability in the face of a material change in one of its key cost elements. Similarly, plans and forecasts were able to be rapidly adjusted for the scheduling and load changes that occurred following the severe hurricane season in the Caribbean and Gulf of Mexico in 2005. In both cases, the value of timely and focused analysis translates into bottom-line performance.

As these examples show, the financial value of leveraged technology does not always show up in the budget of the finance department; more often than not it will appear in the corporate profit and loss account, the balance sheet, or the company's operational execution. Using technology to focus finance and planning staffs on the right things is a critical element of being able to effectively support a business operating in a volatile and uncertain world—and today that means all businesses.

BEST PRACTICES FOR LEVERAGING TECHNOLOGY

Beyond the specific needs for supporting the planning and performance management process, there are a number of core best practices for successfully applying technology to any business process. Ten of the most important practices are discussed next.

1. Integrate business and technology planning.
2. Break down the functional walls.
3. Set the right priorities.
4. Do not implement new systems just for the sake of it.
5. Avoid automating inefficiency.
6. Get the basics right.
7. Implementation is a team effort.
8. Focus on use, not deployment.
9. Manage complexity
10. Link the return on investment to business value.

Integrate Technology and Business Planning

Many organizations struggle with integrating technology effectively into their strategic and operational planning processes. Technology planning often is delegated to the IT department, resulting in a very tactical and technical set of plans that does not clearly explain how technology will support the realization of the overall business objectives. Explicitly recognizing the pivotal role technology plays in achieving an organization's strategic objectives demands that technology planning is integrated into the overall business planning process. Exhibit 10.4 shows some of the key points of integration.

During the strategic planning process, management should be assessing the likely future trends in the use of technology within the chosen businesses by asking three questions:

1. How is technology likely to impact our marketplace in the future?
2. How are our competitors and customers using technology?
3. What new technological developments are occurring outside of our current business and markets?

Similarly, the IT organization must adopt a customer- or business-centric view in its research and investigation of new technologies. Instead of simply succumbing to the lure of every new technology, an effective IT organization rigorously assesses the potential of each new advance regarding to deliver value to the organization. Three questions help ensure that an appropriate focus is maintained:

1. Can this technology improve the quality of the product or service our organization delivers to customers?
2. Does this technology reduce the cost and improve the productivity of our organization?

Exhibit 10.4   Key Points of Integration

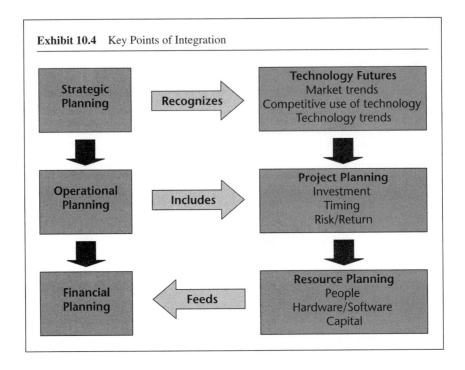

3. Does this technology provide information, tools, or capabilities that will help our people achieve number 1 or 2?

Managers who cannot answer yes to at least one of these questions should query the wisdom of any investment in a hot new technology.

Break Down the Functional Walls

Since computer technology first entered the business world, the prevailing view of business systems has been functional. Business software grew up around the functional department structure of the typical organization. Finance systems were sold to finance people and sales systems were sold to salespeople. The internal systems or IT department mirrored the prevailing architecture with teams assigned to support the different functional departments within an organization. As the network age took hold, the traditional functional view of business systems and technology was challenged. The emergence of enterprise resource planning (ERP) systems moved business computing from a largely functional or departmental focus to an enterprise focus. Technology cut across functional boundaries, raising a whole series of challenges related to technical standards, data definitions, process integration, system support, and, perhaps most significantly, ownership and accountability. The arrival of the Internet poured further oil on the flames of integration.

The need to link systems together in a seamless manner moved beyond the boundaries of the organization into the customer and supplier communities of every organization.

The traditional approach of each functional department defining its own requirements and selecting its own systems was obsolete—or at least it should have been. Unfortunately, the buying process lagged behind the technology; the result was the continued optimization of departmental or functional systems at the expense of the enterprise-wide requirements. These islands of automation are hugely inefficient. Today, business is conducted in real time, and management reporting must be matched to the real-time nature of business processes. Organizations that effectively integrate their management reporting cross-functionally garner a significant advantage. For example, a collection officer who can access customer information residing in a sales force application, or a purchasing officer who can access a key supplier's inventory, can make better decisions faster. It is not the optimization of information flows within a function that drives best practice management reporting but the integration across functions and between different organizations.

Set the Right Priorities

Choosing the right system is a process fraught with frustration for many companies. Investments in IT have grown to be the largest single item of capital expenditure for most companies. Because it is a high-stakes game, most companies expend significant effort to select the right system. The selection process can be exhausting. Typically the first step is to complete an exhaustive requirements definition process that requires the questioning of all potential users of the system about their needs. Background research is undertaken on potential solutions, which invariably requires large numbers of IT staff to attend numerous conferences and trade shows in Orlando, Las Vegas, or New Orleans. The organization now has a laundry list of requirements and a lot of glossy software brochures. Now that the word is out among the consulting and software community that the organization is contemplating a major new system investment, the feeding frenzy begins.

The next step is to organize the information into a requirements specification and select the group of vendors to compete for the organization's business. The requirements specification will pass through a number of iterations as the relative merits of specific features and functions are debated. The completed requirements document needs to be summarized into a request for information (RFI) that will be sent to potential vendors.

Upon receipt of the responses to the RFI, the number of suppliers will be winnowed down. The next step is the development and issuance of a request for proposal (RFP), which details the specific requirements and defines all the required contract terms to enable a prospective supplier to develop a complete proposal. A series of question-and-answer sessions are held for the bidders to help them prepare their response. Once each proposal is received, it is evaluated. References are checked and site visits are made, which yield little since the references and site visits are to organizations recommended by the supplier. The results of the proposal scoring reveal that fewer than 10 points on a 1,000-point scale separate the top three prospective suppliers.

As no clear winner has emerged, the organization completes a second detailed scoring, this time adding in a more precise weighting of perceived functionality gaps. Suppliers assure the organization that all such gaps will be fixed in the next release. After six months, the evaluation team reports back that that the top three offerings can meet two-thirds of the business requirements. At this stage, the chief financial officer eliminates one of the short-listed suppliers because of a prior bad experience. Exhaustive negotiations continue with the two remaining vendors. Desperate to close the deal before the end of the quarter, one of the suppliers throws in a 5 percent price reduction, 100 free training credits, and two tickets to the Masters' golf tournament. Finally, a choice has been made; however, the losing finalist calls on a board member of the client and questions the fairness of the selection process. This last-ditch attempt delays final confirmation of the selection for another three weeks, at which time a letter of intent is signed.

Once the choice is made, implementation moves ahead at full speed. After a couple of years and a few million dollars more than budgeted, the project is finished—or at least the project team is. There follows a period of relative tranquility; however, soon questions are being asked about whether the project delivered the projected return on investment (ROI). The normal answer is at best "We have no idea"; at worst, "No." At the same time, the vendor starts pushing the organization to upgrade to the latest release of the product, assuring the organization that it will definitely fix all the problems encountered since the initial implementation.

The ultimate irony is that the many months spent choosing the right system were probably spent answering the wrong question. Instead of focusing on the question of which system to select, companies should focus most of their time on defining how they are going to use the system. As one chief information officer who understood this crucial fact explained, "There are far more bad implementations than there are bad systems." Time spent on planning how to implement new technology is more valuable than time spent selecting new technology.

Do Not Implement New Systems Just for the Sake of It

One of the phrases clients tell consultants most often is "We need a new system to . . . ." This statement assumes that the answer is a new system. People tend to believe that regardless of the problem, a new computer system is the answer. An example can illustrate the point. In the mid-1980s, a fast-growing London-based securities trading house was building a very strong business in trading shares, options, and warrants issued by Japanese companies. The Japanese economy was the strongest in the world at the time, and Japanese companies were increasingly using global markets to raise capital. Even then securities trading was one of the most technology-intensive businesses in the world; timing and information were everything. Few of the major financial information services provided fast, in-depth information on Japanese companies at the time. Companies had to rely on local Japanese information services, which were targeted at local Japanese players and broadcast their information in Japanese. An English translation followed 15 to 20 minutes later. In the fast-moving and volatile world of securities trading, such a delay meant English-only speakers could not compete.

A colleague and I were working with the company on developing their overall information systems strategy. During a planning session, several traders raised the issue of the delay in making English translations available. After some discussion, it was agreed that the company could gain a significant competitive advantage if it could access an English translation faster. Inquiries to the information service provider indicated that a simultaneous Japanese/English service was three to five years away. After further research, a proposal to develop an in-house system that would translate the incoming Japanese feed into English with a delay of 30 to 45 seconds was presented. The cost was £3 million (about $4.8 million at the time). Based on the potential upside to be gained by having up to a 15- to 20-minute advantage on the rest of the market, the cost was not a problem, so the project was given the go-ahead. To my colleague and me, the technology solution seemed to be overkill. We agreed that a more rapid English translation would be valuable, but we questioned the need for a technology solution. When big news broke on the Japanese-language version of the service, traders told us that usually a Japanese-speaking colleague picked it up and shouted over to them. This worked well for the big news, but the colleagues did not know the details of all the companies each trader was tracking. We summarized the situation: "What you really need is not just a faster English-language version but also a mechanism to highlight news that is directly relevant to the companies you are tracking." The traders agreed with our assessment. After some further discussion, we offered an alternative solution. Instead of relying on traders who had their own job to do, we suggested that the company hire two or three of the brightest bilingual English-Japanese students it could find. Set them up in the trading room with a dedicated terminal from the Japanese information service. Ensure they are briefed on the companies each trader follows. When they see news that is relevant to a particular trader, they can call him or her up or shout the news out. That way, the traders would get rapid translation, selectivity in what was translated, and personalization of the information to each trader's needs without spending a penny on a new computer system or having to throw away their existing system. Another advantage was that they could implement this solution in less than a month.

Three weeks later, two bilingual business graduates had been hired, and the company had achieved a major lead on the market. Management estimated the innovation contributed almost £4 million to profits in the first year at a total annual cost of approximately £150,000. The moral of this story is not that technology is bad. The point is that technology is only one potential solution to a business need and that effective use of technology is as much about deciding when it is not the right answer as deciding when it is.

Avoid Automating Inefficiency

Flexibility has been a key word in the marketing lexicon of all technology suppliers for a long time. Suppliers emphasize their product's ability to adapt, scale, configure, and integrate with users' business in a seamless manner. Flexibility has been universally accepted as a desirable attribute for a technology. The problem with this line of thinking is that it allows an organization to perpetuate bad practices and thereby miss the golden opportunity presented by the implementation of a new computer system to improve performance.

A large chemical company determined that it needed a new computer system to support its overall management reporting process. The company had been wrestling with multiple different reporting systems that resulted from a series of acquisitions and lax enforcement of common standards in prior system implementations. The new system would bring together all the data required for management reporting into a single data warehouse. During the requirements definition process, many business unit managers expressed concern that they would lose critical information as a consequence of the rationalization process. Senior management insisted that no one organization should be worse off in terms of information after implementation of the new system.

The project team cataloged the reporting requirements of every business to ensure that the new system would fully meet its requirements. The design specifications mushroomed as the team documented each business's needs and then added the new requirements. Upon completion of the project, the organization conducted a postimplementation review and found that there had been no discernable improvement in the efficiency of the overall process. In fact, costs had gone up, as the organization now had to support the massive new data warehouse. All the organization had succeeded in doing was putting all its inefficiency in one place and automating it.

To date, there have been two main approaches to implementing new technology: process driven and technology driven. The process-driven approach follows a traditional methodology of defining requirements, designing a process, and then developing technology to support it. The technology-driven approach gained a lot of support in the 1990s as organizations leaped from technology bandwagon to technology bandwagon and simply deployed new tools as they appeared with little thought as to how the processes or organization needed to adapt to realize the full potential. Software suppliers poured fuel on the flames with false promises that simply implementing their systems would guarantee best practice performance. Many drank the Kool-Aid, and spending on ERP systems mushroomed; however, a research report by AMR Research published in July 2005 indicated that half of the ERP licenses purchased remain unused, indicating the cost and complexity of deployment.[2] In addition, most organizations have also developed a data warehouse, and two-thirds have implemented a balanced scorecard. Information technology budgets grew but management's satisfaction with its technology investments did not. A new approach began to emerge that blended the best elements of the process-centric and technology-centric model and added a third ingredient: best practices. Making best practices the heart of the process provides organizations with much greater assurance that the resulting changes will deliver the expected benefits. Exhibit 10.5 compares and contrasts the three approaches.

Each approach has its advantages and disadvantages, but the best practice approach provides the most attractive option. If it is done right, it is faster and less risky and delivers more certain benefits.

Get the Basics Right

It is easy to lose focus when addressing large, complex technology implementations. The plethora of tools and technologies can create a confusing set of choices, and it is easy to be blinded by the apparent sophistication and sexiness of many of the offerings. Staying focused on the objectives and getting the basics right is essential. Doing this means:

- Identifying the areas where technology can have a positive impact
- Defining the right requirements

Exhibit 10.5   Comparison of the Three Approaches to Implementing Technology

	Advantages	Disadvantages
Process approach	• Explicit integration of process improvements into the design stage • Reduced risk of relying on technology to fix process or organizational problems • Maximizes benefits stream	• Uses internal requirements as the baseline, which may not align with best practices • Can take longer to implement • Compromises or customizations made between the design and configuration stages can drive up costs and reduce benefits
Technology approach	• Minimizes configuration and setup costs • Lower implementation risk	• Higher operating costs/lower benefits • Higher risk of automating inefficient processes • Does not always address organizational issues
Best practice approach	• Uses best practice as the baseline for redesign and requirements definition • Greater assurance of achieving best practice benchmark performance levels • Lower risk and shorter cycle time	• Requires disciplined project management and effective teaming between functional and process experts • Third-party partners need to commit fully to the approach

- Selecting the right tools
- Making them easy to use
- Getting people to use them
- Measuring the return on investment

Implementation Is a Team Effort

There is no such thing as an IT project anymore. Recognizing that successful implementation of any new technology is a team effort is crucial to the chances of realizing an acceptable return on investment. Implementation requires the right combination of a number of different skills: leadership, planning, change management, process simplification, organization design, and systems design and implementation. Convergence demands an integrated team-based approach by following a few basic guidelines:

- Projects are evaluated for both strategic fit and economic return. Scope is precisely defined, and a rigorous process for agreeing changes is agreed on up front.
- From the outset, project teams are jointly staffed by technical and functional resources that report through a single project management structure and share the same goals and incentives.
- All third-party partners, such as hardware and software vendors and consultants, are integrated into the project team.
- Project plans explicitly address the change management requirements and tasks around process redesign, organizational alignment, education, training, performance measures, and incentives.
- Multiple projects are coordinated by a program management office (PMO), which is staffed with a blend of functional and technical resources.
- Project reporting extends beyond simple measures of budget and task completion to track the development of the organization's capability to use the new systems successfully.

Delegating systems projects to the IT organization alone is a good sign that an organization still treats technology as if it were a remote back-office rather than a business-critical resource. Organizations that blame IT for failed projects get the systems they deserve.

Focus on Use, Not Deployment

Systems are only as good as the uses to which they are put. As leading companies revamp their planning and reporting systems, they are changing their focus with respect to the types of data and the relationships between data that are required to support decision making. For the designers and builders of management information systems, the opportunity exists to leverage this vast new reservoir to:

- Focus on the identification and reporting of leading indicators that are predictive of future events/financial results
- Incorporate external measures of customer, competitor, and market behavior into routine management reporting
- Leverage the digitization of data that relate to upstream and downstream activities beyond the boundaries of the enterprise
- Leverage the low-cost ubiquity of the Internet and related communication technologies to deliver meaningful information directly to all interested parties, not just managers

One of the liberating effects of the speed required to be competitive is the devolution of decision-making power to the front line. The Internet is empowering front-line employees, and the impact is dramatic. Employees who may have little familiarity or aptitude for using computer systems are making key business decisions. A major design consideration has become making systems easy to use in a wide variety of operating conditions.

Technology can be a powerful tool for improving information delivery when it is designed in the context of how the information is used. Boeing has been able to improve productivity in its factories significantly by providing complex technical information to its engineers through a wireless network that allows workers to access the information on hand-held devices at their work location. Providing management reporting tailored to the specific needs and situations of the user is one of the most potent opportunities presented by convergence.

Manage Complexity

In many companies, the investment in new planning and reporting tools has made the overall technology environment more complex. The proliferation of new database systems, stand-alone analytical tools, and other platforms has added another layer of complexity to the morass of legacy systems supporting operational activities. The issues with leveraging technology appear to be largely self-inflicted. Organizations that have failed to successfully deploy technology in support of their planning and reporting processes tend to share the same characteristics.

- They fail to fully implement the technology that has been purchased across all business operations.
- They are unwilling or unable to enforce standards.
- They grant business unit autonomy in the acquisition and development of systems.
- They are unable to convince employees to use new tools and technologies.
- They have an inadequate focus and investment in user education and training.

Link Return on Investment to Business Value

Measuring the return on technology investment has been the Holy Grail for chief executive officers and chief information officers for the past 30 years. Much effort has been expended on trying to quantify the returns in terms of sales growth and cost reduction from the tens of millions of dollars invested in each new wave of technology. Generally, the results have been inconclusive and often are restricted to broad statements about productivity increases being somehow tied to technology investments. This loose causal relationship has been discomforting to many business leaders.

Some are now beginning to question the value of the exercise. The pervasive impact of technology now means that, in many cases, information technology is so inextricably intertwined with people and processes that the identification of specific technology-related benefit streams is of marginal value.

Only the combination of the judicious use of technology, optimized business processes, and suitably trained and motivated people can realize the true value of a technology investment. Isolating a single input and attempting to measure its impact is akin to assessing the direct contribution of cheese to a pizza. This does not mean that ROI measures are ignored; quite the contrary.

How should IT investments be evaluated? As discussed earlier, you must abandon the idea that there are IT projects; there are no such things anymore. There are only projects targeted at improving business processes, developing new products or services, delivering more efficient customer service, or improving some other aspect of business performance. The ROI evaluation must match the total investments with the total returns regardless of the source of each. Doing this leads to the utilization of broader investment criteria than traditionally used for IT projects. For example, consider the investment in a new customer relationship management (CRM) system. Typically the expected benefits from such investments are framed in terms of improved customer satisfaction leading to increased retention and/or use of products and services, together with an improved ability to target customer needs. However, the implementation of the new system is only one element in ensuring that full value is realized. Having perfect customer information without adequately trained customer service representatives to interpret and act on that information or without providing the insights derived from the CRM system to the sales force or product development organization ensures that the ROI is not maximized.

Companies are now beginning to value ROI investment by addressing four elements: people, process, technology, and information. In the CRM example, the investment evaluation would first address the returns to be gained from implementing a new CRM system (technology). The next step addressed would be the need to develop a set of processes to communicate the insights gained from better customer information to the sales force so they can close more deals and to the product development team to refine and design better products (information and process). And finally, customer service representatives would be trained both to interpret and to respond to the new customer information to deliver better service (people). Once investments are viewed in this context, it becomes easier to define expected benefits and subsequently measure those returns.

Measuring Return on Investment at a Finnish Bank

A few years ago, I was consulting to one of Finland's largest banks, which was evaluating a potential investment of $45 million in a new asset management system to support its ability to provide personalized wealth management and investment services to Finland's richest individuals. The bank had a 30 percent market share and believed the new system would allow it to increase its share to 50 percent. Management felt the system could provide real breakthroughs in account management, online service, and execution efficiency and was perfectly in tune with Finland's emerging high-technology reputation. I had been asked to provide an independent view of the project's viability. Traditional ROI calculations showed an attractive return, but I was concerned by some of the assumptions that had been used. The number of high-net-worth individuals in Finland was not that large. I evaluated the investment in terms of the market impact that would be required to justify it. I estimated the total cost over and above the $45 million for hardware and software to include the costs of the project team to implement the system, ongoing support costs for the system, training for bank staff, education for customers, and the marketing costs of promoting the bank's new capabilities. This came to almost $75 million in total. I reduced the results of my evaluation to a single slide as shown in Exhibit 10.6.

The project would add $15 million in expenses for each of the next five years. To offset that investment, the bank would need to add 700 new customers each year or grow its assets under management by $400 million each year simply to break even. After viewing the slide, management decided that there was little probability of either of the two events happening. By relating the total investment to the business results that would be required to justify the investment, management was able to move beyond the pure technology appeal of the proposed system and make a rational decision.

Exhibit 10.6

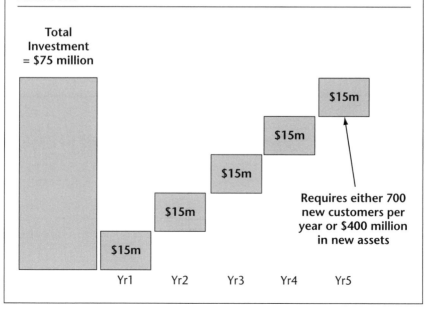

Over the next few years, it is likely that boards and senior executives will increasingly seek to better understand the total expected returns from projects where technology is a major component. Adoption of broader, more business-based evaluation methods should be one result.

BEST PRACTICE SUMMARY

- Eliminate, simplify, and then automate.
- It is not what technology you buy but how you implement it.
- Optimizing the application is less important than integrating the application.
- Performance management systems and ERP systems are not the same; they have different objectives, different structures, and different measures of value
- The general ledger is not a data warehouse, a management information system, or a budgeting system.
- Standards work only if they are enforced.
- There is no such thing as an IT project anymore. Because the costs and benefits of new systems cannot be separated from the process or people elements that make up every project, you must value investments holistically.
- Technology that is not used has no value. Measure usage, not deployment.
- Training is more than providing user manuals; effective training simulates the real-life business processes including the exceptions
- Systems must deliver the right information, not just more information. Selectivity, focus, and timeliness are key.

NOTES

1. Gartner Inc, "Global IT Spending Forecast," May 2005. IDG News Service, May 2005
2. AMR Research, The Enterprise Resource Planning Spending Report, 2005–2006, July 2005.

Part Three

Moving from Data to Decisions

Chapter 11

Implementing Best Practices

People never improve unless they look to some standard or example higher and better than themselves.

—Tryon Edwards

Measurement alone changes nothing; however, it is almost impossible to track progress toward some objective without a basis for comparison. Our environment is constantly being measured, and the number of measures we consume on a daily basis keeps growing. As I write this, I am sitting on a Boeing 767 traveling from Houston to Honolulu to start a vacation with my wife and two children. The video monitor in front of me is bombarding me with measurements. We are flying at 31,000 feet; traveling at 506 miles per hour; have 1,788 miles to travel. In addition, the local time is 11:28 A.M., the time at our destination is 10:28 A.M., and we are expected to arrive at 2:18 P.M. rather than the scheduled arrival time of 2:10 P.M. Before booking the flight, I was able to compare flight schedules and prices for multiple different airlines, review the on-time arrival statistics for each flight option, and even look up the safety record for each type of aircraft. Which of these metrics matter?

It depends on the type of decision you are trying to make or problem you are trying to fix. For me it is our arrival time in Honolulu, since my vacation won't really start until the first cocktail at Waikiki as soon after 2:18 P.M.. as possible.

GETTING STARTED

All changes start with some form of trigger. Triggering events can be of many types, from a major process failure that demonstrates the need for change to a casual discussion between two chief executive officers on the golf course that causes one to return to the office with the notion that things can be improved. When Jack Welch was at the helm of General Electric (GE), his then wife's use of the Internet alerted him to its potential. Not long after his epiphany, e-business had become a core GE strategy. At Nationwide Insurance, it was the impending initial public offering (IPO) of its life and annuity business, Nationwide Financial Services. At Bank of America, the impetus was the need to create sufficient financial visibility and hence flexibility to pursue attractive acquisition opportunities such as FleetBoston and MBNA. The first three steps focus on defining whether an improvement opportunity exists:

1. Identify areas of opportunity.
2. Quantify the opportunity.
3. Understand the drivers creating the opportunity.

Using the metrics in Chapter 3 may show that an organization's financial planning process takes twice as long to complete as that of a best practice organization; further investigation can provide insight into the likely causes of the extended cycle time, such as level of detail, the clarity of the up-front target-setting process, or the effectiveness of the systems that support the process. Combining multiple points of view also can help identify gaps between management's perception of the current level of performance and quantitative reality (see Exhibit 11.1).

Identifying these issues allows an organization to tackle the real drivers of the problems that are being experienced instead of simply implementing Band-Aid solutions. The objective is not simply to identify symptoms but to secure acceptance and commitment to act on the root causes of pain. Developing an understanding of where the improvement opportunities lie provides a sound foundation for identifying those opportunities that are focused primarily on operational efficiency and those that are focused more on business value. For example, extended cycle times are more of an operational efficiency opportunity, whereas the sandbagging of budgets is related more to business value. Plotting the opportunities that arise against each of these two dimensions allows an organization to prioritize the total set of opportunities and then select the portfolio that offers the greatest benefit.

Exhibit 11.1   Requirements for Building a Case for Change

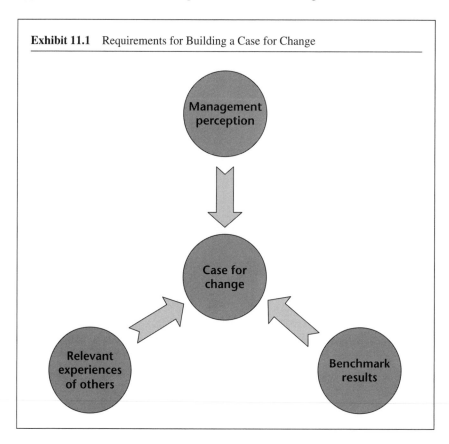

The gaps identified after comparing current processes to best practices not only size the opportunity but also provide a vision of the end state to be achieved. Translating opportunities into results requires focus and commitment. Focus comes from taking the collective results and prioritizing those opportunities that can be tackled over the near, medium, and long term. Commitment is demonstrated through management support and the allocation of appropriate resources to implement the agreed-on changes.

Once a decision has been made to make changes, there are two steps to getting started:

1. Prioritize and select the opportunities to be addressed.
2. Mobilize the resources.

Prioritizing the opportunities based on the benefits that can be derived and selecting those opportunities that can be practically tackled forces management to define a meaningful and manageable scope against which specific targets and accountabilities can be identified. It is important to ensure that the momentum built up is not dissipated. Sponsors need to set out the process for transitioning from a series of identified improvement opportunities to a series of approved, funded, and resourced initiatives.

Guidelines for Developing an Action Plan

- Set the expectation that changes will be implemented based on the results of the assessment.
- Focus the discussion on the drivers and solutions.
- Focus on those opportunities that have value for the largest number of stakeholders.
- Remember that policy and process changes can be implemented more quickly and cheaply than organizational or system changes.
- Do not hesitate to refine or redirect existing initiatives where resources have already been committed.

MOVING TO IMPLEMENTATION

There are many different ways to implement a best practice performance management process. What follows is a simple, logical framework for design and implementation that draws on my experiences of working with many different types of organization. The approach consists of 3 phases divided into 10 steps:

Phase 1: Design

1. Understand the overall strategic goals and objectives.
2. Define the critical success factors and drivers.

3. Define the appropriate performance measures.
4. Link measures to the overall strategy.

Phase 2: Build

5. Define the reporting dimensions.
6. Detail and source the performance measures.
7. Design the user interface.
8. Design and build the management reporting process.

Phase 3: Execute

9. Integrate the reporting and planning processes—align incentives.
10. Develop the required skills.

UNDERSTAND THE OVERALL STRATEGIC GOALS AND OBJECTIVES

The first step is to develop a clear and concise understanding of the overall goals and objectives around which operating and financial plans will be developed and against which performance will be measured. Typically a strategy can boil down to between two to five statements of strategic direction. If no documented strategy exists, the best approach is to facilitate a discussion among the leadership team to agree on the basic objectives that can guide further design work.

At one client, this yielded unexpected and interesting results. During interviews with the chief executive officer (CEO) and his eight direct reports, I asked each executive to list and rank the top three strategic objectives for the company. After nine interviews, I had a list of 19 different strategic objectives. The leadership team got the point. The absence of even the most basic documented statement of strategic direction was creating significant confusion among the leadership team, never mind the rest of the organization. The lack of cohesion made it very difficult for the group to prioritize initiatives and make effective resource allocation decisions. The following week the whole executive management team convened for two days to agree on a minimum of two but no more than five strategic objectives.

The team agreed on five goals and committed to use them as the basis for all future decision making. Less than 30 days later, the effect was noticeable. Fifteen projects had been canceled since they did not directly support any of the agreed-on goals. Three new projects were given the go-ahead, and discussions started with three possible acquisition targets that could help meet another of the objectives. In addition, the tone of the discussion at the weekly leadership team meetings changed noticeably. Instead of fruitless arguments over priorities with each individual pushing his or her own agenda, the discussion was sharply focused on the specific efforts needed to meet the agreed-on objectives. The debate had moved from what to do to how to do it. Not surprisingly, morale and results improved quickly.

Exhibit 11.2 Strategic Objectives Defined

Strategic Objective	Target
Achieve superior returns for stakeholders	Deliver average earnings per share of 15% per annum or 2% higher than a peer group of four competitors, whichever is greater
Achieve superior revenue growth	Achieve growth of 20% per annum
Achieve excellence in all key operating processes	Sustain productivity improvements of 4% per annum in every process
Constantly innovate	At least 35% of revenue must come from products less than 3 years old

The outcome of this step should be a crisp definition of strategic objectives with the accompanying performance targets (see Exhibit 11.2).

DEFINE THE CRITICAL SUCCESS FACTORS AND DRIVERS

An agreed-on set of goals with quantifiable targets provides the basis for developing the operational and financial plans and defining the management reporting requirements. The next step is to translate each goal into the major actions that the organization will need to take in order to be successful. These components often are termed critical success factors (CSFs). Each CSF is made up of one or more drivers. Defining the CSFs and drivers is the first step in translating what needs to be achieved to how it will be achieved. Both CSFs and drivers provide the framework for defining the right performance measures, developing operating plans and budgets, and assigning accountability for results. The most effective approach to building the relationships among goals, CSFs, and drivers is to construct a performance management model. Each goal is supported by one or more critical success factors, which in turn are influenced by one or more drivers. Exhibit 11.3 shows an example of defining the CSFs for the goal "Grow revenue by 20 percent" defined in step 1.

This organization has defined two critical success factors associated with its ability to meet the goal of growing revenues. It needs to be able to attract new customers and sell more to existing customers. Although the process used to define the CSFs and establish the relationships among them varies, I advocate developing an initial list of candidate CSFs for each goal. Ideally no more than four CSFs are supplied for each goal to ensure that adequate focus is paid to each one and that operating plans can be developed at a meaningful level. After developing a list of candidate CSFs, meet with each executive either individually or collectively, depending on the style and culture of the organization, and go through a process of rationalizing the list to those who are most important.

Exhibit 11.3   Grow Revenue by 20 Percent

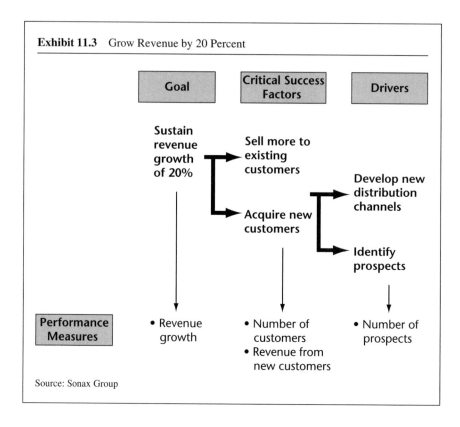

Source: Sonax Group

While these discussions can be done through interviews, a more effective approach is to develop a performance management "game room." Some people prefer to call it a war room, but I prefer the term "game room" since it is designed to be nonthreatening and experimental. Set up the room in this way:

- Remove all the tables. Leave a few chairs or, better still, a couple of sofas in the center of the room.
- Write down a description of each goal on a large sheet of paper.
- Stick each goal description about halfway up its own wall on the far left-hand side.
- Write out each candidate CSF on its own sheet of paper and stick them all on the walls in a column to the right of their respective goals.

You are now all set for round one. Bring in each participating executive, either individually or as a group depending on their preferences, and explain the objective of identifying the CSFs for each of the goals agreed on by the leadership team. The objective is to allow the executives to move around the room developing their own hierarchy of goals and CSFs. Initially let each person move around the room at his or her own pace with minimal guidance or interruption. As people start arranging the CSFs, ask them why they are making certain choices and occasionally challenge them. After 45 minutes to an hour, most people have a pretty good first draft of the goal-CSF framework. After each executive has passed through the game room, you will be able to develop a good picture of the true CSFs for each goal.

You can now begin to rationalize the overall model and develop three to four alternatives based on the preferences of each executive. Once a set of CSFs for each goal has been defined and agreed to, repeat the process for the drivers. This time broaden the number of people who are engaged. As you move to the driver level, there is often a disconnect between what executive management believes are the true drivers of the business and what operational management knows them to be.

The game room allows people to visualize and manipulate the relationships. Some companies have found the game room tool to be so valuable that it remains in use long after the original design process is complete. It becomes part of the on-going process for ensuring that the performance management process remains aligned with the goals and objectives of the business. Exhibit 11.4 shows an excerpt from a partially completed performance management model for a retailer that displays the relationships between the goals and their attendant CSFs and drivers.

DEFINE THE APPROPRIATE PERFORMANCE MEASURES

The completed performance management model provides a structured view of the business that links the overall strategic objectives to the key areas a business must plan on and execute to deliver the required results. The next step is to identify appropriate measures for each goal, CSF, and driver. Doing this establishes the management reporting requirements of the organization.

Each goal, CSF, or driver may have multiple measures associated with it. However, to ensure appropriate focus and minimize confusion, define one as being the primary measure and the others as being supporting measures.

Do not expect to get all the measures right during the design phase. The only valid test of whether the set of measures is right is to use them in practice. Experience suggests that between 15 and 20 percent of the initial set of measures will need to be changed during the first year of use. It is also normal to expect that 10 to 15 percent of the measures will change each year thereafter as the business and market environment evolves over time.

LINK MEASURES TO THE OVERALL STRATEGY

The next step is to link the measures that have been defined back to the overall strategy. This is a check to make sure that the top-down approach has not become disconnected from the strategy.

An example of this type of misalignment occurred at a large manufacturing company that was implementing an extensive total quality management (TQM) program in its manufacturing operations. During the development of the performance management model, new drivers were identified that related to the basic principles of

Exhibit 11.4 Performance Management Model

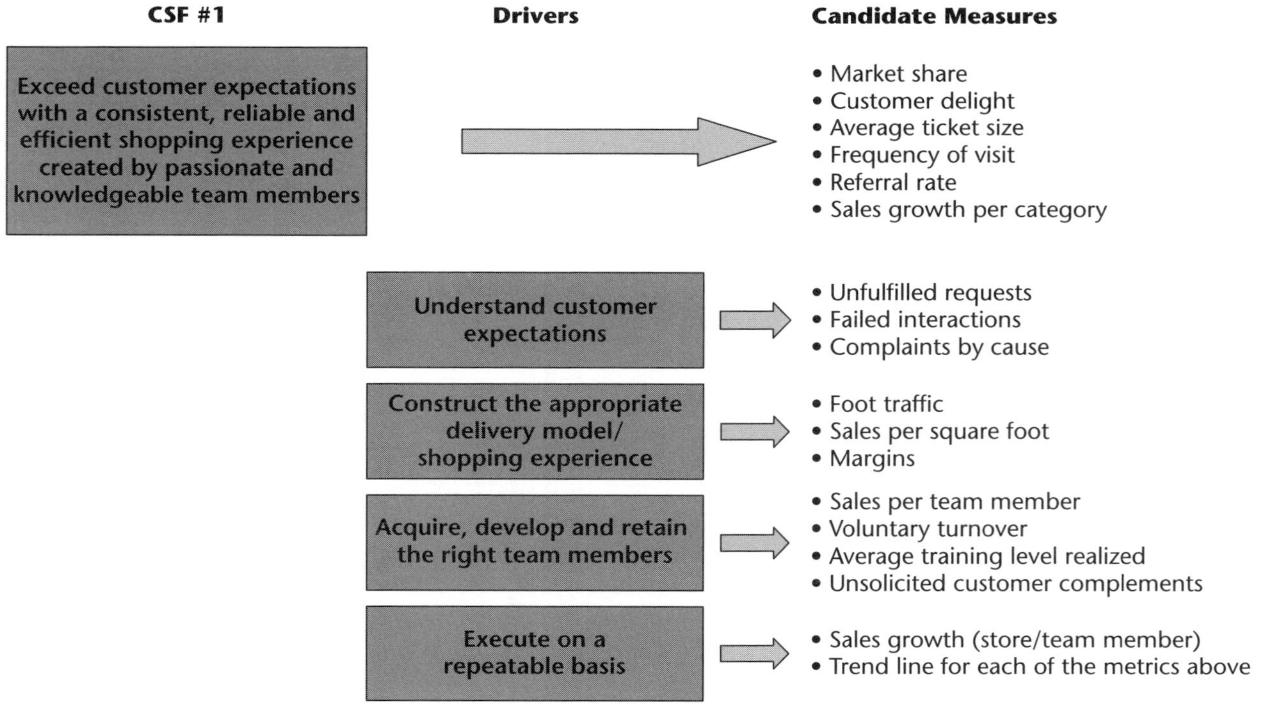

CSF #1	Drivers	Candidate Measures
Exceed customer expectations with a consistent, reliable and efficient shopping experience created by passionate and knowledgeable team members		• Market share • Customer delight • Average ticket size • Frequency of visit • Referral rate • Sales growth per category
	Understand customer expectations	• Unfulfilled requests • Failed interactions • Complaints by cause
	Construct the appropriate delivery model/ shopping experience	• Foot traffic • Sales per square foot • Margins
	Acquire, develop and retain the right team members	• Sales per team member • Voluntary turnover • Average training level realized • Unsolicited customer complements
	Execute on a repeatable basis	• Sales growth (store/team member) • Trend line for each of the metrics above

building quality into every step of the process. However, when it came to developing the measures, the people in the business reverted to measures that they had been using and were comfortable with, measures that tended to be biased more toward a process of checking quality at the end of the process rather than throughout it.

To test whether the right measures have been identified, ask three questions of each measure:

1. How do we determine whether the measure is on or off target?
2. What actions are we likely to take if the measure is off target?
3. Are those actions consistent with meeting the agreed-on strategic goals and objectives?

DEFINE THE REPORTING DIMENSIONS

Defining the dimensions around which each measure needs to be reported is a crucial and often-forgotten step in the process. The value of the information will be severely limited if it cannot be reported around the right dimensions. Reporting dimensions are the parameters that define how the raw data need to be aggregated to derive the required information.

The easiest way to think about reporting dimensions is to take a measure, such as sales, and then define the ways in which you want to view it: for example, sales by month, sales by region, sales by customer. Month, region, and customer are all dimensions around which the measure sales can be reported.

The mapping of measures to dimensions can be easily accomplished by drawing up a matrix where each row represents a measure and each column represents a dimension. The completed mapping defines the data required to support the reporting of all the defined measures.

DETAIL AND SOURCE THE PERFORMANCE MEASURES

Using the measure/dimension mapping as the start point, the next step is to identify where in the existing processes and systems the data can be found. Before starting the sourcing exercise, it is helpful to group all the measures that are likely to come from similar processes and systems together. All sales-related information is likely to come from the customer relationship management (CRM) or the sales order processing systems. All employee-related information will likely be collected from the human resource information system (HRIS), payroll, and time collection systems.

Once like data have been grouped together, the design team can meet with the owners of the processes and systems to identify the type of data available for each measure/dimension. Exhibit 11.5 shows the typical classifications that result from the data sourcing activity.

Completing a preliminary data sourcing analysis allows the project team to get a good sense of whether the performance measure requirements can be met and of

Exhibit 11.5   Data Sourcing Classifications

Availability	Description
1	All required data available with the frequency and dimensions required.
2	All required data available with the dimensions required but not at required frequency.
3	Some dimensions missing.
4	Data available but definitions vary across multiple sources.
5	Data not available.

the likely complexity of building the management reporting systems. Complexity is largely a function of two things: the number of different data sources that need to be accessed and the consistency of the data definitions across the different data sources. It is easier to go to a single source for all the data required; however, this is not feasible except in the smallest businesses. Even organizations that have fully deployed an enterprise-wide enterprise resource planning (ERP) system will have many other systems supporting different aspects of the business.

Today external data are playing a crucial role in best practice performance management, and these data must be sourced. Typically, doing this requires accessing data from the Internet and from customer or supplier systems, each of which may have different standards and protocols. The issue of data definitions has bedeviled the designers of management information systems for years and shows no sign of abating. The crux of the problem is when two processes or systems appear to capture the same data element, but it is defined differently in each system.

For example, two systems may both capture the dimension customer associated with each order that is processed, but in one system the customer field may relate to the customer's billing address, which may be the corporate head office, and in the other system it may relate to the shipping address, which may be at a subsidiary or plant location. Such seemingly minor differences can create major problems in the design of management reporting systems. Addressing issues of definitional consistency is a prerequisite if the substantial investments made on systems are to pay off. This is dirty work, and it is all too easy to let it slip in favor of the more attractive tasks of designing reports and screens and selecting sexy decision support tools and systems.

Despite the exponential increase in the amount of data available, it is not unusual for some of the data needed to not be readily accessible. Where the data are incomplete—a rating of 3, 4, or 5 on Exhibit 11.5—a decision needs to be made. Typically, there are three options:

1. Build the required data collection processes to close the gap. Do this only where there is demonstrable payback on the investment required; the measure must be really important with no suitable alternatives.

2. Identify a surrogate measure. Doing this involves defining a different measure that, while not exactly meeting the need, offers an acceptable substitute. This could involve calculating the measure by using sampling or some other statistical technique.
3. Accept the deficiency until such time as the data become available as part of another change, such as replacing the source system.

There must be a compelling business reason to invest significant effort to close the gap, particularly if an alternative measure is readily available. Sometimes the design team becomes so wedded to the complete set of requirements that it is loath to sacrifice anything. It is important to guard against this behavior and to ensure that objective decisions are made.

After completing the data sourcing, the team has a good picture of the total information and data set required to support the management reporting process and the probable sources of the data. Now it is ready to start building the delivery process.

DESIGN THE USER INTERFACE

The acid test for any management information system is whether it is used. The reporting of measures around the goals, critical success factors, and drivers of the business must be designed so as to allow its intended users to fully leverage the information in support of making better business decisions. There are two steps: content and format. The first step is to identify who needs what information and when. Generally speaking, information needs follow a common pattern. The farther away an individual is from a specific decision, the less detail and the less often he or she needs it.

Senior management generally needs a broader set of less detailed information whereas operational staff needs more detailed but more narrowly focused information. Of course, some managers appear to have an infinite desire for detail in every situation. Often this causes problems for the project team, which is fearful of telling the CEO that he or she cannot have the information requested. After many years of trying to address this issue, I have concluded that fighting this particular battle is a distraction that is not worth the effort. If senior executives want access to lots of detail, that is their prerogative. As long as performance does not suffer, it is simply not worth fighting over. This is a useful axiom for all best practices. Best practices will not necessarily make great managers better or make already great companies better, but they raise the performance of average performers.

Format is more than just designing the screen layouts and reports; it includes designing how the information fits into the recipient's role and situation. No standard format is better than others. The advent of low-cost, Web-based reporting tools has allowed for much greater creativity in the design of the user interface. A number of companies mimic the layout of popular Internet sites such as Yahoo; others seek to replicate existing interfaces that people are comfortable with, such as the spreadsheet. The key is to match the interface to users' preferences, responsibilities, and situation.

Focusing on the user means designing the interface from the user's perspective rather than looking at the total set of information and working out how to design reports. Good user interface design does not compensate for bad information, but bad design can destroy the value of good information.

DESIGN AND BUILD THE REPORTING PROCESS

The measures have been defined, the data have been found, and the user requirements agreed to; the next step is to define the process that will be used to actually get the data from their source to the end user. This subject merits a book all of its own, many of which are available. Chapter 10 explored the technology best practices that support the information delivery process. This activity takes the five steps of the information delivery process—collect, structure, store, transform, and use—and details the wiring diagram to make that happen: Functional and technical requirements are agreed on, technology choices are made, roles are defined, and systems are implemented.

INTEGRATE THE REPORTING AND PLANNING PROCESSES— ALIGN INCENTIVES

The completed performance management model does not just define the performance measures that need to be reported; it also defines those elements of the business that need to be planned and forecast. The management reporting process should allow the user to see the specific tactics against each driver for that CSF, identify the total resources that have been committed, and forecast the impact of material changes in the current or future business environment and their impact on progress. The target measures that are defined during the design process become the primary measures that make up the organization's scorecard and around which management will make decisions.

The goals and CSFs form the table of contents for the planning process. Initiatives, resources, and results should be aligned around them, and management should be held accountable for performance against them. The performance management model must infuse all aspects of planning, reporting, and forecasting and also provide the basis for defining incentives and compensation. The relationships established in the performance management model define the goals, major strategies, tactics, and performance measures that will be used to judge success. Identifying those measures that should be used as a basis for evaluating individual and organizational performance and rewards is a critical step if behavior is to be aligned with plans.

DEVELOP THE REQUIRED SKILLS

Last but by no means least, the move to a best practice process requires not only redesigned processes and new technologies but also appropriately skilled and trained people. The change in skills and focus needed to support a best practice process is significant (see Exhibit 11.6). In the finance department, individuals who used to spend all their time processing transactions, reconciling accounts, and mining for data are suddenly expected to provide insightful, action-oriented analysis to senior executives. If that is not significant enough, the impact on the broader organization is even greater. People now have access to a much richer set of information and tools than ever before. The move from managing through gut instinct alone, due to the relative lack of good information, to combining gut instinct with useful information is not an easy change for many. In addition to traditional training methods (classroom, self-guided tutorials, and help screens), many best practice companies have combined a range of tools to prepare managers and staff for the advent of the new processes, systems, and information.

Examples include:

- *Collaborative design sessions.* Any opportunity to involve intended users helps to increase awareness and acceptance.

- *Role-playing simulations.* A powerful way of explaining the performance management model is to use a series of business game- or role-playing scenarios that illustrate how the relationships were developed and how they relate to different aspects of the business process.

- *Coaching.* For senior executives, the most effective approach can be to assign a coach to work one-on-one with each executive to help him or her tap into the power of the new tools and systems. Coaching has the advantage of allowing training to be scheduled in a more flexible and consultative way consistent with the executive's schedule. General Electric assigned mentors or coaches to its entire executive team to help them first use and then understand the potential of

---

Exhibit 11.6   Changing Focus of the Finance Professional

Typical Focus	**Required Focus**
• Cost optimization	• Revenue enhancement
• Certainty	• Risk
• Precision	• Accuracy
• Budgets	• Forecasts
• Cost accounting	• Cost elasticity
• Operational execution	• External threats
• Criteria for success	• Criteria for abandonment
• Calendar driven	• Event triggered
• Silver bullets	• Portfolio of skills and tools

the Internet. Another less often touted benefit of coaching is that it avoids executives embarrassing themselves in a more formal training environment.

- *Postimplementation reviews.* These reviews are not the traditional ones of a new system after implementation but formal debriefing sessions scheduled at periodic intervals after implementation, typically after completing the first planning sessions using the performance management model, after the first set of scorecards is delivered, and after completing the first forecast. Each session focuses on the success or lack thereof of the process and the need for any improvements or changes to the process. The more engaged, enthused, and involved the intended user community is about the process and systems, the greater the success. Education is not simply about learning how to use the process and system; it should inspire users to investigate for themselves, experiment, and adapt the tools to suit their own style. A best practice performance management process does not guarantee great decisions, but it does reduce the risk of making uninformed decisions. The educational tools that are used to stimulate appreciation and use are vital if the organization is to realize the full return on its investment.

Successful completion of these 10 steps should result in a best practice–compliant process. Sustaining the process over time will require constant attention and fine-tuning as the organization changes. The next chapter reviews the critical success factors for implementation and ongoing management of a best practice process.

Chapter 12

Implementation Secrets

It's good to have an end to a journey; but in the end it's the journey that matters.

—Ursula K. Le Guin

Given the preponderance of project work in today's organizations combined with the almost constant merger and acquisition activity, it is disturbing to see that most studies estimate that between 40 and 60 percent of information technology (IT) projects fail to deliver the expected benefits and that two-thirds of all mergers are deemed failures. Michael Hammer and James Champy estimated that "as many as 50 percent to 70 percent of the organizations that undertake a reengineering effort do not achieve the dramatic results they intended."[1] Clearly, successful projects are the exception rather than the norm. How do you increase your chances of success?

LEARN FROM THE MISTAKES OF OTHERS

There has been a distinct evolution in how companies approach best practice deployment. There have been four distinct phases (see Exhibit 12.1).

Phase 1 was the desire of organizations simply to understand how they stacked up relative to the best performers. Up to that point, the relative paucity of any credible benchmark measures made it virtually impossible to know whether an organization was spending too much or too little on a particular process. Cost reduction was the number-one objective of most organizations.

Phase 2 was allied to the growth of the reengineering wave of the mid-1990s following the 1993 publication of Michael Hammer and James Champy's manifesto, *Reengineering the Corporation.*[2] Hammer and Champy championed a radical redesign of processes that often entailed blowing up the existing process and starting over. The catchphrase "Work smarter, not harder" became a rallying cry; however, as organizations moved down the reengineering path, many were daunted by the prospect of having to radically redesign their business processes without a clear understanding of the desired end state. By this time, most organizations had some awareness of best practices.

Questions moved from "How do I stack up?" to "What do best practices look like?" Organizations now wanted to know what best practice processes, technologies, and organizational secrets they should be implementing; they could quantify the improvement opportunity and wanted to understand the target or end state solution. While the combination of these two pieces of information triggered major cost and productivity improvements in many areas of business, organizations often

Exhibit 12.1   Evolution of Best Practice Benchmarking

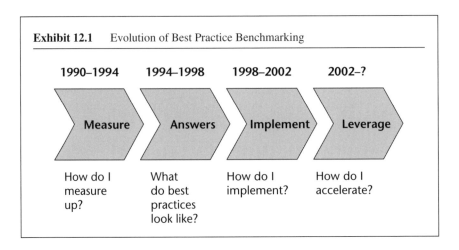

1990–1994	1994–1998	1998–2002	2002–?
Measure	Answers	Implement	Leverage
How do I measure up?	What do best practices look like?	How do I implement?	How do I accelerate?

found it very difficult to implement all the best practices. Projects took longer to complete, systems failed to support best practices adequately, implementation costs were greater than projected, and benefits fell short of expectations. Research into the causes of these problems uncovered some interesting conclusions. Although some of the problems were related to technical issues, such as the complexity of the solution or the failure of new computer systems to perform as expected, by far the dominant category of problem was those associated with people; more specifically, these problems related to the change management issues faced in first securing a commitment to change and then ensuring that implementation resulted in improved execution.

In phase 3, organizations sought to add the missing element of "How do I get there?" They wanted to go beyond identifying the opportunity and knowing the answer to understanding how to effect the change. A new type of best practice was defined that focused on implementation. Disciplines such as program management and change management became popular as organizations strove to deal with the challenges of implementation. Exhibit 12.2 highlights some of the key implemen-

Exhibit 12.2   Implementation Questions

- How do we define a manageable scope for our transformation effort?
- How do we sell the need for change to all the different constituencies within our business? How do we sustain that commitment?
- What sort of resources and time commitment is required?
- How should the project be organized?
- How do we get IT to work as part of the overall team?
- What role should consultants play?
- How do we implement as fast as possible?
- Can we just implement the new technology and use that to force us to best practices?
- How do we manage employee morale throughout the process?
- What types of incentives do we need to provide to ensure successful implementation?

tation questions that organizations began to ask before embarking on a major transformation effort.

The last few years have seen the pace of best practice deployment pick up significantly as organizations faced a new set of challenges. Although they recognized the power of a best practice–driven transformation approach, organizations did not have the luxury of time. Costs had to be cut, organizations had to realign to a harsher operating environment, and technology investments had to deliver measurable returns fast. Instead of following a traditional measure-plan-act cycle of improvement, organizations wanted it all immediately. Coupled with the advances in technology, organizations are now seeking simultaneously to implement best practices processes, realign themselves, and deploy new technologies—in short, leverage all the investments and learning of the previous three phases. Instead of two- to three-year programs, the objective is to complete the transformation in 6 to 12 months.

The cumulative impact of moving from a sequential to a parallel approach increases the pressure on organizations to accept and adapt to more change, more quickly. Organizations must understand the relationship between the amount of change they need to make and the amount of change they can make before embarking on any major project. This capability gap—and it is usually a gap—is a key factor in determining whether a transformation project will be successful. Unless an organization has a completely new management team, it must face the reality that the very processes that it is trying to change are the ones that enabled the current management team to reach its present position. Understanding the relative acceptance among the management team of the need to change and the willingness to lead by example are key factors to consider during the planning of a major change project.

Developing strategy, executing operational plans, and managing performance is a process of continuous change. From major strategic shifts to minor midcourse corrections, everything revolves around the identification of a course of action and the implementation of that action. Managers continuously refine resource allocations in pursuit of their overall objectives. Understanding how to change the way an organization behaves is the single most difficult challenge to be faced in implementing best practices.

EFFECT CHANGE AND THEN SUSTAIN IT

Designing and implementing a new performance management process requires a two-step process (see Exhibit 12.3). The organization must effect a change in direction and also sustain the change. The skills required to effect change are very different from those required to sustain change. The best managers quickly learn that effecting a change is far easier than sustaining a change. If you are in doubt, reflect on the ease of starting a diet versus the challenge of sticking to it.

Effecting a change can be accomplished in many ways ranging from inspiration, through coercion or mandate, on to taking over control. Inspirational change is the stuff from which legends are made. The combination of a truly compelling idea broadly propagated is the Holy Grail of change management. Think Sony Walkman,

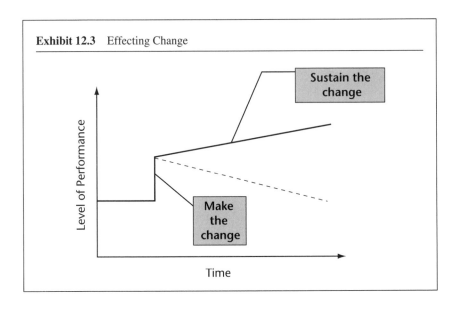

Exhibit 12.3   Effecting Change

the Egg McMuffin, the drive-through window, or the TV remote control. If you can develop an idea that possesses the attributes of any of these innovations, sit back and watch. Unfortunately, inspirational change is rare; most change requires a little more effort. Few remember Apple's failure with its Newton PDA in 1990s, which presaged the phenomenon of the iPod just a few years later.

Coercion is probably the most prevalent method for effecting change. It is perhaps more politically correct to describe this approach as "selling change." Coercion combines elements of inspirational change with a more forceful approach that recognizes that the change agreed on must be sold aggressively. Mandating change tends to be used in two situations:

1. The change requires immediate action and there is no time for debate or dialogue. In this case, the individuals with the most power simply mandate the change to speed implementation.
2. Senior leaders lose patience with more collaborative methods and adopt a "just do what you're told" attitude. Phrases like "They just don't get it" typify situations in which mandates are likely.

The most important element to remember about mandated changes is that they require constant effort if the change is to be sustained. People by their very nature tend to resent being told to do things. Unless the mandate rapidly sells itself, there will be continuous pressure to regress to the old way of doing things. After an initial burst of activity, performance will tend to regress unless the direction mandated quickly delivers a return in excess of the effort required. Sustaining commitment to change is a continuous process that must be fueled constantly. In many cases, open acceptance of a mandate is used to mask covert avoidance. In such situations, the most effective option can be just to take control. Jeff Henley, chairman and former chief financial officer (CFO) of Oracle Corporation, related a story of the frustration Oracle experienced in implementing standard practices across the company in the late 1990s.[3] Oracle grew at a phenomenal rate for much of the 1980s and 1990s. As a consequence, numerous different approaches to conducting business had emerged across its many business units and geographies. After a study identified the cost of these inconsistencies, management resolved to drive much greater standardization across critical business processes in areas such as marketing, finance, and IT. Oracle's chief executive officer (CEO), Larry Ellison, has a reputation for being a strong leader, and he hit the road to communicate the required changes. The inefficiencies were so obvious that management believed that Ellison's inspirational leadership combined with a not-too-subtle mandate would do the trick. All went well with the road show. No one disagreed with Ellison's "guidance," and all pledged their commitment to implement the changes.

Some months later, Ellison told Henley that he believed a number of people were "blowing him off." Although outwardly they accepted all the recommendations and vowed to implement them, in reality, nothing was changing. Ellison, being the forceful leader that he is, did not tolerate such behavior. His response was not to reenforce his directions; he went one step further. He removed all three functions from the control of the businesses and made them report into a single executive at corporate headquarters. Mandate had not worked, so the only option left to effect change was to seize control.

Despite the universal acceptance of the importance of change management, often it is seen as somehow soft and woolly. Many executives cite the critical importance of change management while at the same time shying away from seeking to understand how to effectively make change happen. Often change management is oversimplified and represented simply as being about communication, which is only part of the story.

The ability to motivate people to change is perhaps the defining quality of leadership. As Harry S Truman said, "Leadership is the ability to get men to do what they don't want to do and like it."

Change management has taken its place in the pantheon of management disciplines and spawned its own vast library of research. What follows is a brief overview of 12 of the critical success factors (CSFs) for best practice implementation.

#1: Do Not Count on a "Silver Bullet"

I have referred a number of times to the tendency for organizations to seek a quick fix or silver bullet as a solution to their problems. At various times, enterprise resource planning (ERP) systems, data warehousing, executive information systems, balanced scorecards, economic value added (EVA), reengineering, rolling forecasts, and the Internet have all been touted as the answer. Unfortunately, the question that they were supposed to answer was less clear.

Each of these tools, along with many others, has a role to play; however, no one solution will by itself guarantee best practice performance. Studies clearly show that a combination of process, organization, information, and technology defines a best practice solution. Implementation requires a delicate blend of many skills, from selling, to design, to training. It is wise to center a transformation program on a powerful focal point, such as a new system or a new leadership team that can serve as a rallying point or selling tool, but make sure that the implementation balances all the requirements necessary for success. Remember, Michael Jordan was acknowledged as the best basketball player in the world some years before his team won the NBA championship. The best team will best the best individual every time. Best practices operate in much the same way: No single best practice guarantees success.

#2: Approach the Program in Stages

Implementing a best practice transformation program is a significant effort. For a company that scores around average in the benchmark, it can mean operating with 50 percent fewer people, redefining the jobs of 80 percent of the people who remain, swapping out most of the current systems, and completely redefining the way in which the executive management team works together. The magnitude of this type of change is not something that can be done all at once. It is simply too great for the organization to digest. The first rule of complex problem solving is to decompose the problem into a series of more manageable chunks. The same is true for large change projects. The timeline for implementation may have to be extended; although this is not always necessary, extending the timeline dramatically reduces the risks of failure. Each stage should have a clear set of deliverables and a checkpoint that must be satisfied before the next stage commences. This ensures that implementation progresses smoothly and factors in the inevitable learning process required in any project. The primary factor to be considered in defining the appropriate implementation sequence is balancing speed of implementation with overall risk.

#3: Plan Comprehensively

Although nearly everyone recognizes the value of effective up-front planning, it is amazing how often planning is ignored as the pressure builds to implement fast. The just-do-it mentality often results in management demanding an immediate payoff. Project managers feel pressured and often respond by curtailing planning in favor of starting implementation. All too often, the result is failure or at best a suboptimal implementation. As Benjamin Franklin said, "Those who fail to plan, plan to fail."

Many of the redundant and poorly integrated systems that companies are now wrestling with are the result of a failure to establish a complete plan as to how technology should be deployed across the organization. The absence of clear guidance allowed individual business units to purchase and implement their own technology solutions with little or no thought to the inevitable integration issues across the organization.

As a general rule, breadth is more important than depth in planning. The ability to identify correctly all the component parts that are required to build a comprehensive plan is more important than great detail in any one area. Taking the time to consider all the possible implications of a major transformation is a wise investment. Identifying all the elements that go into the plan and detailing out those about which adequate projections can be made sets the scene for a successful implementation. As time passes, each element of the plan can be developed in more detail. Planning does not stop when implementation begins; rather, planning is an ongoing activity. The key is to define as many of the components of the plan and the interactions between them as early as possible in the process. Defining milestones, identifying the linkages between different components, and assigning responsibility provide the foundation for rapid execution.

#4: Dedicate the Resources

The progressive downsizing of business over the last 20 years means that few organizations have the luxury of surplus resources sitting around waiting to be assigned to a transformation project. Although it is difficult to find resources, doing so remains a critical success factor. Too many organizations seek to staff major change projects with the resources they have available rather than the right resources to get the job done. In some organizations, no matter how many resources are requested, only 80 percent will ever be made available. The consistent understaffing of projects simply induces project managers to inflate their resource requests. Doing this adds no value and risks the nonapproval of a viable project because of artificially inflated resource demand. The prorating of resources across projects can be equally damaging. It is much better to fully staff all the projects that the available resources allow. When resources are prorated arbitrarily, all projects are understaffed and none succeeds.

Effective project staffing is about both quantity and quality. Best practice organizations assign the absolute best resources they have to major change projects, no matter how critical the individual's current role. They understand that it is a lot harder to change something than it is to sustain the current process. If necessary, they promote the number two to fill the current role or backfill with a temporary reassignment from another organization to ensure that the right caliber of person is assigned to the project. The caliber of resources assigned to a project sends a very powerful message to the organization about the relative importance of the project and management's commitment to its success. The assignment of the best people to a project tells the rest of the organization that management is serious.

Equally important is to ensure that the resources assigned to a project can actually dedicate the time needed. A popular technique for managing resource allocations is to convert a request for a six-person project team into six full-time equivalent resources. The term "full-time equivalent" (FTE) is used to represent a single unit of labor. This unit can represent a single full-time person or assignment of two or more people on a part-time basis that notionally equates to a single full-time resource (e.g., two employees each dedicating half their time to a project or activity). Partial resources are not as effective as full-time resources, for a number of reasons:

- Rarely does each person's other job suddenly shrink by 50 percent the moment that person is assigned to the project.
- Scheduling part-time project team members can be a nightmare. The difficulty of assembling the full team handicaps collaboration and teamwork.
- Two part-timers will not be as productive as one full-timer. Too much time will be spent updating individual team members on progress or seeking to keep other team members apprised of what will be happening while they work their other job.
- If project team members retain their day-to-day responsibilities and, perhaps more important, their reporting line, their first loyalty will be to their normal boss who writes their year-end review. This can create conflicting priorities that need to be managed carefully.

This is not to say that part-time resources cannot be used—practical considerations often make it inevitable. The most effective model is to form a dedicated core team that spends all its time working on the project with a common reporting line and shared measures and incentives. If the team cannot be fully resourced with full-time people, then a smaller core team can be supplemented with additional part-time resources. There are some ground rules for making this work effectively.

- Define the specific blocks of time that part-time team members will work on the project, and secure the commitment of their bosses before the project starts.
- Define and communicate up front to part-time team members and their bosses the process for including feedback and rewards for their work on the project into their performance review.
- Communicate any failure to fulfill agreed-on commitments to the individual's boss and to the project steering committee as soon as it impacts progress.

Managing the initial staffing of a project and then sustaining the appropriate staffing to complete the project are two of the most critical tasks of the project leader and project sponsor.

#5: Build Commitment through Involvement

Building commitment to change is always cited as one of the top two or three critical success factors for any project. Less clear is exactly how commitment will be secured. Commitment requires an individual or an organization actively to support and embrace the changes that a change project seeks to implement. Securing the commitment of individuals who are impacted by the changes or who are essential to implementation is a major component of an effective change program. Keep in mind these seven points when seeking to secure commitment:

1. *Commitment is earned, it's not an entitlement.* Just because one person believes that a radical redesign of the planning process is compelling does not mean that everyone else will agree. To secure the commitment of others, all the attributes of an effective sales and marketing program must be brought to bear. Nationwide Insurance went so far as to assign a marketing professional to its planning and management reporting redesign team expressly for this purpose. The project had a well-defined marketing, sales, and communication plan that ensured that the project team balanced the development of the best solution with the selling of that solution.

2. *In the early stages of a major change program, seek out people across the organization who "get it."* They can see the problems with the current process and are eager to help effect change. Engaging this group early in the process creates a cadre of "evangelists" who can serve as the program's sales force out in the organization. Through a program of periodic working sessions, frequent conference calls, and other forms of interaction, equip your evangelists with the knowledge and tools to educate and sell the changes being proposed within their own organizations. More important, they can serve as a vital communication link to senior management, ensuring sustained support for the program and helping remove barriers to progress as needed.

3. *Once earned, commitment must be sustained.* All too often, during the planning and mobilization phases, project teams focus significant effort on an initiative on building commitment. All the right tools are brought to the table, and great excitement is generated.

   Unfortunately, as the realities of implementation manifest themselves, much of the initial effort dissipates itself. Time that should be dedicated to communication and educational activities is the first to be sacrificed as deadlines approach and budgets become strained. Many projects start out with town hall meetings, video presentations from the management team, Web sites, and newsletters, but the silence becomes deafening as the months pass by. Doing a great job at the beginning of an initiative in creating excitement and energy and then allowing it to dissipate can be more damaging than adopting a lower-key approach but sustaining it throughout the project.

4. *No single method works in isolation.* Different people respond to different messages and media. Matching the right messages and the right medium to each audience is at the heart of successful change management. Some people will be inspired by the goal of building a world-class management process; others will just be happy to go home at 5 P.M. during budget season. Motivations often vary by level in an organization. Senior management is always intensely

focused on the return on investment from any initiative. Middle management presents a very different set of challenges. Middle managers usually do not get fired when the processes they manage run smoothly. Their biggest fears are that any change will disrupt the status quo or impact the people within their organization, thereby increasing the risk of process failures and creating personnel issues. While it is impossible to allay these concerns—any change program will impact processes and people—with middle managers, focus on the steps that will be taken to manage these risks during the transition and the benefits they will feel once implementation is complete. These messages need to be reinforced constantly during implementation.

5. *Contrary to what many people believe, money is not the principal concern of most operational staff.* Job security and the overall work environment consistently rank higher than compensation in most surveys. Securing commitment from operating staff is primarily a function of honesty. People do not fear change so much as the uncertainty about how it will impact them individually. Experience shows that even those individuals who may lose their jobs value honesty and consistency in communication. For those whose roles will be changed, communicating clearly how and when the changes will occur and what the benefits will be to the organization as a whole and to them individually mitigates fear.

6. *Communication by itself does not secure commitment.* How often have you heard the phrase "Communicate, communicate, communicate, and then communicate again" cited as a best practice? Although communication is the most powerful tool for securing commitment, it is not the only tool. Communication is very effective at explaining the nature of the change and the positive and negative impact on the organization and the individuals, but it is no substitute for developing a sense of involvement in the process, which can take many forms. Among the most effective are to:

   • Make sure communication is a two-way process; seek input from people during the design and implementation process.

   • Add representatives from the operating staff to the project team.

   • Conduct workshops or pilots to walk people through the new process.

   • Develop full-scale prototypes for people to try out.

   • Engage people in the testing process.

   • Develop a process for soliciting ideas and input throughout the project.

7. *You will never convert everyone.* No matter how effective your change management program, some people will not get it or want to get it. No matter what inducements or other techniques are employed, a small proportion of people will adopt a not-over-my-dead-body attitude toward the change. They will be casualties in any change process. Expect this and plan for how to deal with such stubborn resistance. The best that can be hoped for is to persuade the resistors to keep their concerns to themselves. Beyond that, options include elimination or reassignment to a position that does not impact the success of the

project. Active resistance cannot be allowed to impact a major change project and must be addressed directly and decisively.

Building Evangelists at Bank of America

Upon taking the role of chief planning officer at Bank of America, one of my first tasks was to build a mechanism for building support across a very diverse organization for the changes we wanted to make. While I had the luxury of strong senior management commitment, that alone was not going to ensure broad support and, more important, advocacy of the changes to be made. The approach we adopted built on three very strong mechanisms that the bank already had in place.

1. Ken Lewis, the bank's chairman and CEO, was a strong advocate of six sigma, and these disciplines had embedded themselves in the company's culture.
2. Related to the six sigma tools and methods the bank has an established approach to evaluating the potential of different change efforts. No project or initiative can gain support or funding without clearly demonstrating that the "Voice of the Customer" has been sought and is a driving factor in an initiative's raison d'être.
3. In order to facilitate knowledge sharing across the bank, a number of "Communities of Practice" had been established that allowed individuals to share knowledge and experience across functional and organizational boundaries.

The existence of these three vehicles allowed us to rapidly build a quantitative argument for change. Using the statistical tools that make up the six sigma tool kit, we were able to analyze and isolate the true drivers of forecast and budget inaccuracy as a vehicle for quantifying the impact of improving the processes. Voice of the Customer told us loud and clear that management across the board was supportive of change; and the communities of practice provided a broad forum to create a cadre of evangelists across the organization that combined enthusiasm for change with credibility among their peers.

#6: Gain Momentum Quickly

Getting off to a fast start is essential. Too many projects create a lot of excitement at launch time but deliver little of tangible value for months thereafter. The momentum gained during the project launch needs to be sustained. Momentum is a function of two things: activity and delivery.

A good rule of thumb is to ensure that meaningful, tangible deliverables are produced at least every 90 days. This is not necessarily because the perfect project plan calls for a deliverable in that time frame; rather it is about selling and marketing the project. Simply because the project was approved does not mean the sales job is done. Project sponsors have to continually fight to get the committed resources assigned or prevent them from being reassigned. They have to guide their project through rounds of budget cuts and fend off the demands of newer initiatives that compete for the same sponsorship and resources. Maintaining visibility by delivering a constant stream of benefits to the organization is a powerful tool for sustaining support and commitment.

#7: Make the Investments of Time and Money

"Can you do it cheaper?" is a familiar challenge coming from senior management. Change does not come free. As the old saying goes, "You have to speculate to accumulate." Change projects require that investment be made. It is perfectly acceptable to challenge the assumptions that underpin the investments requested by any project—that is part of management's job. However, once the commitment has been made, the approved resources should be provided. It adds little value to second-guess the investment requirements at every stage of the process; in fact, doing so can have a negative impact on progress. Approval of a project also constitutes the granting of appropriate authority to the project sponsor or manager. Obviously, material new information or a change in circumstances must be addressed as part of the normal planning and project management process.

"Can you do it quicker?" usually follows hard on the heels of "Can you do it cheaper?" Again, this is a perfectly valid question; however, there are limits. Taking adequate time to do it right is important—nowhere more so than with the first major implementation. If the first implementation fails, in all likelihood the project will never get to the second implementation. Taking extra time and overmanaging the first rollout is smart. The extra effort not only ensures that the implementation is a success, it also provides valuable lessons that can be leveraged to allow subsequent implementations to be accelerated at lower risk.

#8: Work Organizational Politics Constantly

Just because a project has been approved does not mean that it will not be the subject of internal political attack thereafter. The smartest opponents of any initiative will read the writing on the wall as the project nears approval and go underground. Their resistance will appear to melt away. Watch out!

Organizational politics is pervasive. The most effective tool for combating political attacks is success. The more successful a project becomes, the more difficult it is to resist. Ensuring that project sponsors are active in blunting such attacks allows the project team to focus on execution. A balanced and rational approach combines successful execution with constant communication.

#9: Be Flexible but Do Not Compromise

One of the hardest balancing acts is to provide a degree of flexibility during a change program without compromising the end objective. Midcourse corrections always are needed during implementation. No matter how good the up-front plan, it is impossible to define all steps in the process and anticipate all the events that will occur during any project. The key is not to lose sight of the program's overall goals and objectives.

It is quite easy to make tactical adjustments that, although they make perfect sense when they are made, compromise the overall objective. As Art Krause, CFO of Sprint Corporation from 1989 to 2002, commented in an interview, "In the early stages we probably moved too slowly and made too many compromises." Sprint achieved top-quartile performance but found that progress was not as smooth as it could have been.

Adopting a mechanism for evaluating changes to any aspect of a project relative to the overall objectives makes it possible to estimate the effects early in the process. Where the impact is material, the change can be referred to the overall project steering committee or executive management team for a decision. It is important to ensure that the description of the change is accompanied by a sound analysis of its likely impact on the project's goals, timeline, budget, and resource requirements.

#10: Do Not Let the Techies Take Over

Technology has become an integral part of almost every project an organization undertakes. Frequently, it is the largest expenditure and the dominant activity on the critical path. However, that does not mean that every project should default to being a technology project. Unfortunately, it is all too easy for confused and fearful business managers to cede ownership and control to the IT organization. This is a recipe for disaster. Not only does it risk compromising the overall business objectives of the project, but in most organizations IT has a lamentable track record for on-time, on-budget delivery of systems that meet requirements.

The business value of any technology investment is not measured in technical terms; it is measured in terms of a service level or value added provided to the business. Results are measured in terms of key business measures, such as increased revenue, reduced operating costs, enhanced customer satisfaction, and better decision making. Ensuring business ownership and accountability is essential if the projected business benefits are to be realized.

#11: Keep Senior Management Informed and Focused on the Goals

Typically, the first bullet point on the list of critical success factors for any project is senior management commitment. Although support from senior executives in general and the project sponsor in particular is important, it has been overemphasized. It is the job of the project team to make change happen; it is the job of senior management to ease the path.

Too often, project teams lament the lack of active senior management support for their program, when in fact they should celebrate it. The last thing a project team needs is for senior executives to become too involved in the details of execution. The inevitable second-guessing and questioning of tactics can derail a project. As one of my clients succinctly put it, "What I want from senior management is their blessing, then I want them to get the hell out of the way."

This approach also recognizes the realities of executive politics. Senior executives are unlikely to risk expending precious political capital on a process improvement or transformation project. They will conserve such capital for really meaningful battles that directly impact their own status or organization. Good project managers attune themselves early to the political environment in which their project exists. They are sensitive to the relative importance of their project to others and the amount of executive credibility that is vested in their initiative. They communicate progress frequently but not exhaustively. They do not hesitate to summon executive support, but they make such decisions judiciously. Effective project managers also understand that executive support is not an entitlement; it is earned and must be continuously reearned. Nothing fosters executive commitment like success. All executives like to be associated with a successful project.

#12: Don't Let the Naysayers Get You Down

Earlier I mentioned the small proportion of people who will never support a change program and the tactics that can be employed to mitigate their negative impact. Far more numerous are the people who at the first sign of trouble start to question the viability of the project or find reasons not to change. Addressing the concerns head-on is essential. Doing this starts with the project team. Look at the 20 reasons for not changing that are listed in Exhibit 12.4. Any team member who uses one of the forbidden phrases should pay a one-dollar fine. At the end of the project, you will have plenty of money for beer and pizza for the whole team, but you will also reinforce a can-do rather than can't-do attitude among the team. Fostering a problem solving mindset will carry over into the team's interactions with the organization as a whole, instead of seeking out barriers to change, they are vigilant in looking for enablers of change.

Managing your own morale is essential. The emotional ups and downs are much greater than with a routine 9-to-5 job. As Price Pritchett comments in *New Work Habits for a Radically Changing World*: "If you put someone else in charge of your morale, you disempower yourself. If you wait around for higher management to heal your wounded spirit, you'll end up hurting longer than necessary. You're far better off to assign yourself personal responsibility for attitude control."[4]

Exhibit 12.4   20 Reasons for Not Changing

1. That's the way we've always done it.	11. The customer wouldn't accept that.
2. We tried that before.	12. That's beyond our responsibility.
3. It's too radical a change.	13. We don't have time.
4. It ain't broke . . . why fix it?	14. It costs too much.
5. We did all right without it.	15. It isn't in the budget.
6. But we would also have to change the . . .	16. It's too hard to sell.
7. It's against corporate policy.	17. Top management will never go for it.
8. Has anyone else ever tried it?	18. Let's shelve it for the time being.
9. It won't work in our industry.	19. We plan on doing it someday.
10. The supplier would never do that.	20. We'll have somebody study the problem.

IT'S ABOUT COMMITMENT AND EXECUTION

Ultimately, successful implementation boils down to two things: commitment and execution. As L.W. Lynett commented, "The most effective way to cope with change is to help create it."

NOTES

1. Michael Hammer and James Champy, *Reengineering the Corporation* (New York: Harper Business, 1993), p. 200.
2. Id.
3. Jeff Henley, speech at the CFO Excellence conference, Phoenix, Arizona, February 2002.
3. Price Pritchett, *New Work Habits for a Radically Changing World* (Dallas: Pritchett and Associates, 1994), p. 38.

Chapter 13

Leading Change

A leader has two important characteristics; first, he is going somewhere; second, he is able to persuade other people to go with him.

—Maximilien François Robespierre

Robespierre eloquently defines two of the most important traits of an effective leader. He himself demonstrated many of these qualities as one of the leaders of the French Revolution that secured the downfall and execution of Louis XVI. Ironically, Robespierre's own downfall only 18 months later was largely caused by his failing to follow his own counsel. Once he reached the pinnacle of power in the new republic, his ability to persuade others to follow him waned rapidly. His response was to resort to the Reign of Terror, which resulted in the deaths of more than 17,000 people but failed to prevent his own execution by guillotine in July 1794. Robespierre is just one example of an inspirational leader who lost focus on what it takes to be a great leader.

Leadership is a much-prized asset. The ability to mobilize and motivate people and lead them to effect substantial change is an essential part of implementing a best practice planning and management reporting process, never mind starting a revolution. Leadership is a complex subject, and a full discussion is beyond the scope of this book; however, a discussion of best practices would be incomplete if it did not recognize the key elements of effective leadership that create the environment essential for successful implementation.

Before the nineteenth century, the predominant business models were that of the farm and the family. Business leaders usually were synonymous with business owners, and most enterprises were family-run. The practice of professional leadership was mostly restricted to the military. It was in the military that the first real separation between ownership and governance or leadership was established. The emergence of professional soldiers—exemplified by famous military heroes such as Marlborough, Wellington, and Nelson—foreshadowed the appearance of the professional manager as leader. During the nineteenth century, the Industrial Revolution triggered a transformation from a largely rural, agricultural economy and business model to an urban, factory-based model from which was born the discipline of professional management and ultimately the role of chief executive officer (CEO).

The twentieth century saw the growth, maturation, and relative decline of the manufacturing-based economy; it was supplanted by a thriving service sector whose growth was fueled largely by economic prosperity and advances in technology and communications.

The increasingly ubiquitous nature of low-cost, reliable computing and communications technologies is revolutionizing the world in much the same way as the adoption of mass production did in the first half of the twentieth century. The latest iteration is the product of innovative and visionary leaders whose names are synonymous with the companies they created, grew, or transformed. The change is also creating a whole new cadre of potential best practices.

Much of the discussion of best practices focuses on the procedural and technological aspects of world-class performance. Both are crucial if a high level of performance is to be sustained; however, the most important element is people. A great process supported by great technology is worth nothing without the right people. Establishing the importance of people starts at the top, with the tone set by leaders within the company. As Jack Welch of General Electric commented: "Getting the right people in the right jobs is a lot more important than developing a strategy."[1] Implementing a best practice performance management process is challenging. It impacts the most senior people in the organization—most of whom probably reached their exalted positions by successfully using the very processes you want to change. If you are to be successful, two critical roles must be filled: the project champion and the project leader.

The project champion should ideally be a "C"-level executive, preferably the CEO. But this person's passion and visible commitment are more important than their title. The champion needs to play two primary roles: principal salesperson for the program and supporter of the project manager. As principal salesperson for the program, this person seizes every opportunity to promote the objectives, values, and contributions required to ensure success. The champion also needs to actively support the project manager in resolving issues that are hindering progress. Often the champion must break deadlocks regarding issues about access to or availability of resources. Ideally, the project champion is active without being intrusive. Champions who become too involved in the minutiae of implementation will distract the project team and also lose their objectivity in providing oversight and direction to the project.

The project leader is the most crucial appointment of all. Projects reflect the personality of their leaders. The project leader sets the tone for communications, team interaction, and morale. More important, the project leader is the most visible representative of a project to the rest of the organization.

LEADERSHIP QUALITIES

Good leadership is independent of role or job title. What follows is a brief description of the principal attributes of effective leaders. These apply equally well to the CEO who initiates a best practice change program and the project leader charged with making it happen.

Business Knowledge

Understanding how the business works or, more precisely, how it makes money is a basic skill. The primary objective of any project is to improve some aspect of business performance. Effective leadership means constantly ensuring that all aspects of the project are aligned with the overall objectives of the business. Keeping those objectives in mind helps project leaders make the trade-offs that are inevitable in any project as decisions are made about changes of scope, resource allocations, and personnel changes. The leaders of all major change projects have to face resistance throughout the process. The ability to understand the reasons for the resistance in the context of the business is essential if the project is to continue moving forward.

One of the most common challenges project leaders face is the "My business is different" or the "You don't understand my business" syndrome, which typically manifests itself when a change program cuts across multiple different businesses. A project leader who demonstrates a sound grasp of each of the businesses being impacted by the change is in a much better position to address such challenges, by recognizing the uniqueness of the business in question and also being able to explain how the project team is taking that uniqueness into account while staying focused on the overall objectives.

Financial Acumen

The track record of budget overruns of large-scale projects points to the critical need to upgrade capabilities in this area. Managing a project without paying constant attention to both the budget and the financial implications of any decision is shortsighted. All projects have to be paid for, and all projects are commissioned in the expectation that they will deliver a return in excess of the investment required. The best leaders make the financial management of their projects a nonissue. Given the poor track record of major projects coming in on or under budget, this is an area to which many organizations must pay greater attention.

Decisiveness

Leadership is all about making choices and decisions. People look to leaders to provide guidance and direction. Leaders do not need to be experts on every issue; they do need to be experts on seeking input, questioning assumptions and ideas, and making decisions. Perhaps more important, they look for those decisions to be timely so they do not impede progress. Good leaders are able to make rapid, but not impulsive, decisions. By anticipating the decisions that will need to be made, asking the right questions, and ensuring the right information is available, good leaders are able to make good decisions, fast.

Some of the hardest decisions for a project leader require careful timing and very precise execution. If one acts too early, the progress of the project may be seriously compromised; if one acts too late, the damage may be irreparable. Making certain decisions requires courage. Requesting more time, resources, or money; replacing project team members; and escalating issues that the team has been unable to resolve to senior management are all difficult decisions to make. In each case, the practical and the emotional must be balanced, and the head, not the heart, must rule. This is where strong project leaders distinguish themselves—they recognize that while they have to make the final call, they do not have to do all the work themselves. The willingness to seek input and counsel on the hardest decisions is one of the principal distinguishing features of effective project leaders. They do not hesitate to discuss big issues with others.

Courage to Change Course

Perhaps the hardest task for leaders is to admit they made a poor decision or that a decision that was correct when made but now needs to be reversed. L.L. Bean chief executive Christopher McCormick came to such a realization in November 2005. L.L. Bean had begun building a call center in Waterville, Maine, only for T-Mobile to announce that it would build its own call center next door. Within days, with bulldozers already at work on the site, McCormick ordered a halt to construction. A few weeks later the company announced it was abandoning the site altogether. McCormick's rationale was that while the location decision made perfect sense when made, T-Mobile's decision to locate in the same small community would put a strain on the available labor supply; as L.L. Bean's needs are highly seasonal, the company probably would lose out to its larger neighbor. A sound but still brave decision after the land had been bought and over $500,000 spent on plans and preliminary preparations.[2]

Communication and Organizational Skills

Leadership is about persuading people to change and then leading them down the path of change. The first step requires communication, and the second requires organization. The most important aspect of communication is to understand that it is a two-way process in which listening forms the most important part.

TIP

The best leaders are characterized by the questions they ask, not the answers they give.

Project leaders have to communicate with three main constituencies:

1. The project team
2. Senior management
3. The organization at large

Each requires a different approach. First the project team members must be recruited and sold on the project, then they must be motivated to execute it. This step requires that the project leader's style of communication change from that of salesperson to that of manager. During the selling process, the discussion focuses on the benefits to the organization and the individual of being part of the project and the expectations of the individual on the project team. Once the team has been recruited, the project leader's task is to keep team members motivated while also providing the necessary guidance and feedback on performance relative to expectations. The change from salesperson to task manager needs to be executed carefully if morale and motivation are to be sustained.

Communicating with senior management requires careful planning. Start by asking these questions:

- Why am I communicating?
  - Is it a regularly scheduled update?
  - Has an event occurred that is triggering the need to communicate?
- What response am I seeking?
  - Is this just an exchange of information, or am I seeking a decision?

If the objective is to provide a progress update with no decisions being made, be sure that the expectation is set up front and keep the communication short and to the point. If a decision is required, make sure that adequate briefing is provided in advance to enable senior management to make a decision. All too often, the project team walks into a meeting seeking decisions and comes away frustrated when none is made. Usually this results in the team complaining about management's inability to make decisions. Although is sometimes the case, more often than not the project team is at fault for failing to equip management with the necessary information to enable them to make a decision. The most effective decisions are those where one knows the outcome before the meeting because one has done one's homework with each of the decision makers beforehand.

Communication with the rest of organization cannot be ignored. Redesigning the performance management processes will impact a broad spectrum of people across all functions within an organization. Success is partly a function of the effectiveness with which the change is communicated. Typically this communication involves five steps that describe:

1. The need for change or case for action
2. The nature of the change
3. The benefits of the change
4. An individual's role in making the change successful
5. The steps that will be taken to equip the individual and the organization with the skills and knowledge to be successful in the new environment

Each step requires planning regarding the messages that need to be conveyed, the timing, the audience, the medium, and the expected results. Managing the project organization is a continuous activity. Unlike an operational team, where the structure remains static for periods of time and stability is a positive, project teams are constantly flexing to meet ever-changing demands. Effective leaders are always fine-tuning the project organization to ensure that the right resources are put against the right tasks. The key is to strike the right balance between flexibility and chaos. High-performing teams are able to realign themselves seamlessly around current priorities without losing sight of the end objective. Leadership is about creating the environment where many of the required changes occur naturally without formal guidance or direction being given. Leaders pay close attention and take personal ownership of the processes for selecting team members, organizing the team, defining the governance structure, managing the evolution of the project organization during the project, and disbanding the team when the project is completed.

Integrity

Underpinning effective leadership is a basic level of integrity that inspires trust and confidence. Integrity always has been an essential attribute of effective leaders—never more so than today. Effective leaders who combine a strong track record of success with high integrity are much sought after. Waste Management, itself a victim of an accounting scandal, gained significant kudos through its appointment of Maury Myers as chairman and CEO in November 1999. Myers was not only a successful leader with a track record in difficult situations; he also brought a reputation of the utmost integrity—both essential requirements for the turnaround at Waste Management.

Inspiration

Leaders represent the passion and soul of the companies they lead. Increasingly, they seek to inspire not just their company's workforce but also their customers and business partners. As Winston Churchill once noted, "I am certainly not one of those who need to be prodded. In fact, if anything, I am the prod."[3] His axiom describes many of today's leaders. For instance, Steve Jobs at Apple, Larry Ellison at Oracle, and Phil Knight at Nike are revered more for being "inspirational" leaders rather than for being "managers." This can be a great asset, but it also can be an impediment. Both Apple and Nike struggled to find effective managers to work successfully with the mercurial founders.

Great project leaders are also capable of creating excitement and energy around their projects. They constantly reinforce the importance and value of the projects they lead, and they celebrate success openly and deal decisively with issues. Team members respect the openness and candor and are prepared to make exceptional commitments, knowing that their efforts will be valued.

Coach

The ability to develop talent is perhaps a leader's most lasting legacy. The ultimate challenge is to make oneself obsolete. For many leaders, this is difficult to come to terms with since it runs counter to many of the attributes that helped get them to the top in the first place. Often projects require different skills as they progress toward full implementation and subsequent operation. Effective leaders plan the leadership transitions that may be required as a project moves from planning, to implementation, to ongoing operational management.

Equally important is preparing project team members for their transition once the project ends. The experience of being on a large-scale project equips team members with knowledge and skills that have tremendous value. Ensuring that this talent is not lost to the organization is essential. Best practice projects often pave the way for a significant role change or promotion for the best performers. At Sprint, the project leader became chief financial officer (CFO) of a business unit; one of the team members became director of the shared services center; and a third became executive assistant to the CFO. At Nationwide Insurance, the project leader moved out of the finance department to become product manager for one of the company's most important product lines.

Focus

If leaders are doing their job right, they will be bombarded by creative and innovative ideas. The trick to managing this process is to maintain the organization's focus while not destroying the creative flow. Often this is accomplished through a unifying mission or theme that gives meaning to employees' everyday activities, demonstrating how they can contribute to the success of the organization. When these values are established, they can be used as criteria for screening ideas and initiatives. Effective project leaders create time and opportunity for team members and others across the organization to bring ideas to the table throughout the project without them becoming a distraction. Leadership is as much about defining what is out of scope as it is about implementing the changes that fall within scope. Defining the process for managing scope changes and being disciplined about the impact of such changes on project progress are two of the most valuable services a project leader can provide to an organization and to the project team.

Change Agent

Change management, like reengineering, has become a business catchphrase, and yet, like reengineering, many people talk about it but few are successful at it. Research indicates that as many as 70 percent of reengineering efforts fail to yield expected benefits. Change management often is seen as being "soft and fluffy" and therefore to be scorned by superhero business executives. Expert practitioners understand that change management is a systematic and focused process for leading an organization forward. It encompasses all the key leadership elements discussed so far plus measurement, rewards and incentives, organization design, skills development, and staffing.

DON'T UNDERESTIMATE THE IMPACT OF LEADERS

Leadership sets the tone for an organization's behavior. Leaders have a significant impact on the values and culture of the organizations they run. Each leader's individual qualities can be seen in the culture and behavior of the organizations he or she leads.

Poor performance often results in leadership changes. There has been a trend for large companies to bring in an outsider in an attempt to improve performance. Doing this certainly removes all links with past ownership. Unfortunately, it removes attachment to the good as well as the bad. For every outsider who succeeds in transforming an organization, such as Lou Gerstner at IBM, there are many others who have failed to live up to the initial expectations despite outstanding track records. Michael Armstrong at AT&T, George Fisher at Kodak, John Sculley at Apple, and Carly Fiorina at Hewlett-Packard come to mind. Each came with an outstanding record of success from Hughes, Motorola, Pepsico, and Lucent respectively but was unable to replicate that success in a new environment. According to Jim Collins in his 2001 book *From Good to Great*, all the leaders of companies that made the leap from good to great were insiders who had the courage to change what needed changing but, perhaps more important, to keep what was working.[4]

Leaders, either insiders or outsiders, are measured by results. The transformation of the planning and management reporting processes should deliver better business decisions at lower cost. The success of the transformation will be as much a function of the leadership skills exhibited by the project sponsor and the project leader as it will be a function of the quality of the process design and the functionality of the new systems.

NOTES

1. Jack Welch, *Straight from the Gut* (New York: Warner Business Books, 2001), p. 383.
2. Scott Thrum, "Seldom Used Executive Power: Reconsidering," *Wall Street Journal*, February 6, 2006, p. B3.
3. *The Forbes Book of Business Quotations,* (New York: Black Dog & Leventhal, 1997).
4. Jim Collins, *From Good to Great* (New York: HarperCollins, 2001).

Chapter 14

Looking to the Future

I think there is a world market for about five computers.

—Thomas J. Watson

In the first edition of this book I rashly made a few predictions about the future. At the time I commented that the only certainty about forecasting is that you will be wrong more often than you are right and predicted that at best only half of my predictions would come anywhere near fruition. How did I do?

Not too bad actually. Exhibit 14.1 shows my predictions for some of the benchmarks that were discussed in Chapter 3. For the future I predict that there will be an acceleration of many of the best practice trends described in Part II, driven by the continued convergence of people, information, computing, and communications. Most notable will be changes in overall productivity and operational efficiency, accounting and reporting standards, the use of technology, the importance of the budget, and, last but by no means least, the role of finance executives and their organizations.

FAST, FLAWLESS EXECUTION WILL BE THE DISTINGUISHING CHARACTERISTIC OF WORLD-CLASS COMPANIES

What I wrote in 2002:

Benchmarks show that the average organization's performance management processes are anything but fast and that execution remains far from flawless. Even today's best performers have significant opportunity for further improvement in cycle times, information quality and availability, analyst productivity, and technology leverage. The next decade will see no let-up in the growth in the amount of data available within an organization. As projections for data storage costs continue to decline, storing the data will not be a problem. The ability to sift through the data and identify that very specific subset that is meaningful and relevant to a particular person in a particular situation will remain a challenge. The same processes and technology that enable a pilot of a Boeing 777 to get just the right information at just the right time to make the appropriate decisions will become pervasive within all organizations. This is not just a technology problem—in fact, it is not really a technology problem at all. Most of the technologies exist today. The problem is one of design and application. Moving from a data-centric to a user-centric view is essential. The promise of online, real-time reporting will finally be realized but not in the way many people envision. The dream of instantaneous access to any and all information will be found to be a mirage.

Exhibit 14.1   Benchmark Predictions

Prediction	Status	Comments
Total finance function costs will decline by an average of 7% a year.	Recent studies show that finance costs have actually increased since 2003, largely as a result of the increased costs associated with Sarbanes-Oxley compliance.	This is a temporary blip as companies throw people and money at the problem to meet the initial deadlines. I stand by this prediction over the next five years.
Planning and decision support will consume over half of total staff time, up from 25%; transaction processing will be less than 30%, down from 66%.	The best companies are approaching this ratio, but there is a long way to go.	Any finance team that does not aspire to this objective is focused on the wrong things.
Planning staffs will be 3 times as productive as today, driven by improved training, tools, technology, and information.	Productivity improvements in planning average about 8% a year.	Staff leverage ratios (see Chapter 3) will continue to improve.
More than half of all organizations will be able to close their accounting books in 1 day or less.	Not even close; again, Sarbanes-Oxley has lengthened many close cycles.	Not sure this is even a relevant target anymore. Closing in less than 5 days is probably adequate for 95% of organizations.
Forecasts will be developed in 2 days or less.	Significant progress made in this area—approximately 30% of companies can meet this standard.	Expect two-thirds of all companies to meet this standard within 5 years.
50% of all management information will be sourced from outside the organization.	Significant increases seen as organizations leverage the Internet and develop more sophisticated market intelligence and risk management processes.	Probably 10 years away.
Leading or predictive information will comprise almost half of all management reporting.	Same trend as the previous item.	Again, probably 10 years to go.
Event-driven or on-demand reporting will drive 80% of all management reporting.	Significant improvements with respect to operational reporting.	The move to dynamic planning and forecasting supports this trend.
Paper will remain one of the primary delivery tools—the paperless office will remain a myth.	Duh!	No need to change this one for many years to come.

Far from deluging managers with more and more information, organizations will develop powerful tools for tailoring content not just to the individual but also to his or her situation at any point in time.

What I think now:

Although some progress has been made in this area, a lot remains to be done. Focus and selectivity are the key challenges as organizations wrestle with exponential growth in data volumes. It is very easy for managers to become paralyzed with indecision as the mountain of conflicting data overwhelms them. The challenges are becoming less technical by the day; more important is the ability to filter information dynamically and automatically so that managers get just the information they need at the time they need it. Success in this area provides the best companies with a distinct competitive advantage as valuable as any new product or service innovation.

GLOBAL ACCOUNTING AND REPORTING STANDARDS WILL BECOME A REALITY

What I wrote in 2002:

I hesitate to make this prediction since it is akin to predicting a simplification of the U.S. Tax Code. It is one of those predictions that everyone agrees with but no one can implement. Ironically, the tax code is one of the biggest causes of inconsistency and lack of clarity in financial reporting. Notwithstanding the barriers to change, there is a compelling logic for simpler and more consistent standards for accounting and reporting business performance. Accounting students learn early on that one of the principal objectives of producing accounts is to present a "true and fair view" of how a business has performed. Much of the reporting available today achieves the exact opposite; it serves to cloud rather than clarify.

Drawing a dubious analogy, the world of accounting has many parallels to that of law enforcement. On one hand, there are people who are continuously seeking to exploit gaps or weaknesses in the existing standards for advantage, and on the other hand, there are people charged with upholding the standards or laws. Generally speaking, in both worlds regulation tends to lag behind innovation, creating windows of opportunity that can be exploited profitably. The difference in accounting is the same: People often play both roles—they are both poacher and gamekeeper, as events at Enron, Tyco, and WorldCom illustrate.

Transparency, visibility, and comparability will become the driving forces behind the harmonization and simplification of reporting standards. The inconsistencies in policy, both within individual legislative domains and, more important, between them will be addressed. This does not mean that all policies need to be standard—that will never happen with tax law, for example. It does mean that common global reporting standards should provide customers, investors, and regulators with consistent information. This is perhaps more of a hope than a prediction, but who knows?

What I think now:

As with any activity that requires cooperation among many nations, progress has been slow. However, since 2005, all the 7,000 listed companies in the European Union now report their financial statements according to International Financial Reporting Standards (IFRS). Other countries, including Australia, Canada, Russia, Japan, and China, have or are in the process of converting to IFRS. Although the United States is embracing the objectives of IFRS, it is moving more slowly. The Securities and Exchange Commission now accepts financial statements prepared by foreign companies under IFRS accompanied by a reconciliation to U.S generally accepted accounting principles (GAAP). The chairman of the Securities and Exchange Commission (SEC), Christopher Cox, in a February 2006 speech did indicate that the United States is moving in the direction of supporting global standards; thus, my prediction remains sound and desirable. According to Cox:

> The SEC is working diligently toward the goal of eliminating the existing IFRS to US GAAP reconciliation requirement. Achieving that goal depends on various factors, as discussed in the April 2005 roadmap, including the effective implementation of IFRS in practice. The ultimate success of IFRS for the benefit of the global capital markets depends on the contributions of many parties, including investors, regulators, auditors, issuers and standard setters.[1]

THE FOCUS WILL SHIFT FROM BUYING TECHNOLOGY TO USING IT

What I wrote in 2002:

> Most companies have a massive investment in their installed base of technology that they are increasingly reluctant to throw away just to implement the latest hotshot technology solution. Organizations are going to seek avenues that allow them to preserve much of their past investment while also harnessing the benefits of the latest advances. Expecting an organization to discard all its current systems and start again is naive. The ability to secure the benefits of continued technology advances while preserving the investments made to date will become the dominant planning assumption for an organization's technology strategy.
>
> Examples of this approach can already be seen. In the late 1990s, Delta Airlines was faced with a technology infrastructure of bewildering complexity. So dependent was the company on its systems that it could not simplify and upgrade them while keeping planes flying. Delta did not have the luxury of shutting down for a year or so while it retooled. Its response was to develop a strategy of overlaying its enormously complex architecture with a permeable layer of common tools and information delivery mechanisms that sat between the user and the complexity that lay behind. The new layer allowed information to be shared across multiple different systems of varying degrees of efficiency. Not only were users isolated from the complexity of the legacy systems environment; they also were able to gain access to a much richer set of information that took data from different sources and created new information that improved passenger service and operational efficiency. Users

including passengers, management, gate staff, ticket agents, and flight crews all benefited. The ability to build on past investments makes economic sense. Seamless integration will become a reality rather than advertising copy.

What I think now:

Picking Delta Airlines as an example was perhaps not the smartest choice, given that the airline filed for bankruptcy protection in September 2005; however, I stand by my prediction. Companies continue to seek ways to build on their past investments in technology, and the days of the "Big Bang" project to replace all an organization's systems are past—the costs and risks are simply too high. Technology providers are also recognizing this reality and developing solutions that are scalable and extendable at reasonable cost. The ability to build on past investments makes economic sense. Seamless integration will become a reality rather than advertising copy.

THE ANNUAL BUDGET WILL DIE—AND FEW TEARS WILL BE SHED

What I wrote in 2002:

The annual budget in its traditional static, detailed form has consistently proven obsolete for anything other than the one-time approval of spending plans. Budgeting—universally loathed, time wasting, labor intensive, and ultimately of little value—will finally be seen for what it is: an impediment to decision making in an intensely volatile and competitive marketplace. The feeling of false security that a budget provides is increasingly fleeting, but many are frightened to give it up. The truth will eventually become apparent, and change will follow. Over the next few years, managers will finally wean themselves away from this pernicious activity. The biggest driver will be the continued emergence of more effective tools for the continuous but selective reporting of actual business measures and the adoption of more flexible budgeting and forecasting techniques. Instead of trying to fix the budgeting process, best practice organizations will eliminate the process altogether and replace it with a dynamic, continuous forecast process that leverages real-time data flowing through internal and external systems, thereby empowering faster, more responsive decision making.

What I think now:

Less than a month after the first edition of this book was published in March 2003, Robin Fraser and Jeremy Hope published their book *Beyond Budgeting*. In it they commented:

The annual budgeting process is a trap. Pressured by fixed targets and performance incentives, managers focus on making the numbers instead of making a difference, meeting set goals instead of maximizing potential. With their compensation at stake, managers often resort to deceitful—even unethical—behavior. In the end, everybody loses—the employee, the company, and ultimately the customer.[2]

Hope and Fraser went on to propose that companies abandon the fixed annual performance contract and replace it with a more dynamic and continuous process, so clearly I was not the only one thinking along these lines. Today many companies are reducing their reliance on the annual budget, although few have gone so far as to abandon it completely. The tide has turned, and I remain confident in the accuracy of my prediction. As Jack Welch commented, "The budgeting process at most companies has to be the most ineffective practice in management."[3]

FINANCE EXECUTIVES WILL REQUIRE NEW SKILLS— OR NEW JOBS

What I wrote in 2002:

> The concept of self-service will continue to advance. Business managers will become more financially literate, technologically enabled, and hence self-sufficient. Finance will no longer serve as the gatekeeper or intermediary in the planning and management reporting processes; its role will change. Much greater emphasis will be placed on overall business risk management, and finance will play a much more active role in the education and coaching of business managers in using the available information and broad range of analytical tools. Finance traditionally has played a key role in business risk management; however, the increasing sophistication of financial management has made many traditional risk management processes obsolete. Recent high-profile failures will usher in a new era of financial discipline and control. Integrity, transparency, and objectivity will be the watchwords and hallmarks of world-class companies. Finance will play a much bigger and proactive role in building and managing the internal control processes that focus on prevention rather than detection after the fact. Preventive controls and dynamic, real-time risk monitoring will require new skills, processes, and technologies from finance leaders. Regulators, investors, and audit committees will demand nothing less.
>
> Finance executives who are unable to keep up with new realities will find themselves increasingly marginalized in business decision making. Cycle times for closing, budget development, forecast development, and transaction processing will continue to shorten. Even in today's top-performing companies, fully 45 percent of total finance staff time is still consumed by routine transaction processing. This figure will drop close to zero as full automation and integration take hold. Those organizations that remain wedded to a traditional, historically focused, control-oriented way of working will be left behind by best practice–enabled, forward-looking organizations that have leaner, more skilled, and more technology-enabled finance organizations.

What I think now:

Although many chief financial officers (CFOs) have complained of the extra burden placed on them and their organizations by Sarbanes-Oxley, in many ways it has been a powerful boost to their visibility. Boards of directors, investors, and managers all now look to the CFO to provide the assurance that an organization's operations are appropriately controlled and that policies are correctly framed and applied. In many cases the CFO's role is being redefined as that of strategic advisor to the CEO and board as well as the chief risk officer. This in turn is providing a powerful incentive for companies to refocus the finance team on the areas of risk management and decision support, which is wholly consistent with the best practice model.

CONCLUSIONS

I remain optimistic. In fact, the pace of progress and understanding has accelerated over the last few years as companies begin to understand the power of best practices and finally learn to leverage technology effectively to support their implementation. Forums for sharing knowledge and experience provide organizations with unparalleled access to best practices insights that can accelerate implementation, reduce risk, and increase returns. The latent potential of technology will be realized. The rest of the world will not stand still while this happens. Competition, globalization, and integration will continue to drive radical changes in the way organizations operate and structure themselves. The next few years should be exciting.

NOTES

1. Christopher Cox, U.S. Securities and Exchange Commission, February 2006.
2. Robin Fraser and Jeremy Hope, *Beyond Budgeting* (Boston: Harvard Business School Press, 2003), p. 12.
3. Jack Welch with Suzy Welch, *Winning* (New York: Harper Business, 2005), p. 189.

Index

3M, 96

A

AMR Research, 212
AT&T, 11, 14, 183, 189
Accountability, 107
Accounting restatements, 3
Adams, Scott, 78
Affleck, Ben, 172
Alcoa, 10, 61, 82, 135, 154
Allied Signal, 10, 13
Amazon.com, 7, 68
American Express, 169
American Management Association
    (AMA), 80
Ameritech, 12
Ameritrade, 7
Apple, 11, 256
Ariba, 5
Armstrong, Michael, 258
Armstrong, J. Scott, 159
Arthur Andersen, 21
Ashe, Rob, 149

B

BP, 195
BHAGs, 94
BMW, 43, 97
Balanced Scorecard, 148
Baldrige Award for Quality, 189
Ballmer, Steve, 84, 90, 140
Bank of America, 14, 99, 128, 166, 184,
    221, 245
Bank of International Settlements, 182
Bank of Thailand, 28
Barnes and Noble, 8
Basel Capital Accord, 182
Bay, Michael, 172
L.L. Bean, 33, 254
Benchmarking,
  evolution, 236
  predictions, 260

value of, 37
Bennis, Warren, 81
Berkshire Hathaway, 89
Bernstein, Peter L., 179
Best Buy, 15
Best practices,
  application, 31, 61
  definition, 26–30
  implementation, 35
  metrics, 55
  selection of, 63
  types, 30
Beyond Budgeting Round Table (BBRT),
    163, 169
Blair, Tony, 12
Blockbuster, 183
Body Shop, The, 83
Boeing, 7
Bogan, Christopher, 60
Bond, James, 59
Boo.com, 74
Bossidy, Larry, 13, 48, 74, 90, 92, 99, 110
Bozigian, Greg, 205
Briloff, Abraham, 148
British Airways, 11
British Telecom, 189
Buffett, Warren, 89
Bush, George H. W., 82
Business bankruptcies, 4
Business drivers, 119
Business life cycle, 64
Business Performance Management
    (BPM),
  definition, 24, 203
Business Risk Management (BRM)
  definition, 26
Business Week, 131

C

CNN, 68
COSO Framework, 185
Cameron, James, 172